Principals in Action

The Reality of Managing Schools

Van Cleve Morris
University of Illinois at Chicago

Robert L. Crowson
University of Illinois at Chicago

Cynthia Porter-Gehrie
Field Consulting Company
Northfield, Illinois

Emanuel Hurwitz, Jr.
University of Illinois at Chicago

Consulting Editor: Raphael O. Nystrand, University of Louisville

Charles E. Merrill Publishing Company
A Bell & Howell Company
Columbus Toronto London Sydney

Published by Charles E. Merrill Publishing Company
A Bell & Howell Company
Columbus, Ohio 43216

This book was set in Century Schoolbook.
The Production Editor was Jeffrey Putnam.
The Cover Designer was Tony Faiola.
The cover photographs were taken by Jean Greenwald.

ISBN: 0-675-09790-8

Library of Congress Catalog Card Number: 83-42954

1 2 3 4 5—88 87 86 85 84

Printed in the United States of America

Clockwise from the top: Crowson, Morris, Porter-Gehrie, Hurwitz.

Van Cleve Morris received his Ed.D. from Teachers College, Columbia University in the administration of higher education. Following a year of study on a post-doctoral fellowship underwritten by the Ford Foundation in 1953-54, he devoted his scholarship to educational philosophy and has written extensively in that field. From 1969-76, he served as Dean of the College of Education at the University of Illinois at Chicago, and has recently published *Deaning—Middle Management in Academe,* an analysis of academic administration. Since returning to the professorial ranks, Morris has used his knowledge of philosophy and administration to focus on public policy analysis as it relates to educational leadership.

Robert L. Crowson is Associate Professor of Education at the University of Illinois at Chicago. He received his Ph.D. in Educational Administration from the University of Chicago and has served as a public school teacher, college instructor and administrator, and state department of education official. Crowson has writen numerous articles and papers on educational planning, the politics of education, and the school principalship. His current interest is educational policy analysis and organizational theory in education. His honors include the senior Fulbright-Hays research grant for the study of educational planning in Germany in 1975

Cynthia Porter-Gehrie, with a Ph.D. from Northwestern University, is a writer and research specialist in the use of ethnographic methods. She has applied these skills in a variety of research settings including non-institutional adolescent social groups, the criminal justice system, and the public school system. Her primary areas of expertise are developing case material from field data and training practitioners to conduct field research. She is president of Field Consulting Company of Northfield, Illinois.

Emanuel Hurwitz, Jr. is Associate Professor of Education and Assistant Dean of the College of Education at the University of Illinois at Chicago. He received his Ph.D. from Northwestern University in Educational Administration and his research and writing have been in the areas of educational foundations and the politics of education. Recently he has focused his attention on the role of the principal in large-city school systems. Hurwitz is the co-author and co-editor of several books in the foundations of education field. His book (with Charles Tesconi) entitled *Education For Whom?* has been used by preprofessional teacher education students to examine the question of equal educational opportunity. Hurwitz has also given workshops for school administrators on management skills and staff development.

FOREWORD

The school principalship is, by all accounts, a critical position in American education. In recent years, a number of studies have confirmed the conventional wisdom which holds that the climate and effectiveness of a particular school are influenced by the leadership which the principal provides. For a long time, we have known that teachers, students, central office administrators, and others often differ in their expectations for principals and that these differences render the principalship a very difficult position. The nature and implications of these differences have been the subject of considerable conjecture, as have the ways that principals can and should deal with them.

Morris and his colleagues provide an important addition to our knowledge regarding the challenges of the principalship and how these challenges are met in real life. The outstanding strength of the book is its basis in what principals actually do. Unlike most texts, which rest primarily upon reviews of literature and the experiences and viewpoints of its authors, this one draws upon research done by the authors in the Chicago public schools. Their open-minded and sustained observations produced a picture of the principalship which is at some variance with the traditional view. They found, for example, that principals typically spend less than half the work day in their offices. They are administrators "on the run" who conduct most of their business in face to face situations. Perhaps most important, they found that the position affords a great deal of discretion to those who hold it.

The picture of the principalship which emerges in this book gives new and fuller meaning to Weick's description of schools as "loosely coupled" systems. The authors discuss the implications of managing such systems for principals themselves, as well as for those who train and select them. Their analysis and suggestions warrant careful consideration by all who recognize the pivotal importance of building level leadership to future school improvement.

Raphael O. Nystrand
Louisville, Kentucky
May, 1983

PREFACE

Among scholars of school administration, the school principalship has remained an enigma. The job is still quite unlike its textbook descriptions and this lack of symmetry between theory and practice continues to puzzle us.

In the research that led to the writing of this book, we have detected a latent cause for this condition. We believe that the principalship must be analyzed and understood not according to some received canons of professional conduct but rather in terms of what actually goes on during the principal's work day. In designing the investigations leading to this volume, we were interested first in a direct, uncluttered look at what principals actually do. We arranged for an observer to be with the principal and share directly in the principal's work, for up to twelve full work days. We were interested in whom the principal interacted with and by what means (verbal face to face, written word, telephone, etc.). We wanted to know which party initiated each interchange, whether it was planned or spontaneous, how long it lasted, and where it took place. Most important, we wanted to follow the changing subject matters of these conversations, not only to see what topics consumed the principal's time, but also to trace the rhythm of the principal's working hours.

Out of these findings, we were able to piece together the texture of a school administrator's typical work day. We discerned at first faintly, but then in greater detail, the ways in which the work is driven by expectations that are conspicuously missing from most job descriptions. For the first time we obtained a kind of "movie documentary" of the school principal at work, and the documentary revealed things never before shown in the catalogue of administrative occupations.

We were also curious about a more subtle characteristic of administration: discretionary decision making. Much of any administrator's work is by the book, but we discovered that a major segment of the principal's time is devoted to behavior which is ad hoc and "situation specific." Principals, like other managers, must often work without the book; they must make up rules and precedents as they go along. How, we asked, does a principal act when the guidelines for action are missing or are so unclear they offer no guidance?

Out of these observations of discretionary behavior, we sketched a mode of conduct of the principal which revealed an innovative and imaginative side of the job. This in turn led us to see more clearly how the principal's behavior affects four distinct "constituencies":

1. Associates and clients (teachers and students in the school building itself)
2. The lay constituency (parents and others) in the community

3. The hierarchy of superiors at district headquarters
4. The principal as a career-oriented professional ("How does my administrative behavior affect *me?")*

This book is an account of principaling *in action.* It is a picture of the principalship that, for the first time, systematically takes into account how the principal, the primary actor, defines the job not by writing it down somewhere, but by acting it out daily.

*   *   *   *   *

The book is organized into four parts:

Part One, comprising the first three chapters, concerns the study and practice of school administration, with special emphasis on the principalship. We offer here a review of the development of the discipline itself, and an extended discussion of how modern research techniques, especially ethnographic approaches, are providing new insights in the field. Part One concludes with a "bench mark" chapter, providing a general context for the discussions to follow.

Part Two examines the discretionary decision making of the modern principal. In Chapters 4, 5, 6, and 7, we analyze the four sectors of effect drawing for each a specific comparison between conventional understanding and what our on-the-scene reporting revealed.

Part Three, comprising two chapters, studies the implications of these findings for the administrative profession, specifically implications for (a) day to day operations in the occupation, (b) training of principals, and (c) the selection, placement and career development of principals.

Part Four embraces several instructional cases for use in administrator training programs. The cases have been drawn from our research investigations and can be used, for example, as simulation exercises in graduate classes for administrator trainees.

In developing this text, we are indebted to many people:

We recognize, first of all, our indebtedness to the principals who graciously allowed us to be an intimate part of their professional lives for an extended period—up to twelve days over the course of three school years.

We thank the scholars and practitioners in the field of school administration who served as advisors during the course of the research on which this book is based.

We acknowledge the financial support of the Chicago Principals Association, the Spencer Foundation, and the National Institute of Education, each of whom represented a critical source of funds at several stages of our work.

We wish to mention specifically our colleague at the University of Illinois at Chicago, Bruce McPherson and scholarly associates Donald Erickson of the University of California at Los Angeles, and Paul Peterson, Charles Bidwell and Sheppard Kellam, all of the University of Chicago. They offered special conceptual advice in designing and evaluating the investigations which have occupied our attention over these several years.

We especially appreciate the liaison role played by Fritz Mulhauser and Lorri Manasse, formerly of the National Institute of Education, who helped to direct our findings to a national audience of professional educators.

We thank the reviewers of this book, who offered their advice at various stages of the book's progress: Kenneth E. McIntyre, University of Texas; Hampton Williams, University of Southern Mississippi; Raphael O. Nystrand, University of Louisville; and Lonnie H. Wagstaff, Ohio State University.

In a final critique of the manuscript, Catherine Morris reviewed the several chapters from the perspective of a professional teacher who is able to judge principalship services as a "consumer."

In the preparation of the manuscript, we cite Margaret Power, Marilyn Geron, Dawn Surdyk, Lynn Casey, and Merry Mastny—rare stenographers and word processing specialists who can with good humor work for four people at the same time.

Van Cleve Morris
Robert L. Crowson
Cynthia Porter-Gehrie
Emanuel Hurwitz, Jr.

CONTENTS

PART 1

The Study and Practice of School Administration

1

The State of the Art

Through the years the principal has become the quintessential middle manager in education. This middle position is most evident in the principal's placement in the hierarchy of a school system, taking orders from the superintendent and headquarters staff, then relaying (and supposedly enforcing) these orders to department heads, teachers and students.

THE MIDDLE MANAGER

But the middle position of the principal has taken on a more urgent and complicated character. The principal is now not only in the middle of the hierarchy, but in the middle of a political environment that in recent decades has engulfed educational planning and decision making. The principalship is now a vortex created by forces throughout the social order which exert pressure on educators. Some of this pressure comes from legitimate agencies—school boards, parent organizations, community advisory councils, labor unions, government bureaus or courts. But it also originates, sometimes in its most pernicious form, from groups whose legitimacy itself is controversial—student protesters, minority activists, street gangs, textbook vigilantes, and spontaneous, single-issue parent groups.

Today's school principal must be effective not only in dealing with the formal bureaucracy, but also in wrestling with the volatile demands and procedural surprises of these extra-legal, quasi-legitimate associations. A school administrator must manage an institution while he or she walks a political tightrope, brokering between interest groups. The principalship has assumed a public visibility uncommon in earlier educational epochs; the skills necessary for success, or even survival, are manifold.

A natural question is, *How did we get here? What has been going on in the last century and a half of educational history that has brought us to this point in the management of our schools?* In the following sections we trace the evolution of the study of school administration, examining the various strategies employed by the developers of the discipline, and setting forth the widely accepted results of their research.

But despite the acceptance of these findings we face a major curiosity: Do they match what is actually going on in the schools? What is the relationship between the findings of the scholars and the on-the-job reality of principals?

We close the chapter with this last question. The answer is the focus of the remainder of the volume.

THE EARLY YEARS

The profession of educational administration is still in its infancy. In the mid-1800s, long after the emergence of publicly supported education in America, local school boards were managing their own schools on a part-time, hip-pocket basis. When this degree of commitment was seen as insufficient, many of these boards adopted the practice of releasing one of their teachers for part of the school day to attend to the school's clerical responsibilities.[1] As schools grew, particularly in urban communities, the clerical duties of the "head" teacher increased, and the teaching load diminished. By the mid-to-late 1800s, with schools growing still larger, the head or principal teacher began to assume more responsibility for the work of the other teachers, especially those with the least training and experience.[2]

With the continued growth of common schools in both size and number, and with the advent of the secondary school in the 1870s, the need arose for coordination of whole school systems and for an administrator at the superintendent level. Although a few districts, particularly in the larger cities, established the superintendency in the 1835–55 period, the position of general superintendent did not become common until 1900.[3]

Where did these principals and superintendents get their training for these positions? As is true of other occupations, the establishment of specialized university programs in educational administration followed by several decades. Two major founders of programs in the field, Ellwood Cubberley and George Strayer, did not complete their own doctoral studies until 1905. During the next few decades, these and other founding fathers began to create a professional subject matter and a program of study in educational administration, an effort which grew substantially in numbers of students and of universities offering degrees. Hollis A. Moore has reported that by the end of World War II, approximately 300 of the nation's universities offered programs in school administration.[4]

In spite of the establishment of university programs—or perhaps because of it—the profession has not solved a major dilemma of any applied field: linking theory and practice.[5] How well does the study of administration fit the realities of administrative life? How can administrative practice in education be improved through enhanced theoretical understanding?

A BRIEF CONCEPTUAL HISTORY

The dilemma in educational administration concerning theory versus practice was already problematic at the inception of specialized training in the field shortly after the turn of the century. One problem with historical antecedents is the ambiguity surrounding the definition of administrative roles. Just what is the building principal or the school superintendent supposed to do? The principal had been released from teaching to attend to clerical duties. But, as time passed, the principal was also expected to supervise instruction and provide for staff improvement. Later, as the superintendency developed, the principal was expected to fit into an organizational hierarchy, and like a good soldier carry out the demands of bureaucratic superiors. Most recently, the building principal has been expected to take the initiative in interpreting the work of the school to outsiders, and more important, be responsive to the lay community always looking over the principal's shoulder.

The superintendent is expected to manage the school district and to carry out school policy, while the lay board of education ostensibly makes policy. But the superintendent, as a highly trained professional, is also expected to exert "leadership" and provide "initiative." As a result, superintendents typically do a turnabout, ending up making school policy through administrative decisions, while their lay board of education members become heavily involved in problems of how policy should be carried out. This inversion of responsibilities, already manifest at the turn of the century, is still with us in more exacerbated form.

A second unresolved problem, also of long standing, is accommodating conceptual development of the administrative task to a continuously changing and dynamic reality. Translating theory into practice would be easier if reality did not change. But it does, and since Cubberley and Strayer attempts have been made to bring the study of administration into conceptual rapport with life as it is actually lived in the schools. The major conceptual efforts in this direction are worth extended commentary.

The Scientific Management Movement

An initial approach to educational administration was grounded in the scientific management and industrial efficiency tenets of Frederick W. Taylor.[6] This movement grew out of a reform era in which the administrative functions of school districts were being centralized under strong superintendencies. This era, during the early years of the century, was characterized by periodic exposés of educational mismanagement of the nation's children. Large numbers of immigrant children were streaming into the schools to be assimilated into American life through the melting pot strategy. The schools were under considerable pressure to produce.

The scientific management approach asserted that educational organizations, like commercial establishments, could be made businesslike and efficient. Tasks and responsibilities could be carefully defined and fully planned to lead to maximized organizational productivity. Scholars such as Henri Fayol and Luther Gulick suggested that the organization could be systematically structured at its top, with specialized divisions of effort radiating downward through the hierarchy to cause the entire organization to pull together efficiently as a total organic unity. Such concerns as "span of control" were important to the scientifically inclined administrator. Close coordination and control of subordinate behavior were considered vital to overall efficiency, and one was careful not to distribute responsibilities among lower-level employees beyond the bounds of what each manager could fully supervise. One culmination of the scientific management effort was Gulick's master list of things managers do, celebrated in the well-remembered acronym POSDCORB: Planning, Organizing, Staffing, Directing, Coordinating, Reporting, and Budgeting.[7]

Raymond Callahan's book, *Education and the Cult of Efficiency,* provides a thorough, compelling description of the impact of scientific management upon the field.[8] From the management of classroom instruction through the school system hierarchy, educational organizations were engineered for efficiency. Standardized testing, elaborate systems of records and reports, even "score cards for buildings" provided the beginnings of a systematic information system for the educational administrator.[9] Studies of cost economics and time usage, even an efficiency index of pupil study habits, were added to the list of what should be considered in judging managerial effectiveness in education. Standards of behavior, qualifications for entry-level jobs, and detailed instructions for job performance were all incorporated into specifications for teachers and administrators.

Bertram Gross has labeled the working doctrine of the scientific management era the "gospel of efficiency," since the dedication of its adherents was of a quasi-religious intensity.[10] It was fervently believed that educational administration could best be improved by the scientific application of managerial expertise. This included carefully planned schedules for work, the instructions for doing it, and the expected standards of performance.

It was a movement perfect for its time in education because it indicated the critical importance of managerial officialdom. To a newly developing profession, the gospel of efficiency offered a raison d'être, a role to be filled, a goal to be accomplished, and a methodology. Getzels, Lipham, and Campbell reviewed one of the earliest textbooks in educational administration, Ellwood P. Cubberley's supremely influential *Public School Administration,* 1916. They point out that to Cubberley, the school administrator was the organizer, the executive, and the supervisor of work. The educational executive was told to exercise "large powers," to apply his "broader knowledge" and "larger insight" to educational needs, and to plan all policies even though "the details might be best kept to himself." The importance of the school executive was not diminished by Cubberley's added admonition to be "a man of affairs," honest and square, clean and temperate, honorable, and "able to look men straight in the eye."[11]

The Human Relations Approach

Scientific management had its heyday in the 1920s. A counter movement, the human relations view, gained wide appeal during the depression-ridden 1930s and continued through the 1940s. The optimistic view of a neatly ordered administrative world, fully amenable to a rational, scientific approach to school management, was quickly seen to be out of touch with a nation and an educational system in distress.

While scientific management was a production-oriented concept of administration, the new human relations perspective was widely advertised as people-centered.[12] With guidance from the scholarly work of Mary Parker Follett, Elton Mayo, and Chester Barnard, the management literature turned its attention to the relationship between groups and individuals within the organization. The legitimacy and expertise of administrative officialdom were no longer assumed to be good; rather, the superior-subordinate relationship was to be a focus of managerial examination. Employees were to be motivated by persons with skill in communication, interaction, and conflict management. Employees were to be led to good performance; the ideal was not authoritarian, top-down management but more democratic approaches to goal attainment.[13]

In the organizational atmosphere of our public schools in the 1930s and 1940s, this message found a receptive home. Effective school administration could easily be envisioned as a process of good leadership that featured democratic decision making, the motivation and coordination of worker (i.e., teacher, pupil) participation, and well-developed communication skills. The essential understanding was that the leader and the led must be brought into productive harmony. Proper management was no longer considered an exercise in engineering the work place; it was now a task of somehow integrating everyone in an organization into a cooperative whole. People who worked together as partners were likely to be much more productive than those who functioned only as the director and the directed. To educational administrators the central message of the human relations movement was the charge to develop democratic methods of school management. Authoritarian administration was to be replaced by managerial styles that allowed employees, especially teachers, a fully shared voice in any decisions that affected them.[14]

In the universities, the stress upon democratic leadership became very popular in the training of educational administrators; modern textbooks still point out that "the most promising leadership style for effective school principals or supervisors is the democratic style."[15] A democratic educational leader is neither a laissez faire administrator nor an autocrat. The democratic educator follows neither a hands-off policy toward subordinates nor a top-down, no-communication style. Rather, a democratic leader strives to become a friendly advisor and consultant to his employees.

The Interdisciplinary or Theory-based Approach

Soon after World War II, investigations into leadership roles in a variety of organizations suggested that effective management could not always be best defined as democratic. In fact, it appeared that good leadership combined authority with democracy.[16] Studies at The Ohio State University in the late 1940s suggested that successful leadership merged "initiating structure" and "consideration." Initiating structure meant the more direct style—establishing goals, defining limits, detailing procedures. Consideration provided the democratic dimension—showing employees warmth, trust, and respect. An administrator who emphasized one dimension without the other would generally not be as effective as one who rated high in both categories.[17]

During the 1950s and 1960s, research continued to show that good administration blends what formally had seemed to be simple truths about organizations and human behavior. In this period management theorists turned to the basic sciences, particularly psychology and social psychology, in an effort to base theories of educational administration on a foundation drawn from academic disciplines.

Some theoretical developments in general management theory came from the writings of such persons as Herbert Simon, Talcott Parsons, and Robert Merton. In the field of education, such scholars as Roald Campbell, Jacob W. Getzels, and Andrew Halpin were instrumental in moving the study of educational administration toward an approach that would be theory-based, interdisciplinary, and adaptable to hypothesis-testing styles of research.

A significant contribution, as well as a weakness, of this mode of conceptual development was its emphasis upon what Campbell has termed "structuralism." Much was learned about organizational structure, the interactions of organizational participants within social systems, and the interplay between organizational structure and human behavior. Scholars learned, with Barnard's help, to be aware of the difference between formal organization and informal organization.[18] A school system's organization chart and its written regulations may be far less instructive in explaining the behavior of its members than its informal patterns of communication between friendship groups, employees with shared interests, or people who really wield power within the organization. Similarly, scholars learned that the well-meaning and even rational actions of employees may not always fit the avowed aims of an organization. Occasionally, purposeful activity actually leads to what Merton called a "displacement of goals," where real outcomes are not at all what managerial leaders intended, or where means have somehow become ends in themselves.[19]

As Campbell noted, the central concern of theorists and scholars at this time was finding ways to predict and control organizational behavior—that is, to structure organizations in ways that would enable management to "establish the premises and conditions under which decisions in the organization" can be made.[20] In this position, educational organizations were viewed as essentially hierarchical, ordered, goal-directed, and amenable to intelligent and informed administration: the presumption was that they could be planned, programmed, and improved if studied carefully and redesigned systematically. Special attention was given to the important managerial function of decision making. Based on the authority of Herbert Simon, the acts of choosing a course of action from among possible alternatives, and making sound choices with limited information and circumscribed authority became recognized as the central tasks of organizational behavior. The administrator's prime responsibility was to influence and direct the decision making process—to establish the parameters surrounding the choices that would occur throughout the various offices of the organization.[21]

The movement erred in its essentially closed-system orientation and its overly rational approach to management, failing both to consider the impact of an organization's outside environment, and appreciate the fact that an organization, like an individual, may actually be a blend of the rational and irrational. While the movement directed attention to the characteristics of organizational structures as a starting point for effectively managing human behavior, the approach failed to reach either the level of theoretical understanding or the goals of prediction and control that excited scholars in the 1950s and 1960s.

The interdisciplinary, theory-based approach also failed to come to terms with administrative reality. Despite the movement's interest in predicting and controlling, it seemed more concerned with the deductive development of systematic theory than with the inductive translation of practice into theory, and back into improved administrative behavior. As Campbell noted, theoretical concepts may be very helpful in providing insight, but they do not often "give a prescription for what to do."[22] Knowledge of decision theory or leadership behavior may be helpful conceptually, but of little assistance in dealing with everyday problems of student control, poorly trained teachers, or angry parents.

The Open-Systems Perspective

The failure of the theory-based movement to lead to useful prescriptions for school management became agonizingly apparent during the turbulence of the late 1960s and the 1970s. In this period, extraordinary pressures built up on the public schools. Battles over community control, desegregation, and compensatory education made the profession aware of the inadequacies of its closed-system perspective. How could a system be considered closed when it was faced with militant teacher unionism, the requirements of federal and state regulations, the expanding casebook of school law, as well as the paradox of declining enrollments and escalating costs? Events forced a new recognition of the complexity of organizational structure and administrative behavior. Far from being neatly hierarchical and efficient, educational organizations were found to be "loosely coupled," ambiguous in intention, chaotic in design, and defined internally through their interactions with an uncertain, unpredictable external environment.[23]

In response to these findings, a new, open-systems perspective on educational administration developed in the 1970s. Instead of focusing on the strictly in-house tasks assigned to the administrator, scholars began to take a more cosmopolitan view of the organizational landscape, surveying the total social environment of the manager, both inside and outside the organization. Taking their cue from social science research generally, and from political science and organizational theory literature particularly, scholars directed their attention to the client-publics with which a school administrator must deal—the people the principal works *for, with,* and *against*—in performing the managerial function. These are the constituencies to which the administrator is expected to respond: teachers, students, superintendent and central office staff, board of education, parents, community groups, government agencies, courts. This array of client-publics constitutes the spectrum of relationships which every school administrator eventually encounters. Understanding these constituencies, argued the scholars, would provide a more situational, less technical definition of a school administrator's performance area. Such a focus would provide a more realistic portrait of administrative responsibility.

The open-systems perspective is still under development. It has been instrumental in creating an improved systems analysis of education based on two fundamental propositions: (a) the school system and its environment are linked together in necessary interaction, and (b) the world of the educational administrator, characterized by loosely coupled, chaotic, unpredictable, and fragmented elements, is far more complex than has been perceived. A critical understanding for educational administrators has been the realization that the scientific prediction and control of organizational behavior is still a long way away. Since what happens within schools is vitally linked with unknowns outside schools, and since bureaucratic structures are as disconnected as they are connected, the naive, optimistic assumption that the administrative world is easily explainable and controllable has given way to a more sophisticated appreciation of managerial complexity.

An early, laudable effort to make some managerial sense out of open-systems understandings is found in the development of contingency theory as an approach to school administration.[24] Contingencies are situational forces that surround the working manager, demanding a variable and flexible response.[25] As E. Mark Hanson has pointed out, a key contribution of contingency theory is the understanding that "there is no best way for designing organizations, jobs or tasks; the particular circumstances of a specific situation determine the best choice or decision."[26] Persons who are competent administrators, it is claimed, are likely to be those who are skilled in conflict management, adept at the accomplishment of direction in uncertainty, and well trained in the artful balancing of competing interests.

A Summation

The scientific management approach provided a dominant motif for educational administration through the first few decades of our century. The emphasis was on productivity and efficiency through an intelligent and authoritative manipulation of wage incentives, the careful planning of work, and the application of key management principles covering span of control and division of labor. A counter viewpoint was the human relations approach. Through the 1930s and 1940s, in reaction to the economic determinism of the scientific management school, the emphasis was upon employee-centered rather than production-centered management, and democratic rather than authoritarian leadership. In the 1950s and 1960s, educational administration attempted to move toward an interdisciplinary synthesis of these earlier movements, offering a concept of school management that (a) unified the scientific efficiency and human relations perspectives, and (b) moved into research and theory, drawing heavily upon the social and behavioral sciences. The result was, to use Campbell's terminology, an interdisciplinary, structured view of organizations, with a focus on the organization as a closed system, paying very little attention to the environment in which an organization existed.[27] In the 1970s a more open-systems view of educational administration led to an improved recognition of the importance of the school's exchange with its environment and an appreciation of education's organizational complexity.

THE CONVENTIONAL WISDOM

Each of these conceptual developments in the evolution of educational administration has left its legacy in the conventional wisdom of our field. This wisdom is a composite of expectations, a system of beliefs of what the principal should do.

The Principal as Instructional Leader

Foremost among these beliefs is the notion that the building principal should provide instructional leadership. A holdover from the evolution of the principalship out of a head teacher role, the demand for instructional leadership has been perhaps the most enduring element of the belief system surrounding the job. Over time, with changing theoretical perspectives, prescriptions for leadership behavior have changed from the authoritarian model, including time-motion studies of teacher efficiency, to the democratic model, characterized by the sentiment that the relationship with teachers is that of a senior colleague and counselor, "rather than an 'overseer' or boss."[28] Simultaneously, the how-to literature has delineated the leadership role as (a) a combination of both authoritarian and democratic management styles;[29] (b) the development of effective managerial skills in organizing, planning, and evaluating the school's instructional program;[30] and, (c) the ability to take a dynamic, systems view of organizational relationships between constituent groups "instead of the narrow view from inside the organization."[31]

Throughout this evolution of ideas on leadership, a central, long-surviving tenet of the instructional leadership role is that the principal should devote by far the largest portion of the day to direct supervision of instruction and to staff development. As much as three-quarters of the principal's time should be given to the improvement of instruction.[32] In allocating time, classroom observation and teacher evaluation are at the heart of the instructional leadership role. The conventional wisdom stipulates that building principals should assist each teacher in identifying learning goals, selecting activities, and assessing results. Observations should culminate in an end-of-year evaluation conference with each teacher to identify strengths and weaknesses, and "to encourage professional growth and improved competency."[33] Additionally, principals should provide help throughout the year to each teacher in individualizing instruction, selecting curricular materials, developing tests, checklists, and other evaluation instruments, identifying the best way to communicate with parents, and sharpening strategies for maintaining pupil control.

The Principal as Decision Maker

A second convention is that the building principal should be education's foremost decision maker, problem solver, and agent of change at the school site. With roots in the scientific efficiency movement, the decision making expectation reached full flower in the search for interdisciplinary understandings in educational administration. The decision making model could be adapted nicely to assumptions of organizational rationality and hierarchical, downward-flowing authority. Principals should clarify problems, identify possible solutions, choose the best from the alternatives available, plan and implement this solution, and evaluate its effectiveness. As the human relations aspect of decision making developed, an attractive view of administration as "a social process" became popular. It was recognized that decision making and problem solving must attend to both the personal, individual dimensions of behavior and the institutional, role expectation dimensions.[34] The effective decision maker should blend institution and individual into a productive, symbiotic harmony, and should know how to balance organizational goal attainment with employee job satisfaction.[35]

Later, with the development of the systems approach in the 1960s and 1970s, the decision making vocabulary was extended through the use of such terms as input-output analysis, feedback, management information systems (MIS), program evaluation and review technique (PERT), and management by objectives (MBO). Decision theory strategies of increasing sophistication were developed. A popular contribution was Lipham and Hoeh's "Model of the decision making process" in *The Principalship: Foundations and Functions.* (See Figure 1.1.)

In their Lipham model, the first step in the decision making process is the development of an awareness of a "problem state," perhaps a sense of uneasiness between what is and what should be. The principal formulates and weighs competing decision alternatives, as filtered through the available information as well as through societal and organizational values. The decision maker's own values, intellectual ability, training, prior experience, and creativity all provide an additional "perceptual screen" that affects the decision. Each competing alternative is weighed for its probable consequences, particularly regarding those groups most affected, and for its degree

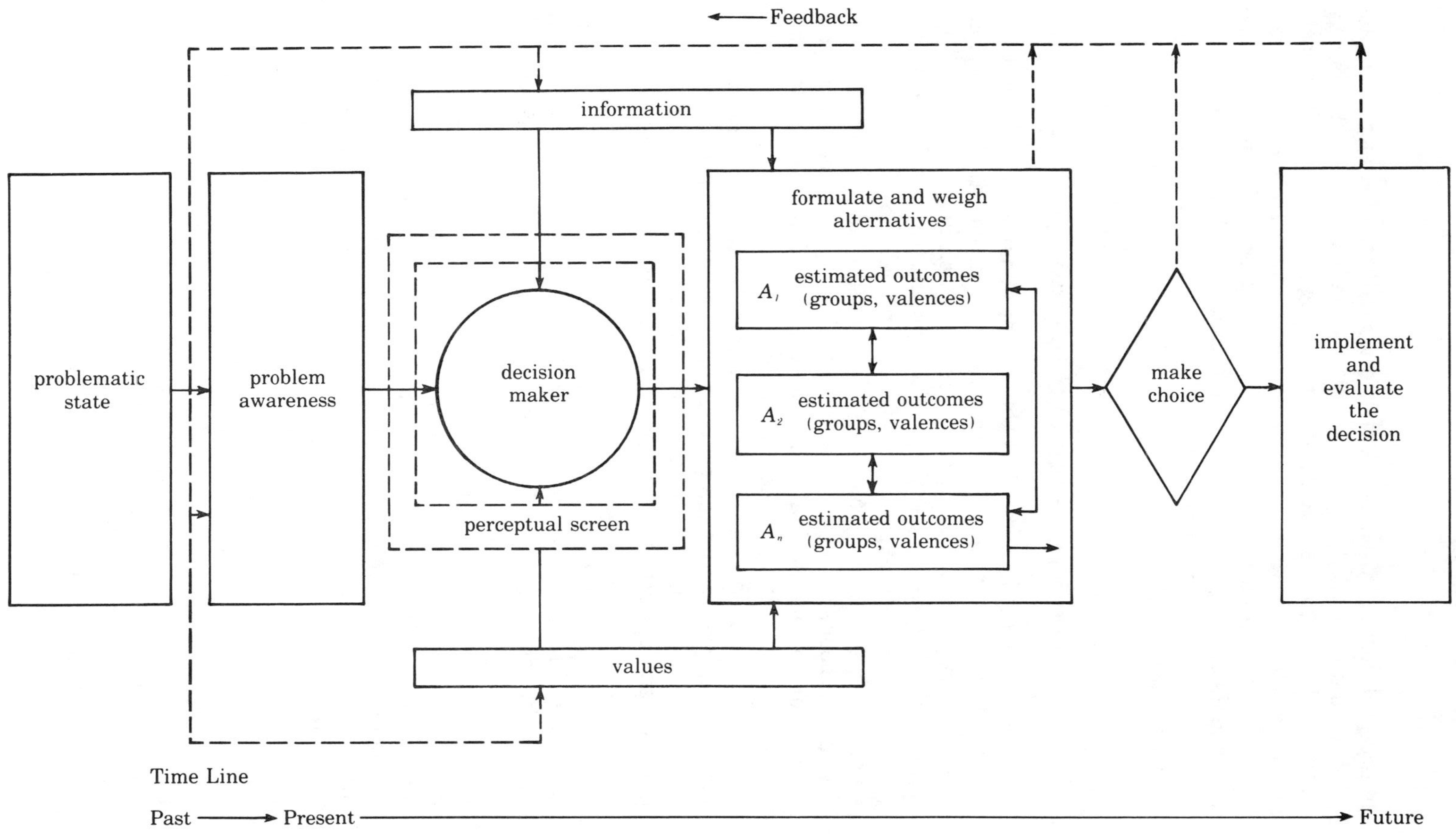

Figure 1.1 Model of the decision-making process (Source: Reprinted with permission from James M. Lipham, "Making Effective Decisions," in Jack A. Culbertson, Curtis Henson, and Ruel Morrison, eds., *Performance Objectives for School Principals* Berkeley, California: McCutchan, 1974. © 1974 by McCutchan Publishing Corp., all rights reserved.)

of acceptability or "valence." A choice is made, the decision is implemented and evaluated, and the results are fed back to the beginning of the decision process.[36] Although it is recognized that such a neatly patterned cycle of managerial action seldom works so well in practice, since there are almost always unintended consequences of action, the proponents of decision theory point out that with skill and experience such models of administrative behavior can significantly improve managerial performance.[37]

The Principal as Site Manager

A third element of the conventional wisdom is that the principal is the key individual in school management. The principal continues to perform the clerical role for which he or she was originally released from teaching. Although instructional leadership remains the central expectation of the principalship, the scope of the school-site management role has grown substantially over the years. Recent textbooks on the principalship indicate the principal's responsibility for: (a) monitoring school facilities and finances; (b) developing and overseeing the school's communication system of bulletins, briefings, records, and meetings; (c) recruiting, selecting, and assigning staff; (d) overseeing the provision of ancillary school services; (e) scheduling school programs, and assigning or grouping pupils; (f) organizing student activities in sports, drama and music; and (g) overseeing student discipline.[38]

With the increasing number of services provided by local schools, the management of the school site is now a complex undertaking. In addition to pupil instruction, the school now oversees such ancillary services as the nutrition, physical health, psychological well-being, and transportation of its youngsters. Adding to the complexity are programs for the handicapped, bilingual, gifted, and programs on sex education and remedial reading. Similarly, school management is now surrounded by regulations or contractual constraints affecting sexual equality, class size limitations, the placement and disciplinary treatment of pupils, and the dismissal of teachers.

The expectation over the years has been that the building principal, as manager, is the person in control. Although leavened by the human relations perspective into the frequent suggestion that the principal should carefully construct a school-site management team, the conventional wisdom also recognizes that the burden of responsibility for the school rests with the principal, the person formally delegated by board of education and superintendent with the care of the local school site.

The burden of the school principalship often reveals the tension between two historically determined roles. Blumberg and Greenfield suggest that the twin demands of instructional leadership and managerial control are in some ways mutually dysfunctional, and their simultaneous pressures pose a dilemma for the principal as to what balance to strike between change and stability. While the principal may wish to be innovative and shake things up, he or she is also expected to maintain good management by avoiding conflict and engendering an ordered school environment.[39]

The Principal as Mediator

A fairly recent addition to the conventional wisdom is the notion that the principal is a prime mediator between education's many constituencies. For some time, school administrators maintained a four-walls-of-the-school philosophy—a belief that the school should be effectively walled off from outside interference and that the professional educator should stay well above the politics of the surrounding community. With the turbulence of the 1960s and changing conceptual requirements of the open-systems perspective, the gatekeeper model of the principalship has changed into the notion that the principal should lead the school into close cooperation with its various constituencies. Recent textbooks on the principalship urge the building administrator to establish a carefully planned program of school-community relations through such efforts as needs assessments, community advisory councils, meaningful rather than pro forma student government arrangements, communications vehicles such as newsletters and parent nights, and extensive outreach efforts through adult education and shared-time programs.[40] Principals are urged today to establish enlightened school-community relations and negotiate and compromise with neighborhood groups.[41]

Dale Mann has proposed a principal's handbook to "help building principals to create, support and utilize neighborhood involvement in school decision making." Principals are urged to share control and respond to the unique combination of needs, goals, and resources of their immediate environments. Shared control can produce help from the community and can further the achievement of the school's goals. Principals should not fear conflict, for the working out of differences between factions and blocs can strengthen the school. Nor should principals fear parental intrusions upon the guarded province of the educational expert, the school curriculum, because the lay community can express preferences and make suggestions without taking over technical and professional domains of responsibility.[42]

The Principal as Creator of a Learning Environment

The most recent addition to the conventional wisdom is the notion that the principal can somehow establish an ethos or climate for learning in the school that will facilitate opportunities for student progress.[43] At present only a developing hypothesis, this concept is a derivative of the contingency or situational approach to administration. However, little attention has so far been given in the how-to literature to strategies the principal might employ to generate an organizational ambiance of learning success. As an outgrowth of research into the implementation of change in schools, Gersten and Carnine have suggested that careful administrative attention to school support functions can be a key element in school improvement. Among these may be the provision of emotional support to teachers, the communication of a managerial commitment to school success, and the creative use of the organizational incentive system to encourage top performance.[44] Other than these tentative probes, there is little research on the ethos/climate question.

* * * * *

In summary, the conventional wisdom drawn from sixty years of scholarship on the role of the principal yields the following: The principal is the instructional leader of the teaching-learning community inside the school building and conducts this function through the direct supervision of instruction and the development and training of the teaching faculty. The principal is expected to be the central decision maker of the school site, with emphasis upon planning, problem solving, and the fostering of innovation. The principal, further, is to be the authoritative manager of an increasingly complex educational enterprise, with a variety of noneducational sectors of responsibility included in the jurisdiction. The principal must become the key, site-level mediator between the school and its surrounding publics in the neighborhood and in the wider community. Finally, the principal is expected to create that intangible something, that ambiance of mind and spirit which encourages effective teaching and learning.

CONVENTIONAL WISDOM AND THE REAL WORLD

The conventional wisdom describes a shared understanding of what the school principal should do. But what is the job really like? How do building administrators use their time, day by day, minute by minute? What is education's middle manager actually doing?

Surprisingly, until recently there has been little attention given to this question. It is reasonable to assume that in view of its importance, the school principalship would be the most thoroughly investigated and best understood administrative position in education. Although the literature on the principal is voluminous, it tends to be normative and prescriptive rather than descriptive. The conventional wisdom has developed without a clear understanding of what school principals do during their working day.

How good is the match between conceptual framework and professional experience? Do principals experience on the job what scholars have been describing for the last several decades? Is the principal really the instructional leader of a teaching faculty, or is he doing something else most of the time? If so, what? How, if at all, does it connect with the educational program? Are principals as actively engaged in school-community rapport as the textbooks sermonize? If not, why not? What are the barriers to effective liaison with external agencies and groups and what are the political and emotional resistances among principals themselves which discourage these bridge-building initiatives? Principals usually have an idealized notion of their job. But why aren't they performing it that way? What compromises do they make between the ideal and the real, between what should, and what actually does, occupy their attention? What is lost and gained by these compromises? Is the ultimate client, the student, worse or better off because of it?

The profession needs answers to these questions. In this textbook, we intend to initiate the discussion leading to these answers. We wish to turn the conventional wisdom on its head, to approach the training of principals by starting with description before proceeding to prescription.

THINGS TO DO AND THINK ABOUT

1. In reviewing the chronological development of the study of school administration, this chapter details four epochs, each with its own particular approach. Each of these approaches is still valid, at least to a degree. Which characteristics of today's schools are best understood by each of the approaches? Which approach helps the most in understanding how today's schools are run?

2. The open-systems perspective is currently the most popular among scholars and researchers in school administration. Do you think this perspec-

tive will be replaced by a fifth theory? If so, what will such a theory look like?

3. Half a century of research has yielded a conventional wisdom of what a principal is: instructional leader, decision maker, site-manager, mediator, environment-creator. Which of these roles do you consider most important? Are there conflicts between them? Are there other roles of the principal that everybody takes for granted? What are these roles, and to what extent do today's principals perform them?
4. A notion gaining currency is that the principal is a creator of the learning environment, the architect of a mood or ambiance for maximum teaching and learning. In your judgment, what activities should be studied to determine the presence or absence of this function? What specific behaviors of principals have a measurable impact on school climate?

NOTES

1. P. R. Pierce, "The Origin and Development of the Public School Principalship," Unpublished Ph.D. dissertation, the University of Chicago, 1934.
2. Ibid. p. 214.
3. Joseph M. Cronin, *The Control of Urban Schools* (New York: The Free Press, 1973), pp. 52–57.
4. Hollis A. Moore, Jr., "The Ferment in School Administration," in Daniel E. Griffiths, ed., *Behavioral Science and Educational Administration,* Sixty-third Yearbook of the National Society for the Study of Education (NSSE), Part 2 (Chicago: University of Chicago Press, 1964), p. 12.
5. Roald F. Campbell, "The Professorship in Educational Administration—A Personal View," *Educational Administration Quarterly* 17, no. 1 (Winter 1981), p. 1–24. See also Wayne K. Hoy, "Recent Developments in Theory and Research in Educational Administration," *Educational Administration Quarterly,* Vol. 18, No. 3 (Summer 1982), pp. 1–11.
6. Raymond Callahan, *Education and the Cult of Efficiency* (Chicago: The University of Chicago Press, 1962); also, Cronin, op. cit. pp. 90–122.
7. Roald F. Campbell, "A History of Administrative Thought," *Administrator's Notebook* 26, no. 4 (1977–78), pp. 1–2.
8. Callahan, op. cit.
9. Ibid. p. 67.
10. Bertram M. Gross, "The Scientific Approach to Administration," in Daniel E. Griffiths, ed., *Behavioral Science and Educational Administration,* Sixty-third Yearbook of the National Society for the Study of Education (NSSE), Part 2 (Chicago: University of Chicago Press, 1964), pp. 33–72.

11. Jacob W. Getzels, James M. Lipham, and Roald F. Campbell, *Educational Administration as a Social Process: Theory, Research, Practice* (New York: Harper and Row, 1968), p. 29.
12. Campbell, "A History of Administrative Thought," *Administrator's Notebook* 26, no. 4 (1977–78), p. 2.
13. Elton Mayo, *The Human Problems of an Industrial Civilization* (Boston: Graduate School of Business Administration, Harvard University, 1946).
14. Getzels, Lipham, and Campbell, op. cit. pp. 30–39.
15. Charles L. Wood, Everett W. Nicholson, and Dale G. Findley, *The Secondary School Principal: Manager and Supervisor* (Boston: Allyn and Bacon, Inc., 1979), p. 35.
16. Campbell, "The Professorship in Educational Administration", p. 8; also, Caroll L. Shartle, *Executive Performance and Leadership* (Englewood Cliffs, N.J.: Prentice-Hall Inc., 1956).
17. John K. Hemphill and Alvin E. Coons, *Leader Behavior Description* (Columbus: Ohio State University, 1950); also, Andrew W. Halpin, *Theory and Research in Administration* (New York: Macmillan, 1966).
18. Chester I. Barnard, *The Functions of the Executive* (Cambridge: Harvard University Press, 1938).
19. Robert K. Merton, "Bureaucratic Structure and Personality," in Robert K. Merton, et al, *Reader in Bureaucracy* (New York: The Free Press, 1952), pp. 361–371.
20. Campbell, "A History of Administrative Thought", p. 3.
21. Herbert A. Simon, *Administrative Behavior* (New York: MacMillan, 1947).
22. Campbell, "The Professorship", p. 14.
23. Karl E. Weick, "Educational Organizations as Loosely Coupled Systems," *Administrative Science Quarterly,* 21, no. 1 (March 1976), pp. 1–19; also, James G. March and Johan P. Olsen, *Ambiguity and Choice in Organizations* (Bergen, Norway: Universitetsforlaget, 1976); and P. R. Lawrence and J. W. Lorsch, *Organization and Environment* (Homewood, Ill.: Richard D. Irwin, 1961).
24. E. Mark Hanson, *Educational Administration and Organizational Behavior* (Boston: Allyn and Bacon, Inc., 1979); also Thomas J. Sergiovanni, Martin Burlingame, Fred D. Coombs, and Paul W. Thurston, *Educational Governance and Administration* (Englewood Cliffs, N.J.: Prentice-Hall, Inc., 1980).
25. Hanson, *Educational Administration and Organizational Behavior*, pp. 163–164.
26. Ibid. p. 164.
27. Campbell, "A History of Administrative Thought", p. 3.

28. Wood, Nicholson, and Findley, op. cit. p. 35.

29. James M. Lipham and James A. Hoeh, Jr., *The Principalship: Foundations and Functions* (New York: Harper & Row, 1974), pp. 188–199.

30. Larry W. Hughes and Gerald C. Ubben, *The Elementary Principal's Handbook: A Guide to Effective Action* (Boston: Allyn and Bacon, Inc., 1978).

31. Lipham and Hoeh, Jr., op. cit. p. 200.

32. J. Lloyd Trump, *A School for Everyone* (Reston, Virginia: National Association of Secondary School Principals, 1977), pp. 66–71.

33. Hughes and Ubben, op. cit. p. 171.

34. Jacob W. Getzels and Egon C. Guba, "Social Behavior and the Administrative Process," *School Review* (Winter 1957).

35. Lipham and Hoeh, Jr. op. cit. pp. 195–199.

36. Ibid. pp. 155–161.

37. Ibid. p. 174.

38. See, for example, Hughes and Ubben, *The Elementary Principal's Handbook;* also, Wood, Nicholson, and Findley, *The Secondary School Principal.*

39. Arthur Blumberg and William Greenfield, *The Effective Principal: Perspectives on School Leadership* (Boston: Allyn and Bacon, Inc., 1980), p. 21.

40. William H. Roe and Thelbert L. Drake, *The Principalship* (New York: MacMillan Publishing Co., Inc., 1980), pp. 32–52; also, Lipham and Hoeh, Jr., *The Principalship: Foundations and Functions,* pp. 320–347.

41. Hughes and Ubben, op. cit. pp. 282–294.

42. Dale Mann, *The Politics of Administrative Representation* (Lexington, Mass.: D. C. Heath and Co., 1976), pp. 129–159.

43. Wilbur Brookover et al., *School Social Systems and Student Achievement: Schools Can Make a Difference* (New York: Praeger, 1979); also Ronald Edmonds, "Effective Schools for the Urban Poor," *Educational Leadership* 37 (October 1979), pp. 15–24.

44. Russel Gersten and Douglas Carnine, "Administrative and Supervisory Support Functions for the Implementation of Effective Educational Programs for Low Income Students," *Eugene, Oregon: Center for Educational Policy and Management, College of Education, University of Oregon, September, 1981).*

2

A New Look at the Art

As noted in Chapter 1, the study of school administration in general, and of the principalship in particular, have evolved through several stages. The pioneers, the scientific management advocates, eventually yielded to the human relations partisans, who in turn ceded the field to the interdisciplinary theorists; these have recently seen their approach displaced by the open-systems people. At each passage from one strategy to the next, we detect a growing dissatisfaction of the new advocates with the older view. The "new wave" activists assess the older view as unsatisfactory, out of date, or merely unable to explain newly identified features of managerial activity. Inevitably, the new wavers advance the claim that their approach, unlike all its predecessors, is able to reveal a wider spectrum of phenomena and to thus generate a more sophisticated analysis of administrative performance.

LIFE AMONG THE NATIVES

As in other social sciences, no strategy or theory is ever completely replaced; each supplanted theory remains relevant. With each new strategy of inquiry, something has been added but nothing has been taken away. The supplanted view still sheds some light, even though the new view sheds still more. The discipline needs all four of the foregoing strategies to guide professional understanding of the school administrator's role. In this sense, all four strategic approaches are still true. They provide necessary, accurate and complementary perspectives on educational management.

Why, then, is yet another book on the school principalship needed? We do not offer a fifth summarizing strategy designed to bring the research to a fitting climax. On the contrary, what we offer is not a new theory at all, but rather a refocusing on the subject. We need to change the lenses on our cameras. We need to experience the administrator's world from a different vantage point, not merely add new phenomena to the catalogue so far yielded by the four theories. We need to look at everything all over again from the viewpoint of the lead character—the principal at work in the daily routine of running a school.

An analogy drawn from anthropology may be instructive. During the nineteenth century, American scholars and journalists became interested in other people around the globe. They traveled to foreign countries and wrote accounts of local manners and customs. Working with documentary materials of alien cultures, they were able to piece together a picture of life as it is lived in other lands.

Something was missing. Although these accounts bore some resemblance to actual fact, they were written, necessarily, from the perspective of the outsider. The researchers were unable to capture the ambiance of the foreign culture as it is actually lived, from breakfast to bedtime, day after day, by the inhabitants. Accordingly, these accounts were only marginally useful in understanding an alien culture.

During the early years of the twentieth century, systematic field work in anthropology began to change this. The study of culture, alien or otherwise, came to be dominated by direct immersion in the target society—what might be called the "Margaret Mead School" of social science. Although not the originator of the method, Dr. Mead became one of its most skilled and articulate practitioners. Her prescription was simple: Live among the natives.

Many anthropologists traveled to remote enclaves of isolated peoples and joined the culture as regular members. They lived their hosts' lives, shared their experiences, felt their sorrows, exulted in their triumphs, and participated as fully as they could in the life of the people. When the extended visit ended, they came home and put together a vivid, first-person account of the life lived in that place.

In trying to better understand the principal's world, we have adapted this strategy to institutional education in the United States. True to the anthropologist's dictum, we have "lived among the natives" in American schools. We have brought back this account of what life is like in that remote enclave, the principal's office.

In developing the account that follows, we intended a fresh and unorthodox look at what the theories have been trying to describe for the last sixty years. We were eager to see if the textbook accounts of a principal's life matched up with "tribal reality." We wanted to find out whether the routines described were as neat and orderly as the literature claimed them to be, whether the problems faced were as solvable as the scholars intimated.

Accordingly, we went into the schools with no hypotheses, no agenda of what would count as evidence for a theory's legitimacy. We went in with as open an attitude as any professional can bring to the study of something in which he or she is passionately interested. *Curiosity* perhaps best describes our collective state of mind as we began the data-gathering which culminated in this book. We were curious about what life was like there, how people reacted to one another, and how they translated their perceptions of their jobs into actual behavior. We were interested in what they understood their purposes to be, and how those purposes were revealed in their conduct.

All four of us have taught university courses for school administrators. In addition to a grounding in theory, these courses provided the study of nuts and bolts tracts authored by practitioners in the business. We occasionally invited the practitioners themselves, in order to provide our students, and ourselves, with eyewitness versions of "life in the trenches." Invariably, these personalized accounts vivified the course syllabus, stirred lively discussion, and illuminated the emotional intensity of the administrator's world.

When we got into the schools ourselves, we began to comprehend the full complexity of the administrator's life; we began to assess more accurately the large number of different subject matters with which the school principal must deal during the typical work day. In retrospect, we realize that the picture of school administration which we had the privilege of witnessing bears only indirect resemblance to the sketch that had been provided by half a century of scholarship on school management. What we offer is a new kind of data on a well studied occupation. We invite you to come into the field and share and evaluate the insights we have gained.

It should be added that we went into the schools with a neutral mind regarding the competence of the people we were studying. All understood that we were not present to decide who was doing a good job and who was not. We went to observe and record, to witness what happened and record it as objectively as we could. When one becomes involved in a situation, even as a detached observer, it is possible to take on some of the perceptions and attitudes of the participants, and "go native" to some degree. No one can claim to be a completely value-free observer. Our task, as we saw it, was to blend in without being taken in. Given these caveats, we acknowledge that ours can be considered a sympathetic account of administrators on the job. We also recognize that the following observations inevitably raise questions about how principals should do their jobs; that is the underlying purpose of any text on the subject. But the point we wish to make at the outset is that the primordial data gathering was designedly free of a priori judgments about what was good or bad about the administrative behavior unfolding before our eyes. We tried to make sense of what was going on, and then we wrote it up in descriptive form as a literal account of day-to-day activity.

Our target sample consisted of twenty-six men and women serving as principals of a like number of elementary and secondary schools in the Chicago Public School System. These schools were selected to represent a wide spectrum of educational conditions: size of enrollment, mobility of student body, racial mix of students and faculty, socio-economic status of attendance area, sex and race and years of incumbency of principal. These twenty-six principals were accompanied on their administrative rounds for up to twelve days each. In all, more than 300 hours of observation were logged by the research team.

Since the data were gathered from an urban sample, we were mindful of the possible bias of our findings because of a presumed unrepresentativeness of the schools we chose to study. Accordingly, we shared our findings with several national audiences. These included the American Educational Research Association; the American Educational Studies Association; the Urban Superintendents Network (a national group); the American Association of School Administrators; the National Association of Elementary School Principals; the Illinois Association of School Administrators; the Florida Council on Educational Management; the Public Education Association (New York City); the Division of Educational Policy and Management of the University of Oregon; and the staff of the National Institute of Education.

In each of these contacts, either in writing or in personal presentations, we received unsolicited acknowledgements of the generalizability of our findings. Audiences nodded in agreement as we detailed the behavior patterns of principals. At every public presentation of our findings, we concluded our remarks with a question: Do you recognize this pattern of behavior? Do principals in your part of the country exhibit these modes of conduct? Without exception, our listeners answered *yes;* some supplied vivid illustrations of the behaviors we had reported. Since our listeners typically came from all sections of the country, from rural and suburban as well as urban school districts, we concluded that the story we tell in this book is representative of principaling as it is practiced throughout the country.

THE NEED FOR THIS BOOK

The fundamental research leading to this book has differed from previous approaches and is intended to provide fresh data on an already well examined subject. The fresh data have a dual purpose:

On the one hand, the data reveal that all of the previous theories may, in one way or another, continue to illuminate the field. There *is* scientific management occurring when the principal tries to rationalize the work day by attempting to control the events in his or her personal schedule; there *are* human relations concepts at work when the principal interacts with hundreds of individuals in a day; there *is* an interdisciplinary reliance on social science concepts when the principal orchestrates the psychological and social vectors inside the school building; there *is* an open-systems dimension operating when the principal is politicized into relationships with community leaders, politicians, policemen and social workers. Thus, what the four theories have already accounted for through a conceptual approach to the study of school management, the on-site visitor can verify by direct observation through an experiential approach. This in turn means that all four theories continue to enjoy an explanatory function which is, after all, the purpose of any theory.

But the other purpose seems to us far more important than examining the soundness of extant theories. This purpose is to reveal phenomena not yet accounted for by the four theories. The reality-immersion strategy is a way of opening up spheres of conduct which have eluded theoretical explanation. There is a good deal of principaling behavior left over after all the theories have had their say. What are we to make of this residue? Especially, what are we to make of the fact that this residual body of behavior is larger than previously thought and, contrary to the conventional wisdom, appears to dominate the principal's behavior?

By presenting new facts about practice, this volume offers new insights into theory. The book is intended to bring both the theorist and the practitioner into a common understanding of what actually happens in administrative life. Once this understanding is shared, the gap between what is and what ought to be will be narrowed. Principaling is not just offering suggestions and getting compliance, bearing good news and presenting awards. There is much that the conventional textbooks do not talk about—confrontation, manipulation, guile, political flattery, dissembling, genteel retaliation, sometimes outright deception. Our experience indicates that much of this conduct is well meaning and of ultimate benefit to the student. But we also know that conventional theories of administration have been silent on this kind of behavior. The factual accounts presented in this book will help us blaze a trail to the kind of administration where this kind of conduct becomes unnecessary.

There is another, perhaps more pragmatic, value of the reality-immersion version provided here. Few books on the principalship have presented an unretouched portrait of the job, warts and all. This book does that. Viewed in this light, it can be a more useful screening instrument than earlier publications, offering the reader a more sanguine version of administrative life, which will help him or her make a career decision. While reading this book, you may ask yourself "Do I really want to get into this line of work? Are the stresses and satisfactions described here compatible with what I want to become as a person?"

Some features of this book will take a little getting used to. And if the book causes enthusiasm for administrative service to flag, it should be said that the preponderant response of our early readers—those who reviewed the manuscript on its way to publication—has been bold and positive. Having lived through this unexpurgated, unedited, unsanitized view of the principal at work, they continue to view an administrative career as a live option, with personal challenge written all over it.

DISCRETIONARY DECISION MAKING

To make the most of our time in the schools and to concentrate our attention on the most lucrative, data-rich phenomena, we decided to focus our gaze on discretionary principaling behavior. Administrators in any organization function partly as transmission boxes; they transmit information from higher echelons to the school, and, in reverse, transmit information from the school to higher authorities. For this phase of their work, principals forward written or oral instructions to their faculties and student bodies, mimeograph newsletters on the regulations of the board of education, and post on the bulletin board the latest guidelines on established policy. They collect information from teachers, students, and parents, organize this information, fill out forms, prepare reports, and generally shuffle paper in both directions, up and down. But since performance in this area is, by definition, pro forma, it is not susceptible to the school manager's discretionary judgment.

Accordingly, we concentrated our attention on *everything else* a principal does: the spheres of activity which are not routine or merely clerical, not dictated by strict rules, mandatory procedures, or the severe, even if unstated, expectations of immediate superiors. We wanted not to deny the existence of pro forma behavior but to assume it. We wished to fix our attention instead on those spheres of managerial conduct to which each principal brings a discretionary attitude and an idiosyncratic flair including the determination as to when a putatively strict rule can be bent or ignored.

Although in our data-gathering we observed and reported both pro forma and discretionary conduct, we oriented ourselves to the latter for the following reasons:

First, we wanted to investigate the notion, which has gained some currency in administration literature, that the school principal has no power. According to this view, the principal is closed in at the lower fringes of the bureaucracy and, because of low status in the managerial apparatus, is unable to act and, more important, unable to be creative and innovative in the operation of a school. Many writers have come to view principals as highly paid clerks, whose function is to transmit messages back and forth between the headquarters staff and the school's personnel. Since our investigation would take us directly into the schools, we were in an ideal position to either verify this conception or understand why it is wrong.

Second, focusing on discretionary behavior would illuminate a relatively unstudied phenomenon: the degree to which a building principal operates in an organizational context, within the larger social system in which he or she performs the managerial role. The exercise of discretion raises the obvious questions as to where discretionary behavior comes from, what its motivations are, and how it supplies the ingredient that is missing, i.e., a rule, a policy, a guideline or precedent. Discretionary behavior is a form of free action; but what is it free *of*? We believed that an examination of this question would give us new insights into the nature of school organizations.

Third, a focus on discretionary conduct provides an entree to the free-flowing dynamic of human interaction. It provides a working glimpse of the traffic between individuals concerning their affective response to what is a preponderantly cognitive enterprise—formal schooling. Much of administrative theory has dwelt on the removal of feeling from managerial performance, as if there were some implied Weberian obligation to eliminate all purely personal, irrational and emotional elements from administrative calculations. A close tracking of discretionary conduct, we anticipated, would reveal the degree to which personal considerations—animus, warmth, delight, exasperation—figure in a principal's performance.

Finally, in planning our observations, we were mindful of the growing interest in principal *effect,* that is, the degree to which the overt behavior of the principal makes a difference in the learning achievement of students. In decades of research, scholars have examined all sorts of variables for their possible linkage to learning—class size, homogeneous grouping, teacher training and experience, home background of classmates. Is it possible that the ambiance of the school, beyond these quantifiable elements and for which the principal is chiefly responsible, has more to do with student achievement than any other single feature of a school's environment? Although not employing any explicit measures for tracking this possibility, we did come to appreciate in a general way the influence that the principal's behavior has on the total learning community. Our experience tells us that this question of principal effect is ripe for investigation, and that discretionary behavior is the place to start.

THINGS TO DO AND THINK ABOUT

1. As anthropologists have discovered, there are serious shortcomings to the research strategy of "living among the natives." What do you think these shortcomings might be? Consult a professional anthropologist in your university to see if he or she agrees with you.
2. We make a distinction in this chapter between pro forma and discretionary behavior on the part of the principal. Give three examples of each. Consider your own job. How much of what you do is pro forma and how much discretionary? Is a principal's job more or less discretionary than yours?
3. As we went into the schools to gather our data on the work activities of principals, we kept an open mind about what was important to look for and what was good or bad about managerial behavior. Would it have been better to make our observations more structured, with some guidelines and specifications worked out in advance? If so, what would such a list sound like?

3

The Principal at Work

The research method used to gather material on the principal's work activities is formally known as ethnography, a variation on the anthropologist's field-based strategy of living with the subjects. Ethnographic techniques require direct on-site observation; the researcher must be present at all times. Each of the principals studied was accompanied by one member of the research team and directly observed on the job for up to twelve working days, not necessarily sequential, over the course of three school years. Typically, the principal's work day begins around 7:45 A.M. and continues until 4:00 or 5:00 P.M. The principal was also followed into the late afternoon and evening if he or she were engaged in professional responsibilities related to the principalship. For work taken home for study over evenings and weekends the researcher relied on reports the following morning.

A NOTE ON PROCEDURE

On the job during the regular work hours, the researcher was privy to all conversations and communications between the principal and those with whom he or she interacted, either face to face or over the telephone. The only exception to this general procedure were those contacts of such a personal or sensitive nature that the researcher's presence would have constituted an unacceptable disturbance. In such cases, and at the request of the principal, the researcher agreed to be absent from the interaction. Throughout the three years of observation, such preemptions of the data gathering schedule represented less than one percent of the total observation time.

During each day's observation, the researcher kept detailed, minute-by-minute notes on the principal's activities—the individuals involved, the nature of the interactions, and the linkage of one interaction with the next to get a feel for the flow of managerial decision making. From these field notes, the researcher then prepared a written log of the principal's work day.

These logs were then differentiated further into separate "events," each event being defined as an interaction or a piece of business which for analytical purposes could be separated from the surrounding activity. Each event, of whatever duration (from five seconds to two hours) was then assigned a number, a typical work day comprising between 50 and 200 separate events. The numbered events were then coded and examined from a number of different standpoints:

1. With whom was the principal interacting (teacher, student, assistant principal, school nurse, etc.)?
2. Which party initiated the interaction?
3. What medium of communication was employed in the interaction (verbal face to face, written word, telephone, etc.)?
4. Where in the building or elsewhere did the interaction take place?
5. What was the duration, in minutes, of the interaction?
6. What was the subject matter of the event?

With these descriptive characteristics available for each event, the research team then developed summations and collations of the seemingly disparate features of managerial activity. From these summations, it was possible to describe in detail the generic workflow of the principal's behavior.

THE ELEMENTARY PRINCIPAL

Interaction Pairings

Most of a principal's work day consists of interacting with other people. In total, our elementary principals spent 83 percent of their work time in this activity. Table 3.1 presents the distribution of these contacts, together with the range of the principals observed.

As a group, our subjects spent more time interacting with students than with any other role category. Most of this time was spent supervising student movement or conferring with students who had caused a disturbance in class or on the playground. Principals spending the greatest percentage of time with students were those who handled all the routine disciplinary cases themselves rather than referring them to an assistant (35 percent), had a special tutoring project with students that lasted nearly an hour each day (30 percent), or were fully accessible to students, with no clerk or receptionist buffering the principal's office from the corridor (23 percent). One principal had little contact with students, apparently due to personal preference. This subject knew few students by name and did not interact with students often (14 percent). The principals with the least amount of student contact had assistants who were freed from other duties in order to handle discipline referrals. Such principals typically interacted with students only in potentially explosive circumstances, in supervising student movement in hallways, or in giving awards and other recognition for special achievements (8 and 13 percent).

The second most frequent interaction concerned contacts with the researcher or with other outsiders, accounting for 19 percent of the principal's time. About one-fourth of these interactions were with individuals other than the researcher. Such conversations were often lengthy because outsiders require explanations of school policy, organization procedures and bureaucratic routines. Also, the principal usually handled these situations personally from start to finish to be sure they were properly taken care of. In one case, a newspaper photographer showed up after a school assembly had been completed. The principal, wanting pictures for the local papers, spent nearly half an hour calling students from their classes to the stage where, once again in costumes, they recreated their portions of the program for the photographer.

Percent of workday (0% – 25% – 50%); Range (low • — | Average — • high)

Principal interacted with:	Low	Average	High
Student	8	22	35
Researcher and other outsiders	17	19	29
Faculty member	10	18	24
Office clerk	6	8	10
Parent/guardian	2	7	12
Superintendent	1	7	10
Other principals	1	4	7
Assistant principal	0	4	4
Central office staff	1	4	11
Teacher aide	0	3	9
Counselor	0	2	8
Building engineer	0	1	3
Social worker/nurse	0	1	3
Community official/police	0	.5	2
Security personnel	0	.5	3

Table 3.1 Elementary Principals' Interaction Pairings

Contacts with the researcher, which took about 14 percent of the principal's time, were comprised of: (a) briefing sessions early in the observation in which the principal acquainted the newcomer with the site; (b) spontaneous commentaries by the principal explaining certain events; and (c) longer conversations in which the principal used the researcher as a friendly sounding board for inner reflections on the job. These interactions provided the researcher an opportunity to obtain the principal's point of view on previously observed events and to catch up on happenings at the school between observations. The relationship that developed between the researcher and subject during these conversations seemed to put the principals at ease and to open access to events that otherwise may have been guarded or excluded from observation.

In one case, however, the time spent conversing with the researcher almost got out of control. This principal was in the midst of a series of difficult professional confrontations (court cases, faculty-union grievance, parent pressure groups). This principal's day was dominated with meetings about this turmoil. Precisely because of the emotional intensity of these events, the principal enjoyed the opportunity to talk with the researcher, explaining what had happened, offering the principal's interpretation of events, and seeking from the researcher (a neutral observer) confirmation and reassurance. Because of the principal's excessive diversion of time to lengthy discussions with the researcher, we decided to remove these exchanges from the time usage analysis. It is important to realize, however, that conflict can escalate until it fills all of an administrator's time. Most principals are aware of this, and have a reserve of strategies that help them cool and diffuse conflict before it monopolizes all their time and energy.

The third most frequent interaction was with faculty members. These included attending faculty conferences, hearing teachers' requests, giving directions, seeking reactions, and holding friendly conversations. The principal with the most faculty interaction was a newly assigned principal who was receiving a large number of disciplinary referrals from teachers. This principal felt that the faculty was using the referrals to "test" her. She was defensive, carefully making a written record of each student conference. The principal with the least faculty interaction was responsible for two schools, thus being forced to divide time between two campuses. In this situation, faculty at both schools relayed requests and other information through administrative assistants at each school. The principal also issued regular lengthy bulletins to both faculties to communicate information that might otherwise have been communicated orally. Finally, the time pressure on this principal meant that informal conversation with staff had to be brief. In this office a brisk and businesslike atmosphere prevailed during individual conferences.

In most schools the headquarters area was physically divided into an outer office where the school clerk, secretaries and administrative aides sat, and a principal's inner office which could be opened to the outer activity or closed off for privacy. Most principals kept their doors to the outer office open and kept an ear cocked for eavesdropping on the routine business that the office handled. Typically, clerks: (a) took charge of the arrival and assignment of substitute teachers; (b) greeted parents and other visitors; (c) ministered to the needs of ill and injured students by examining them and calling their homes; (d) greeted disciplinary referrals, instructing them whom to see and where to wait; (e) gave information to faculty; and (f) made appointments to see the principal. The clerk frequently entered the principal's inner office to give an update on who had stopped by, when the visitor would return, who was waiting to see the principal, who had gone home, and who was going where and for how long. The percentage of time devoted to these exchanges with the clerk constituted 9 percent of the principal's time, spread in small units of a few minutes each throughout the day.

The amount of time principals spent with parents was almost completely devoted to conferences. Frequently these concerned student misbehavior. In a few cases they centered around complaints by parents about a teacher, other students, or a school regulation.

In relating to their superiors, some principals work with their superintendent directly, while others work with the administrative staff at central headquarters. One principal spent only 2 percent of the time interacting with the superintendent, but 11 percent with headquarters staff. Another spent 14 percent interacting with the superintendent, but only .3 percent with central staff.

Our data revealed that principals spent little time interacting with other principals. When they did, the purpose was to exchange information about how to respond to a directive, to learn about a meeting of the principal's professional organization, or to ask a favor (i.e., to acquire a few extra report cards or to borrow a curriculum guidebook). In one case, a principal's contact with fellow principals was increased through service on committees appointed by the superintendent (5 percent). Another principal seemed to enjoy calling his colleagues, passing the time of day and either seeking information or extending resources to his colleagues (7 percent).

Most principals had little contact with teacher aides. An exception was a black principal who made extensive use of a white community aide to establish relationships with white parents who had initially opposed the appointment of a black principal; these interactions comprised 9 percent of this principal's work time. Coordinately, this principal had very little direct contact with parents during the first year at the school (2 percent). A similar situation arose in a black neighborhood where a white principal used a black assistant principal as a conduit for communicating with predominantly black parents and students. This principal devoted more than 11 percent of the time to interactions with the assistant.

Initiatory Behavior

Table 3.2 provides a distribution of interaction time related to the initiator of the contact. Over two-thirds of the principal's interaction time was devoted to contacts that he or she initiated (70 percent). Five percent of the time was involved with interactions initiated by the principal's immediate supervisor. Staff in the central of-

Percent of workday (0%, 25%, 50%, 75%); Range (low – high), Average

Interchange activity initiated by:	Range low	Average	Range high
Principal	51	70	76
Superintendent	0	5	14
Faculty member	3	5	7
Parent/guardian	1	4	8
Researcher	1	4	13
Student	0	3	6
Office clerk	2	3	6
Central office staff	1	3	16
Other principals	0	1	4
Teacher aide	0	1	4
Assistant principal	0	1	2
Counselor	0	1	3
Building engineer	0	.5	2
Social worker/nurse	0	.5	2
Community official/police	0		0

Table 3.2 Elementary Principals' Initiatory Behavior

fice accounted for an additional 3 percent. Two principals exhibited relatively low initiatory behavior (51 and 56 percent). In both of these cases, their superiors at headquarters level were correspondingly more evident as initiators—one with the superintendent-initiating interaction time of 14 percent, the other with the headquarters personnel-initiating interaction time covering 16 percent.

Faculty members, it should be pointed out, initiate many interactions, but tend to do so while the principal is on the run—in the corridors or between regularly scheduled meetings. These exchanges are usually transacted in brief bursts and do not log in as a large percentage of interaction minutes. In contrast, parent-initiated exchanges often stem from a concern or complaint about the school or its personnel. As such, these can blow up into administrative crises if not quickly defused. Parent-initiated exchanges are infrequent, but when one does occur the principal will spend extended stretches of time to calm a parent and establish a cooperative rapport. Most principals know that merely giving a parent a chance to sound off is often adequate to neutralize hostility and disarm the angry mother or father.

Medium of Communication

Table 3.3 provides a time distribution of events employing different modes of communication. Verbal communication, either face to face or by telephone, represented the primary medium of contact (74 percent). For the most part, these interactions were brief. Two principals are representative: the average length of face to face contacts for one is 3 minutes 12 seconds and for the other 1 minute 54 seconds. Telephone interactions for these two principals averaged 2 minutes 54 seconds and 2 minutes 12 seconds respectively. For the entire sample, the average duration of a verbal interaction was under 4 minutes. A few, lengthy interactions of 15, 27 and 105 minutes were recorded, but they were rare.

Principals made little use of the public address system (.5 percent). When it was employed, principals either made general announcements (e.g., reminding teachers to send student council representatives to a meeting in 5 minutes) or called a specific student from class.

The time used by the principal for visual surveys of the school (14 percent) is represented by touring through the hallways, supervising the exits and entrances, cruising the playground, or observing teachers in classrooms.

The principals in the sample devoted about 12 percent of

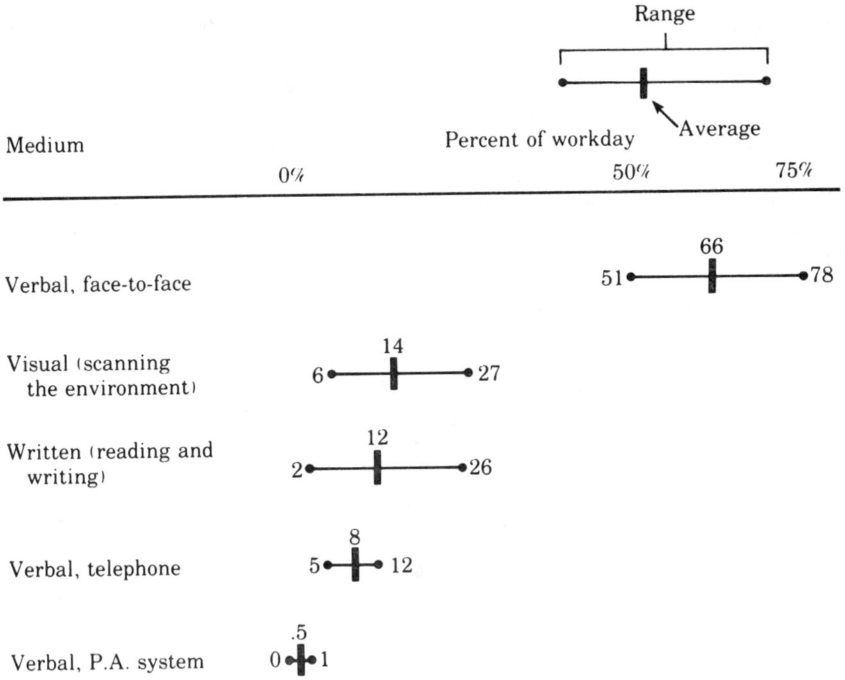

Table 3.3 Elementary Principals' Medium of Communication

their time to written work. This consisted of writing notes to teachers, reading reports from district and central headquarters, preparing brief notices for the teachers' bulletin board, and filling out the flood of official forms.

Considerable variation among principals is reflected in the range for each medium of communication category. The principal with the least face to face verbal contact (51 percent) is also the principal with the most visual communication (27 percent). This principal spent the entire lunch hour each day supervising students in the lunchroom. Most of the other principals devoted the lunch hour to informal face to face conversation with their colleagues, either having lunch with faculty in the lunchroom or eating in their offices where faculty members dropped by to see them.

Locus of Principaling Events

Table 3.4 provides a distribution of principaling time conducted in different parts of the school building or off school

Locus of activity	Percent of workday: Range (low)	Average	Range (high)
Inner office	30	48	56
Off school grounds	0	11	22
Corridor	4	11	17
Classroom	3	9	12
Outer office	2	8	15
Lunchroom	0	4	9
Auditorium	0	3	11
Faculty lounge, restroom, etc.	0	3	11
Other administrative offices	0	2	5
Playground	1	2	6
Gymnasium	0	.5	2
Library	0	.5	3

Table 3.4 Elementary Principals' Locus of Principaling

grounds. The elementary principal, like his or her secondary counterpart (see next section), spends less than half the work day in the principal's office (48 percent). When this total is added to time spent in the outer office and other administrative offices in the school, we see that the principal is in the headquarters area 58 percent of the work day.

The principal moves about the premises of the school building constantly, spending 11 percent of the time in the corridors, 9 percent in classrooms, and 13 percent at other sites outside the headquarters suite.

Eleven percent of elementary principaling time is spent off the school grounds. One principal who was away from the site a great deal (18 percent) seemed to seek out tasks that would require leaving the building. For example, this principal drove a car to the district office to hand-deliver reports and other documents, and before returning, purchased school supplies from a nearby discount stationery store. This principal also spent the most time supervising students in the hallways, lunchroom, playground and auditorium (where movies were shown), and the least time in the inner office (30 percent). This principal represented an extreme form of "away-from-the-desk" style of management, spending most of the work day supervising students, conducting disciplinary conferences at the "scene of the crime," or running school errands to distant points.

Principals did not always use the same location to accomplish the same tasks. During bad weather, for example, different supervision strategies were developed to control students during recess or lunch periods. One principal sent students to their classrooms for indoor recess, and patrolled the corridors peeking into classrooms. Another supervised indoor recess in the auditorium where students went to read books after eating. Yet another principal led students in a bingo game after the tables in the lunchroom had been cleared.

* * * * *

We can see in the tabular material a generic profile of the elementary principal at work. We turn now to a single principal's work day.

A Day in the Life . . .

When Mary Stewart arrived at Blaire Elementary School* at 8:15 A.M., the teachers were stopping by the office to sign in on their way to their classrooms. Stewart removed her coat and boots, hanging them in the closet outside her office. She put on a pair of medium-heeled shoes, explaining to the researcher, "The children like to see the principal a little dressed up." She joined her clerk in the outer office, where the two of them reviewed the list of teachers who would be absent and the steps to be taken to secure substitutes. One substitute, sent by the central office "Sub Center" had already arrived, and Stewart asked the clerk to give her the regular teacher's file containing a class seating chart and lesson plans.

Returning to her desk, Stewart's eyes drifted to the Continuous Progress Program packet and accompanying memorandum

*Note: All individuals and schools mentioned in this book have been given pseudonyms.

from the superintendent's staff which had arrived the previous afternoon. It was a reminder that the next reporting period was imminent and that all forms must be filed by Friday before the close of business. This meant that Stewart would be spending part of each of the next three days buttonholing the teachers to get their reports to her on each child, and then summarizing these figures on an all-school report. Stewart anticipated that she would have to divert some time from other managerial duties to get this paperwork finished on time.

As she reviewed her calendar, Stewart mentally prepared for a meeting with faculty union representatives who constituted the Professional Problems Committee. The union contract provided that this group, elected by the teachers, must meet regularly with the principal. At 8:30, Stewart left her office for the short walk to the school library, where the committee members were gathering. Stewart called the meeting to order about 8:35. High on her list of items was the matter of selecting textbooks for next year. But before this discussion got underway, the teachers wanted to relay questions to Stewart that individual teachers had raised with them: a problem in supervising the third floor washrooms, a question about how next year's faculty advisor to the eighth grade graduating class was to be selected, and a problem in getting supplies during a free period when the office clerk was often not available. After promising to work on these problems, Stewart spent most of the remaining time discussing plans with the teachers to host upcoming meetings with publishers' representatives. Together they also reviewed plans to form faculty textbook review committees, and procedures for selecting a common textbook for each grade level.

After the meeting, Stewart was approached by two teachers with individual questions. Miss La Pointe wanted to know whether Stewart would be available during eighth period. Stewart nodded and invited her to stop by the office at that time. Mr. Fields, the gym teacher, informed her that the basketball team did well at yesterday's game. They came close to beating Doyle, which was one of the best teams in the district. Stewart congratulated him, and asked how Marvin Goth was behaving in class lately. Fields said that Marvin still got "edgy," but in general was "doing a lot better."

As Stewart walked through the hallway back to her office, Mrs. Noyes motioned to her from inside the classroom. The students were already in their classrooms or moving quickly through the halls in the last moments before the class bell rang. Noyes told Stewart that she was scheduled to take the students on a field trip this morning, but that one of the parent volunteers had called at the last minute to say that she would not be able to come, leaving Noyes one parent short. Should she cancel the trip? Stewart remembered that

Mrs. Case would be volunteering in the reading center this morning. She offered to ask her if she would fill in.

On the way to the reading center, Stewart peeked into several classrooms. As she passed the student washrooms she quickly looked into each, checking to see that no students were present and that the rooms were in order. As one student hurried past her, she asked him why he was not in class. He said that he had arrived late. She checked to see that he had a late admittance slip, and urged him to get to school on time in the future.

When she entered the reading center, she nodded in the direction of the reading teacher and motioned that she wanted to speak with Mrs. Case. Mrs. Case quickly joined her and agreed to help with the field trip. On her way out the door, Stewart complimented the reading teacher on a bulletin board entitled "Read for Experience."

Instead of returning to her office, Stewart continued to walk the halls on the second and third floors. On the third floor, she spent a few minutes studying the washroom situation. Then, stopping briefly at each classroom, she asked the teachers to be sure that only one student at a time was excused to use them. On her way back down the stairs, she detoured for a moment on the second floor to swing by a classroom with a substitute teacher, "just to see how he's doing." Finding the students somewhat unruly, she stepped into the classroom, fixing the well-known principal's stare on the children. As expected, her presence quieted the room. She greeted the substitute and inquired whether the regular teacher's substitute file was in order. He said that everything seemed fine, "they're just testing me a little bit."

When Stewart returned to the office, she spoke briefly with the clerk, reviewing the arrival and assignment of substitute teachers. Stewart asked the clerk to inform the librarian that she would have to cover one of the classes during the second period, if the substitute teacher did not arrive by then. Then Stewart picked up the mail that had arrived via the school system's delivery service. She asked the clerk to inform Mrs. Noyes that Mrs. Case would come on the field trip. She also asked the clerk to be sure that a teacher aide was available during seventh period to give out teaching supplies. As they talked, the clerk handed her two telephone messages.

Stewart entered her office, leaving the door to the outer office open. (A second door connecting directly to the hallway was kept closed. In this way, anyone who wanted to see Stewart had to go through the clerk. Stewart usually passed through the outer office in order to exchange information with the clerk on the way in or out of her own private office.) She quickly wrote a note to Mrs. Reynolds informing her that the teacher aide would be available during seventh period to give out supplies. She also wrote a bulletin to all teachers in longhand: "Teachers: It appears that students from different classes are meeting at prearranged times in the third floor washrooms again. When excusing students to the washrooms, please be sure they use the nearest washrooms only. Thank you." She walked to the outer office and taped the bulletin to the counter by the sign-in book. She also placed the note to Mrs. Reynolds in her mailbox.

Stewart returned to her office and placed a call to another principal who had left a message. The principal told her that he was calling a meeting of the district's science fair committee and would appreciate knowing when a convenient time would be for Stewart. They agreed to meet at 10:00 A.M. the following day at Blaire School. After the phone conversation, Stewart wrote a note to the cafeteria director, asking that coffee and some rolls be available the next morning in the conference room adjoining her office. She consulted the teachers' schedule and then also wrote a note to Mrs. St. Antoine, asking her to come to her office during seventh period. She walked to the outer office and placed the notes in St. Antoine's and the cafeteria director's mailboxes.

Returning to her office, Stewart once again picked up the telephone and dialed the number of a representative from a photography company that took students' yearly pictures. There was no answer, so Stewart left a message that she called. She set the phone message at the corner of her desk, so that she "would remember his name when he calls again."

She then began to look at the morning mail and some items the clerk had placed in her "in" box: a personnel bulletin listing several openings in the system for teachers and administrators; an announcement of a conference for reading teachers; a set of rating cards to be completed for each teacher. These teacher rating cards were filled out each year by the principal and placed in the teachers' personal files.

Stewart placed the rating cards to one side on her desk, then got up, taking the other items to the outer office with her. She placed the conference announcement in the reading teacher's mailbox and tacked the personnel bulletin to the teacher's bulletin board. As she did so, the clerk informed her of an incoming telephone call.

Returning to her desk, she picked up the phone and heard the voice of the photographer's representative, glancing in recognition at the name on the earlier phone message. After some preliminary pleasantries, she said, "Mr. Haskins, every year we make a selection from among several school photographers to take school pictures. You say you'd like to be considered this year? Fine, I'll be glad to include you in the group. Could you send me some materials—a list of the size and kind of photo to be included in each student's packet . . . maybe a sample packet, OK? Also the cost to the student, and the amount the school keeps for each packet sold. Also any other items that you make available, such as class pictures and teacher photographs."

Stewart went on to explain to the photographer that the eighth grade faculty sponsor participated in the selection. However, the sponsor for the following year had not been picked out. "I'll make sure that you get the information on the selection process and the date and time of the meeting when we ask all photographers to come to the school to demonstrate their work. However, I'd appreciate it if you would not meet directly with the faculty sponsor, except of course at the demonstration session. I look forward to seeing your materials, and thanks for your interest in the school."

Stewart put down the phone and turned to the researcher: "You know, it's a pleasure dealing with these photographers. They really enjoy coming to the school, and I must say, the kids get a kick out of these sessions too." Then, turning to another subject, Stewart explained to the researcher that she had gotten a hurry-up phone call from downtown headquarters a day or so ago calling her to a special meeting on the Access to Excellence program.[1] "It's scheduled for Friday at eleven," she explained, "and that's just when I'll be putting the finishing touches on the Continuous Progress materials. I hope I can get them done in time. But, you know, these meetings . . . they're having more and more of them. They want to turn this school into an 'academy', whatever that is. And we've got to go downtown and sit around for a couple hours to be told what it is. Then, no doubt, there'll be more meetings at headquarters setting it up. Seems as if I spend more and more of my time away from here, going to meetings, meetings. Hard to keep on top of things here when I'm not around."

The researcher listened intently, and they discussed the possibility of "academy" status and what that would mean for the school and the community.

After a discussion of fifteen minutes, Stewart looked at her watch and saw it was nearly time for the primary grades recess. Breaking off the conversation with the researcher, she walked through the outer office and went to stand by the exit doors to the primary play area. When the bell sounded, the children were escorted through the building toward the exit. In the ensuing commotion, Stewart spoke sharply to a few boisterous children, telling them to "walk, don't run," and "move slowly down the stairs."

She explained to the researcher that her customary practice was to accompany the youngsters out onto the playground where she and the teachers could supervise their play. However, today, she had to get back to the office to prepare a schedule for performance rating conferences with each teacher. Returning to her desk, she assembled the teacher evaluation materials and got from her drawer the teachers' daily schedules. Allowing 20 minutes for each teacher, she began making up a conference schedule. In the middle of this activity, she was interrupted by three boys entering the outer office, with a teacher aide following close behind. One of the boys was crying and holding the back of his head. The aide explained that the injured boy had fallen and hit his head on a patch of ice near the rim of the play area. The other two boys, she reported, had been chasing the injured boy.

Stewart moved to the outer office and told the two chasers to sit down at a bench inside the hallway door. She inspected the head injury and found that it was beginning to swell at the point of impact. Sending a student helper to the cafeteria to fetch some ice, she asked the injured boy for his name, his home telephone number, and his mother's name. She then dialed the number and spoke with the mother. After hearing what had happened, the mother said that she would come pick him up as soon as she could get a neighbor to drive her to the school. The helper soon arrived with the ice, and Stewart wrapped it in a paper towel and gave it to the boy to place on the bump. She told him to sit down on the bench and wait for his mother, and took the two chasers into the inner office. She closed the door. "Now look, you know you're not supposed to run where there is ice, it's too dangerous. Now that someone's hurt, the matter is serious. I want your parents to know about this." She filled out a form that requested a parent to come to school with the boys the following morning. With the boys still at her desk, she telephoned their homes and requested that a parent come to see her the next morning. She explained to the boys' mothers, "There's been an injury and your son was involved. Something must be done about their wild behavior during recess." She then sent the boys back to their classrooms, explaining that she would see them again in the morning.

As she gave them their hall passes, the injured boy's mother arrived. Stewart explained to her that two other boys had been involved and that she would be meeting with their parents in the morning. The mother asked her son, "Who did it?" and he replied it was "Jeff and Michael." "Those boys," the mother said, "why do they pick on him so much? Last week they pushed him in the bushes on the way home from school. Now they've gone too far." Stewart asked the mother to "let me see if I can't work something out." She promised to call her back in the morning, after she met with the other parents.

As the boy and his mother left, Stewart looked up and saw that it was beginning to snow heavily. She went to the public address system and announced that students eating lunch at school would remain inside the building during the lunchtime recess.

Stewart returned to her desk and worked on the conference schedule, but was shortly interrupted by two phone calls. One concerned the placement of a student teacher in the school. The other was from her husband, asking if she would like to meet him downtown for dinner. As Stewart was finishing the schedule, the clerk brought in a master copy of the parents' bulletin for her to approve before it was duplicated. She set aside the schedule and read through the bulletin as the clerk waited to one side. She pointed out two typos and then placed her signature on the copy master. The clerk took it and left. A moment later she returned with the U.S. mail. Stewart took a quick glance at the envelopes before setting them to one side and continuing to finish the schedule. Stewart neatly copied the final schedule by hand and then asked the clerk to place a copy of the schedule in each teacher's mailbox.

Stewart then headed toward the cafeteria, speaking with students in the hall on the way, telling them to "slow down" and "go to your recess areas." She took a tray and moved through the lunch line. Instead of going to the faculty room, she returned to her office to eat. There, she was available for teachers who might want to stop by. As she ate, she looked through the U.S. mail: promotional material for textbooks, school administration booklets, instructional supplies, and also an announcement of a tea at a local Catholic high school for the eighth graders. Stewart set this aside and threw out the rest.

A student asked to see Stewart. As student council president, she wanted to know when the next student council meeting would be (the last meeting had been cancelled because of the snow). They picked a date and the student said that she would inform the council members. Stewart chatted for a few minutes with the girl about her plans for high school.

Getting up from her desk, Stewart carried her tray and the tea announcement to the outer office. She left the announcement in the eighth grade class sponsor's mailbox and returned her tray to the cafeteria. Then she began her tour of the hallways, inspecting the building as the students returned to their classes to settle down for the afternoon's course work.

When she returned to her office, the clerk handed her a phone message. Stewart dialed the phone for an in-house call and reached the building engineer. He told her that a small window at the back of the building had been broken during the lunch hour by some loitering high school students. He said he had covered it with some heavy cardboard, "but I thought you should know about it. Also, you know the art room . . . the shades in there have been damaged. The art teacher just lets the kids go wild in there during seventh and eighth periods. I think you should talk to him." Stewart agreed to check on it.

Miss La Pointe arrived. She had agreed to start a dramatic program in the school and wanted to report to Stewart the plans she was making for a production in the spring. They discussed use of the auditorium, rehearsal schedules, the play La Pointe had selected, and the tryout announcement La Pointe had prepared. Toward the end of the seventh period, the conference was concluded and La Pointe left to return to her classroom. Stewart got up and, checking to make sure that the teacher's aide was on station in the outer office to give out supplies, headed for the art room to see the damaged shades and to make sure the students were under control.

When she returned to the office, Stewart found Mrs. St. Antoine waiting for her in the outer office. Stewart invited her into her own office and asked for an update about the plans for the eighth grade tea, dinner and other graduation festivities. St. Antoine discussed with her the results of faculty and student committee meetings to that point. Then Stewart asked St. Antoine whether she was thinking about remaining eighth grade sponsor next year. St. Antoine seemed a bit embarrassed. She said that she enjoyed working with students very much, but that there was some jealousy from some of the other eighth grade teachers who felt excluded. They discussed how some of the other eighth grade teachers might be brought more closely into the planning, and St. Antoine left agreeing that she would try to mend some of the fences that had been neglected.

Seeing that it was near the end of the day, Stewart checked her desk to see what remained to be done. Noting the stack of material in the in box, she looked through it. It contained several forms that required signing: they pertained to the ordering of supplies, teacher absences, and a field trip permission. Stewart signed all of the forms but one. It was a request to order a film. Stewart was unfamiliar with the film and wanted to discuss its nature and use with the teacher before signing.

Stewart put on her hat and coat and walked to the main exit doors just as the students were beginning to leave. Stationed just outside the exit, she called to the students inside the hallway and out on the playground to "slow down," and "watch out, it's slippery." When the students were gone she returned to her office to find a tiny kindergartner with tear-filled eyes sitting next to a teacher aide. The aide explained that the girl's father was supposed to pick her up from school, but had not arrived. They tried to make some phone calls to find out who was coming for the girl, but could not get an answer. The girl suggested that they call her aunt, which they did. The aunt agreed to take the girl, but said no one could come and get her right now. Stewart agreed to bring the girl by the aunt's house. "There now," the aide told the girl, "the principal will take you to your aunt's house."

Stewart placed a few items in a small brief case and was

ready to leave. She waited as the aide and clerk prepared to leave also. As they put on their coats, she checked the teachers' sign-in sheets to be sure that they were all out of the building. Then she locked the office as they left together. Stewart reached for the small girl's hand and helped her down the slippery steps. Before going to her car, she muttered to the researcher, "I suppose I shouldn't be doing this . . . liability and all. But someone has to."

* * * * *

As the foregoing account indicates, the principal's managerial routine consists partly of responding to demands from outside the school. Principal Stewart sensed an increasing load of paperwork, most of it attributable to the Continuous Progress Program. As with the recordkeeping apparatus in general, the tracking of Continuous Progress statistics was handled by headquarters staff people, and as the Program matured and gradually accumulated a data base, central staff statisticians became more interested in accurate, precise, on-time reports on each child in every school every ten weeks, in order to find out if the Program was working. Accordingly, the principal became the central cog in the machinery for collecting these numbers, organizing them into system-wide forms, checking the forms for accuracy, and then preparing them for delivery to district offices.

The principals examined in the generic profile above devoted about 12 percent of their time to written communications at their desks. Half to three-quarters of this time was consumed in processing documents for headquarters personnel. The principals' general perception was that the load of this type of paperwork was increasing. One principal reported that it was necessary to take work home virtually every night to stay on top of the task. Many principals stayed at their desks after school or reported early in the morning in order to stay ahead of the mail. Others diverted time from other activities during the day to handle data gathering for each child.

Principal Stewart also sensed an increase in the number of meetings calling her away from the building. The school system leadership had been churning out new program initiatives almost without letup for the preceding five years. Most of these programs, as principals see it, had been developed by planners, lawyers, technical specialists and educational politicians who had little understanding of the realities of elementary school management. Once the programs were designed, the principals were called to district or central headquarters meetings where they were instructed how to implement these programs in their schools.

With reference to Table 3.4, the principals spending the

most time away from their buildings (22 and 19 percent) were attending meetings on implementing new programs for their schools, including interviewing faculty candidates, inspecting materials and facilities, and discussing arrangements with superiors.

Although not required to leave their buildings, many principals discovered that their work configuration was sharply affected by decisions made elsewhere in the system hierarchy. One example is the magnet school concept.[2] Vis à vis Table 3.1, those principals exhibiting most parent interaction (12 percent each) turned out to be those wrestling with the conversion of their neighborhood schools into combination neighborhood-magnet schools. Inevitably in such a conversion, many parents contacted the school for information about enrollment and programs, fearing their children would be shortchanged in the transition. Program innovation, especially that originating at central headquarters, is more than an educational enterprise; it is also a political enterprise in convincing a suspicious community.

On occasion, the principal is unwittingly drawn into outright political battles for power, either in the community or the school system at large, and discovers that the school itself becomes the field on which these battles are fought. In Table 3.2 we see that one principal devoted 26 percent of principaling time to written communications. An analysis of this case reveals that some disruptive confrontations between teachers and pupils had occurred recently in the school, and the principal's handling of these disturbances was being challenged by a self-appointed group of teachers and parents trying to engineer the principal's removal. The principal's defensive response to this challenge necessitated much desk work devoted to the preparation of detailed memorandums and other documents that explained the teacher-pupil altercations and defended the manner in which those were adjudicated.

Finally, the principal's relationship to the external environment is complicated by understandable career ambitions. To survive in the hierarchy he or she must be attentive to the administrative reward system, to the power wielded by the immediate superior. Principals know that advancement in the ranks sometimes goes to "the good soldier." Because of this principals try to keep problems off their boss's desk, respond promptly to orders even when they disagree with them, and in other ways exhibit their loyalty to the organization in its encounter with sometimes hostile constituencies.

THE SECONDARY PRINCIPAL

Comparison and Contrast

In most school systems, secondary schools are larger in enrollment, larger in square footage, and programmatically more complex than elementary schools. In some situations, elementary principalships are considered stepping stones to the high school principalship. The high school principalship, because of its administrative demands, is often considered a stepping stone to a staff position at central headquarters. However, since these positions tend to emphasize paper shuffling over personnel managing, many high school principals spurn these promotion possibilities; they believe their site-level positions actually carry greater status in the profession. As in military organizations, the combat colonel has greater credibility than the deskbound bureaucrat.

It is also important to remember that secondary school principals differ from their colleagues at the elementary level in that their students are older, more savvy about grownups, and are feverishly pushing into adulthood with characteristic adolescent feistiness. Being physically larger and intellectually more clever and devious, high school students represent a potential for mischief which is far more threatening to the school's stability than is true in most elementary schools. This means that the principal, as chief manager of an educational program, must also serve as first officer of a control apparatus, a miniature police force whose task it is to keep students in line, maintain surveillance over their behavior, and take corrective, punitive action when necessary. With the great increase in drug use in the wider society, and the growing street wisdom of many high schoolers, the principal's control function, especially in large metropolitan areas, is necessarily magnified. Nowadays, many parents look more to the high school to govern their youngsters' conduct, recognizing that they are gradually losing control at home.

We see then the secondary school principal as the chief administrator of a large, complex organization. The apparent mission of this organization is *education,* but the modern definition of this term is so broad that the school must be thought of, in real-life terms, as a multipurpose institution. It also encompasses:

1. *custody* (baby sitting for parents and keeping young people off the streets and out of the labor market for the benefit of society)
2. *behavior control* (exercising police discipline over adolescent conduct)

3. *career planning* (through guidance, helping young people map out their futures)
4. *psychological support* ("hand holding," and helping teenagers through adolescence)
5. *entertainment* (serving as a production center for football games, band concerts, holiday pageants, dramatic productions, international food bazaars, senior proms)

The modern secondary school is a true center of community life, not only for the young people who attend it, but for their parents, friends and neighbors. It is no wonder that secondary school principaling has now taken on a sociological and political, as well as an educational, dimension.

Interaction Pairings

In managing this large, complicated enterprise, the secondary principal is in contact with many people. The typical on-site work day begins at about 7:45 A.M. and concludes about 4:00 or 5:00 P.M.. In these 500 minutes, the principal is in direct interaction with other people for between 200 and 300 minutes. This means that the principal spends a half to two-thirds of the time talking or listening.

The pace and rhythm of these interactions vary enormously. Sometimes the conversation may be only a snippet; at other times, there is more to talk over and the interaction covers 5, 10, or 20 minutes. On very rare occasions, the interaction covers a half hour or more.

Our clocking of face to face interchanges reveals that principals differ among themselves on the pace of these conversations. For example, over five work days, one secondary principal engaged in 148 face to face contacts covering 789 minutes, for an average of 5 minutes 20 seconds per conversation. Another principal in five days of work engaged in 434 interactions covering 1085 minutes, for an average of only 2 minutes 30 seconds per contact, less than half that of his colleague. For the secondary principals observed over 54 days or part-days of activity, the average duration of a face to face encounter was approximately 2 minutes 50 seconds.

On the telephone, the principal interacts with an unseen party. These interactions are not extended, unless the principal is entangled with a long-winded superior or a voluble parent who is better dealt with on the phone than in person. Over four work days, one principal conducted 36 telephone conversations covering 73 minutes for an average call time of just over 2 minutes. Another principal, over four days, held 40 phone conversations for a total of 140 minutes, or an average of 3 minutes 30 seconds for each conversation. For all six principals, the average duration of a telephone conversation was 2 minutes 35 seconds.

These data of interaction time reveal, perhaps more vividly than any other measure, the fractionated, piecemeal character of managerial life in a secondary school. The principal must absorb, digest, and disseminate information in very small lots to very small audiences, sometimes repeating the same information many times each day to many individuals.

In our research design, we wanted to know the exact nature of these interactions, and which specific individuals in the principal's environment constituted the primary media of managerial activity. Table 3.5 presents in descending order the categories of people with whom the principal interacts.

It is clear from this breakdown that most of the principal's personal exchanges occur with teachers, administrative aides, students and office clerks. Taken together, they account for 60 percent of the principal's face to face contacts during the work day. It is pertinent to point out that the principal spends roughly equivalent time with teachers, administrators and students. Conversely, the principal has very little contact with the building engineer. This is partly because their spheres of responsibility are quite different and, in some situations, their chain of command networks are operationally distinct and separate.

The principal also spends very little of the work day in contact with his staff or line superiors. Only 7 percent of the time is devoted to interchanges with the superintendent or the headquarters staff. We have noted elsewhere in this book that the modern school system is a loose coupling of relatively autonomous units. The infrequency of contact with administrative superiors appears to support this generalization.

Initiatory Behavior

In developing the overall plan of our study, we were interested in learning which of the two parties in these interactions was responsible for initiating the piece of business. Table 3.6 provides a distribution of initiating behavior.

It is clear that the high school principal takes the initiative in the vast majority of interchanges with others in the manageri-

Range: low • — average ┃ — • high (Percent of workday, 0%–25%)

Principal interacted with:	Range low (%)	Average (%)	Range high (%)
Faculty member	13	19	30
Assistant principal	5	18	24
Student	8	15	24
Researcher and other outsiders	5	14	28
Office clerk	4	8	13
Other principals	1	7	22
Superintendent	1	5	14
Counselor	1	3	7
Parent (or guardian or sibling)	1	2	5
Central office staff	0	2	4
Building engineer	0	1	3
Community official, police	0	1	3
Teacher aide	0	1	2
Security personnel	0	1	1

Table 3.5 Secondary Principals' Interaction Pairings

al environment. Considering the principal's leadership role, this finding is not surprising. Once again, there appears to be a rough equivalence between faculty members, administrative aides, and students in the role they play in initiatory conduct. Here also is further evidence of the relative autonomy of the principal; only 5 percent of the work day consists of responding to initiatives from the superintendent or the headquarters staff.

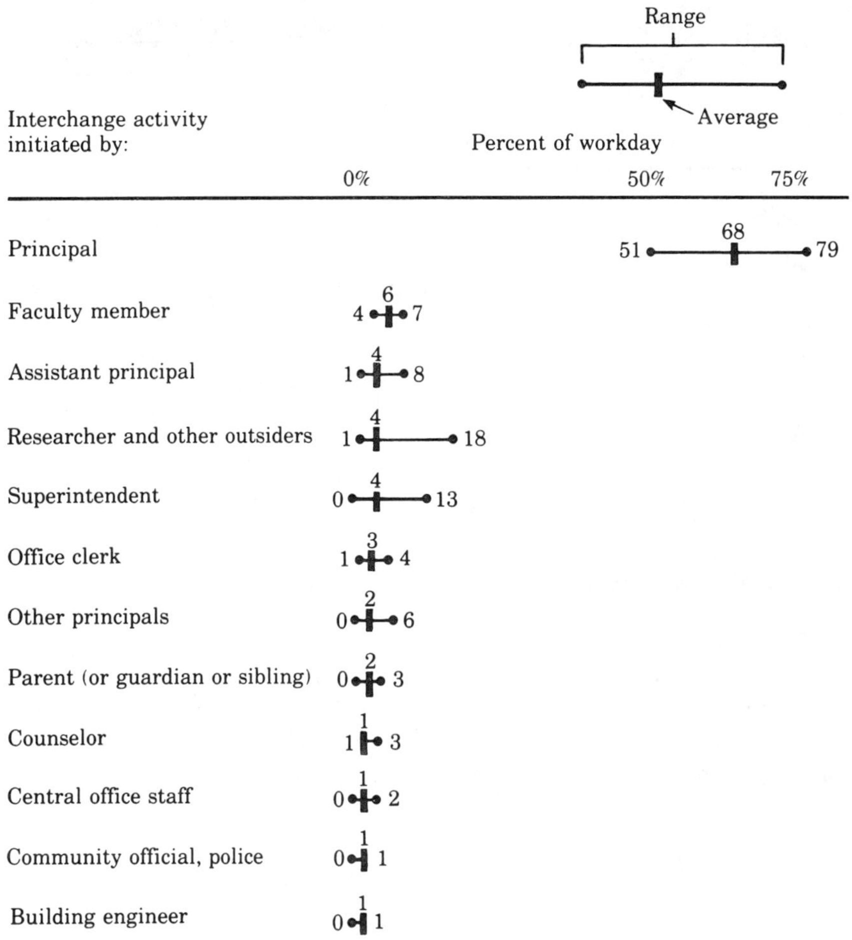

Table 3.6 Secondary Principals' Initiatory Behavior

Medium of Communication

In carrying on the administrative function, the secondary school principal conducts the verbal interchanges face to face. The work day, however, embraces many other means of communication: conversations on the telephone, visual inspection of the environment, reading and writing of memoranda, and occasional use of the public address system. Table 3.7 provides a distribution of time through the five different media.

As noted elsewhere in this report, the principal is a talker and listener. We see from Table 3.7 that up to 83 percent of principaling time is devoted to these activities. Coordinately the principal

Medium	Percent of workday: Range (low)	Average	Range (high)
Verbal, face-to-face	68	75	83
Visual (scanning the environment)	3	10	15
Verbal, telephone	6	7	8
Written (reading or writing)	4	7	9
Verbal, P.A. system	0	1	2

Table 3.7 Secondary Principals' Medium of Communication

does not read or write much during the work day. The principal is a quintessential paradigm of what Marshall McLuhan called the "cool medium" (non-print) communicator, relying almost exclusively on the spoken word in conducting the work of the school.

Locus of Administrative Activity

Where is the high school principal's job performed? We wanted a literal answer: which spots in the school building and elsewhere serve as the principal's work sites? Common sense suggests that the principal, as the chief officer, enjoys the special privilege of a private office, and that most managerial work would be conducted in that place. This is not the case. Table 3.8 provides a breakdown of physical sites where the principal carries on the business of the school.

We see from this table that less than half of the secondary principal's activity takes place in the principal's office. For 55 percent of the work day, the principal is somewhere else. Much of this time is off school grounds altogether, attending meetings, conferring with the immediate superiors, visiting other (feeder) schools, or going directly to central headquarters to straighten out a problem.

About a tenth of the time, the principal is in the corridor. Add to this the time spent in areas frequented by students,—lunch room, classrooms, auditorium and gymnasium—and we see that al-

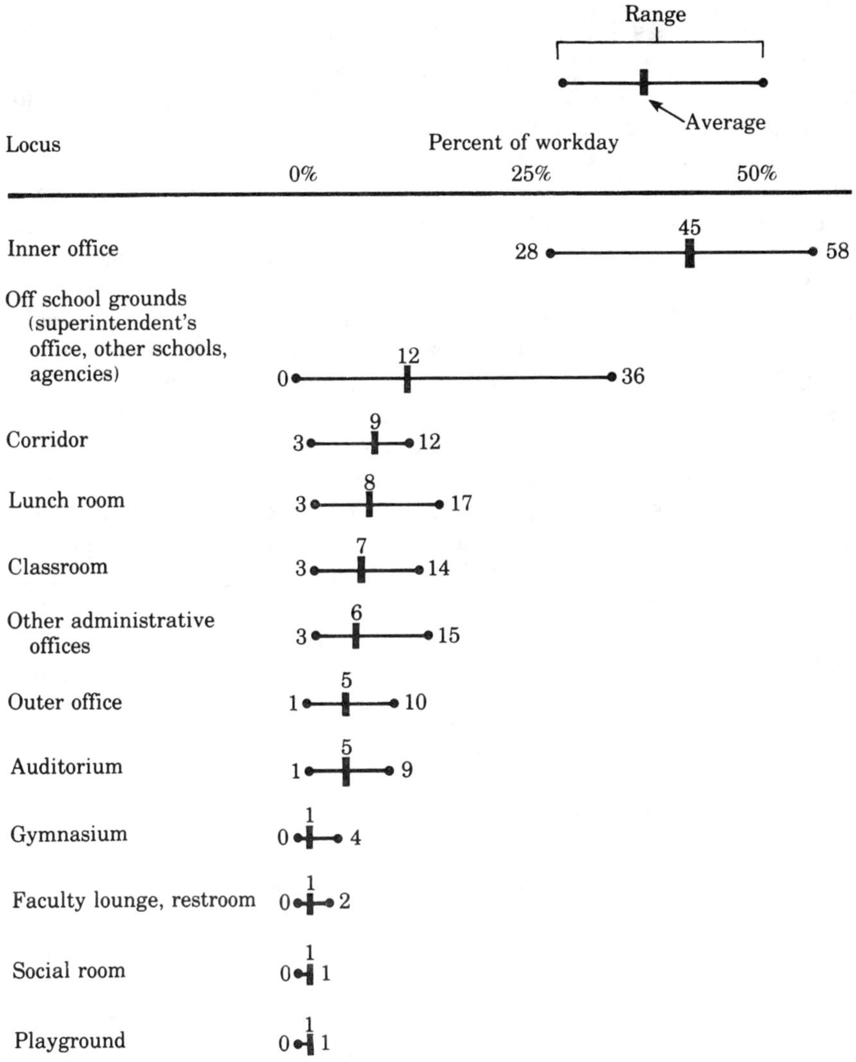

Table 3.8 Secondary Principals' Locus of Principaling

most one-third of the principal's work schedule is around students.

Principals usually avoid the teachers' lounge, apparently agreeing with teachers that this area is a retreat, a sanctuary from both students and administrators. They also spend little time in gymnasiums or on the playgrounds, leaving these large instructional areas to the special faculty assigned for this purpose.

Secondary principals are also conspicuous by their relative absence from the site of teaching and learning, the classroom. In professional circles, it is generally thought that a primary responsibility of the principal is the evaluation and improvement of instruction. However, our field work revealed that secondary school principals do not spend much time doing this. Of course, in large high schools, the principals turn over much of the observation and evaluation of teachers to assistant principals. But the principal knows that evaluating teaching is a generally unpleasant task. Standing in judgment of other people is always difficult, especially when the judgee (the teacher) has attended a teacher training institution and knows as much about pedagogy as any principal. Also, teaching is a highly personal art, and what may work for a teacher may strike the observer-evaluator as unorthodox or, worse, counter-productive. Who, then, is the competent judge?

Principals pointed out to us on numerous occasions that they do not spend much time evaluating teaching because such monitoring has only a marginal impact on the overall quality of instruction in the school. Even in the case of gross incompetence, the principal is required to spend months in carefully staged observations, teacher conferences, consultations with the superintendent, and accumulation of supporting documents. And in most cases the incompetent teacher is simply transferred to another school. The principals' answer is to stay out of the classroom.

A Day in the Life . . .

We can discern from the foregoing sections a generic profile of a secondary school principal. Showing a typical principal in action will bring these statistics to life.

The principal of the modern secondary school is a face to face communicator, a peripatetic commandant over the domain, and a semi-autonomous site-level officer in charge of a unit only loosely coupled with the remainder of the system. He or she usually engenders among the faculty and students that special blend of fear, love, and respect which is the magic ingredient of managerial leadership in organizational life.

The principal, Mr. Geller, is in his forties, a wiry, agile former athlete. Like some other male principals, Geller has come up through the coaching ranks and has served his administrative apprenticeship in several elementary schools. He now oversees a large, complex high school with over 4,000 students and more than 200 faculty and staff. He likes his work, and appears to have an easygoing, comfortable relationship with those around him.

This morning he arrived at his desk around 8 and sat down to glance over some mail placed there by his secretary who had arrived a few minutes earlier. As he studied an attendance report, the doorway darkened with the figure of a youth wearing a distraught look on his face: "Mr. Geller, I've been barred from class. My mom hasn't got here yet to bail me out. They've got me in the 'Bar Room' (a holding area for malingering students). Can you do something?" Geller consoled the boy, informing him that his first step should be his counselor; with a friendly smile, he waved the boy off and returned to his mail.

He soon tired of this activity and decided instead to take his daily first-period stroll through the corridors. He greeted teachers, asked students to produce their I.D. cards, and told a boy to take off his hat. Moving on to the journalism teacher's room, he stopped the teacher and said, "Joe, you know those yearbooks last June . . . we weren't able to unload them because they arrived after the kids had finished school. It's Christmas season. What do you say we put an ad in the school bulletin that we're selling last year's yearbooks for the bargain price of three dollars? Think they'd sell as gifts?" They discussed this briefly, and then Geller continued on his walk.

Checking the walls for graffiti, picking up a stray wad of paper, glancing in an occasional classroom, he moved briskly through the halls for a visual check of the premises. The building, a large five-level structure has been remodeled and expanded frequently through the decades, so he did not expect to cover the entire school. But he got the feel of a new day, and after about twenty minutes eventually worked his way back to the first floor and to his office, where he sat down to open the mail.

An assistant principal came in and said the fire marshal had arrived and wanted to hold a fire drill this morning because the weather was good, even though the temperature was about 30°. This meant that it must be an announced drill, so the students could get their coats. After a brief discussion with his assistant principal and the marshal, Geller announced the drill over the P.A. system and set it for later that morning. The drill would be complicated by the fact that about ten minutes before the drill was to begin, an assistant principal received a telephone call from an unidentified caller informing him that there was a bomb in a girl's washroom. Geller and his aides pondered a course of action, calling downtown headquarters for standard operating procedures. Geller mused aloud, "This is the worst thing that could happen right now. Once they see us empty this building, they'll think they're responsible." The bomb threat turned out to be a hoax and the drill proceeded on schedule.

Geller spent the time before and after the drill conferring with his assistant principals, handling clerical materials with the secretaries, answering questions of students who dropped in unannounced. Geller had his mind, however, on a scheduled meeting of the social studies teachers set for 10:00. They drifted in, one by one, and sat down in the circle of easy chairs. Around 10:15, after some small talk, Geller opened the meeting. The problem centered on the drop in enrollment in traditional history classes, with the students opting for the more "relevant" and presumably easier courses in contemporary problems. If nothing was done about this drain of students from standard history courses, there would likely be budget cuts and some faculty would lose their jobs.

All those present recognized the basic cause of the problem: the school's clientele was changing because the attendance area was changing. More minority students were entering the freshman class, but they were not doing well in the regular, traditional curriculum. If they became discouraged during their freshman year, they tended to drop out and usually did not return. If these students could somehow be kept in school through their first year, argued Geller, there was a good chance that the school could keep them through the full four years until graduation. Could the history and social studies faculty assist in redesigning the freshman offerings to enable the school to hang on to these students?

Understandably, the history teachers in the group were both worried and angry. Why should they be expected to teach courses for which their training did not prepare them? Why should the school change its programs simply because a new type of student was showing up? An hour's discussion focused on different remedies. No consensus was reached, but next week there would have to be some action started on this problem.

The teachers slowly rose from their chairs, grumbling about lowering standards and watering down requirements. But the message had been delivered and they appeared to have understood it. Shaking their heads in resignation, they returned to their classrooms.

With the meeting concluded, Geller conferred briefly with the assistant principals in a post-mortem on the meeting. He assigned one of them the task of following up on this problem and helping the teachers work out with their department head some ideas for resolving the difficulty.

As the aides left, Geller turned his attention to the drafting of his Performance Appraisal Profile (PAP), a document which each principal was expected to submit annually to the superintendent as a guide to a performance evaluation during the coming year. Central headquarters had specified several all-system goals that each principal was to work toward. This year, one of them was the reduction in vandalism. Geller glanced at last year's figure and was puzzled to read "five cents per pupil." He surmised that this was a typo, since vandalism for a school of this type usually ran forty to fifty cents per pupil. As a goal, he jotted down the figure of ten cents.

As he worked on other sections of the PAP, several students dropped in with special scheduling problems, a teacher stuck his head in the door to report that the photocopying machine was broken, a student messenger appeared with an eligibility list for the bowling team which Geller must sign, and an assistant came in for a signature on a crowd control form—a basketball game was about to start and special personnel was required to handle the crowd. As the aide left, Geller returned to his paper work, jotting down ideas for the PAP. Beyond the all-system goals, each principal was to set down personal goals for the coming year. Geller decided on four: (a) implementation of Access to Excellence programs; (b) in-service training for his teachers; (c) implementation of the North Central[2] recommendations from a visit by the Association a year ago; and (d) development of better communications with the community. Geller smiled at the last one; he knew his superintendent was especially interested in it. Furthermore, he knew that it was the kind of goal that lent itself to self-enhancing documentation—schedules of contacts with community leaders, minutes of meetings held, letters from parents and political figures extolling the school, etc. It was the kind of goal that could be supported by a body of "evidence."

As he was choosing the best wording for these goals on his working draft, he was interrupted by a secretary who told him about a man in the outer office asking to put health foods into the lunchroom; could she show him in? Geller waved her off, telling her to send him to the lunchroom director. As the secretary was leaving, a teacher (the student council sponsor) and an assistant principal came in to discuss arrangements for a rock group scheduled to perform at the school next week. This was the kind of event which would require very careful planning. After about 15 minutes, the two left and he turned once again to his desk papers.

He looked at the vandalism item on the PAP. Realizing he needed more information on this, he walked a hundred yards through the back passageways to the engineer's office. The engineer greeted him, and they discussed the graffiti problem and the worsening vandalism of the auditorium. The engineer reported that students were tearing up the balcony seats when they were forced to use that area for a study hall. Since these seats were no longer manufactured and irreplaceable, some existing seats would have to be cannibalized to make repairs on others. This meant that the seating capacity of the auditorium would gradually decline.

Geller returned to his office but left almost immediately for a general tour of the building. His first stop was the "Bar Room," where he spoke to the students briefly about their infractions and his hope that they would shape up, be reinstated and get on with their studies. The students responded with stares and smirks, resentful of incarceration and this pep talk by the man they consider the chief warden. *Sotto voce,* the teacher expressed her frustration "When I call their parents, asking them to come down to school to bail out their kids, they hang up on me!" Geller commiserated and complimented her on her efforts.

Geller departed and continued on the tour of the school, stopping to look at a teacher putting up a bulletin board display, moving on to watch a musical rehearsal in the auditorium, going into a classroom to witness a one-on-one tutorial lesson for a student learning English as a foreign language, and then watching a soccer game in the gym. Geller peeked into various classrooms en route, to see how things were going. At one classroom, he gently tapped on the door and motioned the teacher to step out. He emerged, and Geller whispered in his ear, "Your fly is open."

At the lunchroom, he got his tray and sat with his regular coterie of staff friends in the cafeteria. One of them offered an explanation to the researcher. "We have a rule: No shop talk at lunch!" They discussed the weather, gambling trips to Las Vegas, the fortunes of area football and baseball teams, and the shocking murder of a colleague a month ago. A half hour later Geller took his tray to the collecting point and, with the engineer (one of the lunchroom coterie), he went to check on the progress of some repair work in the boiler room.

About 1:00 he arrived back in his office. Among his messages was one marked "personal and confidential." It was a letter from an irate parent claiming that her daughter had been falsely accused of calling a teacher "f_____g bitch." What was the principal going to do about this?

A clerk came in and reported that a teacher was complaining that twenty-six dollars had been incorrectly deducted from his paycheck. Could Geller look into this? Then a staff person from central headquarters returned a call. Geller said, "Yes, Lucille, I've got this Social Mal (socially maladjusted) kid. He's been suspended, but he's due back Wednesday. Do we open up a special class for him? He's the only one we've got at the moment. Or do we put him in with some other Special Ed classes?" A discussion followed about how to handle the placement of this student when he arrived Wednesday morning.

Geller turned again to his desk work and jotted a note to himself on the twenty-six dollar paycheck deduction. As he turned to the other papers, he interrupted himself, picked up the phone, and asked his assistant principal to step in for a moment. When the AP came in, Geller said, "Joe, remember those fellows ripping out the seats in 204 a couple of weeks ago? Look, here's what they found stuffed into the metal posts holding up those old desks." He handed the AP a piece of old, crumpled notebook paper. In the upper right-hand corner was the notation: "Raymond Voss, March 19, 1930." It was a student's theme on Edgar Allen Poe's story, "The Tell-Tale Heart." Geller continued, "You know, the fiftieth reunion of this guy's class is coming up. Maybe we could locate Voss, if he's still alive... He'd be nearing 70, find out what he's doing now, and have him come to the reunion. I'm sorting out the stuff the men bring me as they tear out these seats. It's quite a collection: a school newspaper from 1948, book reports from the fifties, scrawled notes to classmates."

The AP looked over the Poe theme, and remarked, "This is fascinating. Why don't we get our history department to make a student project out of this . . . get these papers together, track down the people who wrote them, bring them into class to tell the students what has happened to them since leaving high school. It would make a great teaching unit!" Geller pondered this for a moment, then with resignation in his voice, said, "Well, no chance of that, Joe. You know as well as I do the history teachers are not interested in that kind of history. They want to stick with what they've been trained for . . . the English kings, the industrial revolution, the Civil War. You know, history in *books!*" Geller emphasized this last word, but then his voice trailed off as the AP handed the paper back to him. The idea died as Geller returned to his papers and the AP departed for his own office.

Geller returned to his work, then picked up the phone and asked a couple of his assistant principals to drop in. They entered and he showed them the "f____g bitch" letter, asking for some background on the situation. After a discussion on how to handle this mother, he told one of the aides, "Look, you get the mother in here, get the girl, and ask the teacher to come down. We'll talk the whole thing out right here . . . you be here too." As they were leaving, there was a phone call from a parent complaining that her daughter was not allowed to leave school for a family trip. Geller listened, then responded, "Well, Mrs. Kladany, the teacher is absolute boss on excusing students. You know that. I just can't overrule a teacher on something like this." They discussed the problem for some minutes, Geller holding his ground. Then, to ease the tone and bring the telephone call to a conclusion, he said, "Is your leg still in a cast? How's it coming?" She was appropriately disarmed and concluded the conversation so that Geller could get back to work.

The next hour or so was taken up with work on the draft PAP, and with students popping in to have their schedules changed. As he was dealing with these people, Geller received a phone call from a woman in the Mayor's office asking for a room in which to hold a meeting. For most outside groups, the answer would be no. But a room would certainly be found for this caller.

A student came in; she was accompanied by her sister,

not a student in the school. She needed to be reinstated after cutting too many classes. Her sister said, "I'm here in place of my aunt. She can't come in today. Mr. Geller, I know you need a parent here to reinstate, but our father doesn't live with us and our mother is in Central America visiting her sick father. He just had a stroke, and we don't know when she'll be back." Geller interrogated the student, pondered an answer, then wrote a note for the girl authorizing her reinstatement.

Returning to his desk, he jotted a note to the engineer asking him to remove some broken hardware from a swinging door on the third floor; it was sticking out in the hallway and was a hazard. He then took a look at a report from headquarters on alternative programs for job-holding students who want to get a high school diploma in the evening school.

Picking up some papers, Geller walked to the administrative outer office, delivering some end-of-the-day materials and giving instructions to clerks and secretaries. Then he decided to take another short spin through the corridors. Almost immediately, two girls spotted him, and reported that there were cockroaches in the locker room. Could he check on this? After another hundred yards of walking, watching the students put on their coats, he decided to return to his office. He phoned the engineer about the cockroaches and then turned once again to his paperwork. A sealed envelope to "Mr. Geller, Principal" confronted him. He opened it and read a long, rambling memo from a teacher complaining about his treatment the previous day when Geller criticized him for allowing his study hall students to wander out into the hallways. The last paragraph of the letter carried a mild threat: "I am forwarding copies of this letter to the superintendent and to Operation PUSH."[3]

Geller was nonplussed by the letter, coming as it did from a competent, responsible, and cooperative teacher. One phrase in the letter was particularly cryptic. The dissident teacher accused Geller of "abusing my professional experience." This made no sense. Geller wondered, did someone else write this letter for the teacher? If so, what was the motivation? And why the intimidating tactic of involving an outside organization in such a complaint?

Geller knew this kind of complaint should be dealt with promptly. He placed the letter on top of the others on his desk: "I'll get to that first thing in the morning." Geller gathered up some other materials and put them in his briefcase. Then, pondering how he could have abused a teacher's "professional experience," he headed for the parking lot.

* * * * *

We see from the previous sections and from the above case study that the tempo of a principal's work day does not encourage serene reflection. There is a certain tumble of events, one after another, which requires a facility to move abruptly from one subject to another. The principal is expected to keep track of the contents of hundreds of conversations, many of them unrelated, and to retrieve the important elements of these conversations later.

There also seems to be little rank-ordering in the importance of events; everything seems to blend together in an undifferentiated jumble of activities presumably related, however remotely, to the vitality and purpose of the larger enterprise. This principal must deal with a critical problem in the school's curricular program—the freshman history sequence. Yet the entire matter is elbowed aside, denied a position of deserved prominence, by a cascading farrago of other concerns—auditorium seats, a foul-mouthed girl, bomb threats and . . . cockroaches!

Management, whatever else it is, is the bridge between the long view and the nitty particulars of organization life. This truism is well illustrated in the secondary school principalship.

THINGS TO DO AND THINK ABOUT

1. Make a comparison of elementary and secondary principals in the four measures of their contacts with other people: interaction pairings, initiatory behavior, medium of communication, and locus of principaling. Are there any surprises here? Secondary principals spend almost 40 percent of their time with faculty and administrative subordinates, while elementary principals spend only about half this amount of time with these individuals. Is there a reason for this?
2. Ask the principal of your school to look over the eight tables in this chapter and compare these findings with his or her own regimen. If sharp differences show up, what significance can be drawn from your principal's deviation from the norm?
3. Tables 3.4 and 3.8 reveal principals spend less than half the work day in their own offices; the remainder of the time they are somewhere else. What is the meaning of this statistic? What conclusions can you draw from it?
4. Have a principal read over the appropriate section on "A Day in the Life." Would he or she find this account a prototypical representation of the job? If not, how is your principal's work life different? Why is this so?

NOTES

1. Board-sponsored program to encourage inter-school (i.e., commonly interracial) transfers.
2. The North Central Association of Colleges and Secondary Schools, a regional accrediting organization.
3. A local black-oriented civil rights organization.

PART 2

Discretionary Decision Making

4

Principaling and its Effects on the Schools

The encounters shaping the workday lives of principals are predominantly those events directing their attention *inward* toward the school. The building principal is the key administrative official within a dense network of relationships between people of different ages with different roles, goals, and perspectives.

WHAT WE KNOW FROM THE LITERATURE

First, there is the "fundamental dichotomy" between the roles of student and teacher.[1] Students are compelled to enter school and are

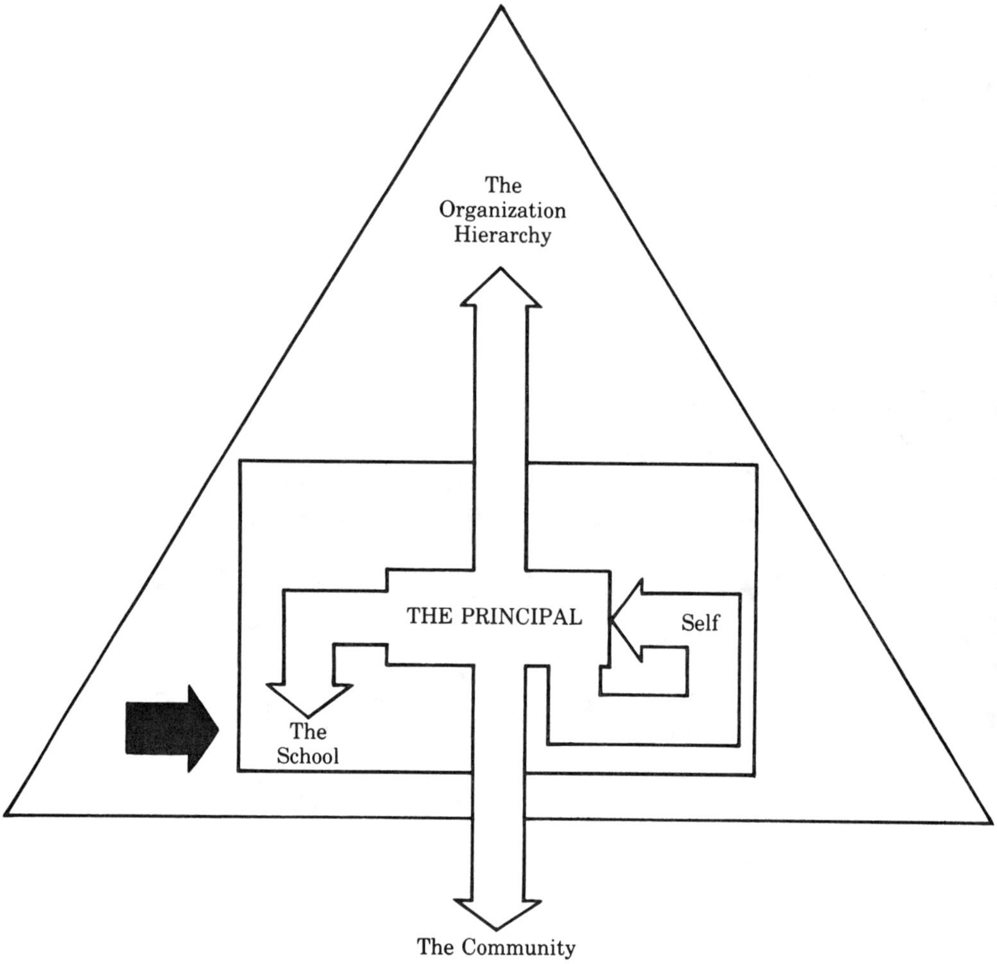

Figure 4.1 Principaling and its Four Sectors of Effect

inducted into adult life through activities not relevant to their immediate interests. Teachers, on the other hand, enter their roles voluntarily, even eagerly, and are provided continuing incentives in return for their professional contributions.

The school also houses another group whose incentives and obligations are sometimes different from those of teachers and students: assistant principals, guidance counselors, Title I coordinators, and department heads. These people are sometimes pressured into a managerial role which can conflict with the pupil-centered role of the classroom teacher.

Still another constituency is the secretaries, clerks, and maintenance workers whose interests differ from those of the adult professionals and students. Although their institutional task is to further the educational program, they may be more concerned with working conditions and job security than with the cultivation of a stimulating and orderly learning environment.

At the center of this world of different "subcultures" sits the principal, whose responsibility is to mold these disparate interests into a working whole, attending simultaneously to individual and institutional needs. In the more volatile school environments, the principal tries to counter the centrifugal forces of divisiveness and diversity. The conventional wisdom as discussed in Chapter 1 stipulated two expectations of principals in overseeing the school: They will effectively manage the school's environment, insuring a controlled setting for learning; and they will offer instructional leadership to the teaching faculty, promoting effectiveness in pupil achievement.

The Principal as Manager

The tasks of the manager in education are similar to the duties of other managers. Records must be kept, reports submitted, supplies and equipment ordered, budgets prepared and followed, and facilities maintained. The principal is also responsible for the flow of work and people in the work area. Scheduling activities, assigning pupils and staff, developing communication channels, and distributing instructional resources to teachers are also important managerial duties in the school.

The manager's job, though, is more than this. In one of the earliest sociological explanations of life in schools, Willard Waller observed in 1932 that the world of the local school is a social world, a "tangled web of interrelationships" between human beings who have much in common but are also in conflict. Teachers, administrators, pupils and parents relate to one another in the confined setting of the school quite often as "antagonistic forces" existing in a state of "perilous equilibrium."[2] Accordingly, perhaps the principal's most important administrative task is conflict management. The effective principal is expected to maintain order, to "keep the lid on."[3]

Research since Waller has extended our understanding of the many opportunities for conflict in the school. A central source of conflict is the tradition of teacher autonomy. Both Howard Becker and Dan Lortie have observed that the "authority system" of the public school provides the principal with formal and legitimate control; however, this control is always compromised by a countervailing norm throughout the educational industry—the teacher should be free to teach.[4] Principals must be able to manage, but teachers must be allowed to manage their own classrooms. In fact, principals must support the professional independence of their teachers in any situation where teacher autonomy is threatened.[5] In contact with the angry parent of a difficult child, the teacher is always supported.

Early research on the role of the principal in providing leadership in such a contentious milieu suggested that effective principaling should include a democratic relationship with subordinates. Teachers should be fully involved in directing the school, their opinions respected, their advice sought. Later, it was suggested that effective principaling should combine an element of managerial directedness with the democracy dimension.

A series of studies inaugurated at The Ohio State University in the late 1940s used the "Leader Behavior Description Questionnaire" (LBDQ) to rate principals along two scales: *Consideration,* or the provision of warmth, trust, respect, and friendship in contacts with members of the school staff; and *Initiating Structure,* or the definition of organizational patterns, channels of communication, and methods of procedure.[6] This instrument was based on the idea that principals were expected to be both directive and non-directive in style, both employee-centered and production-centered, both authoritarian and democratic in behavior. Principals who scored high on both initiating structure *and* consideration were thought most likely to gain the greatest degree of teacher acceptance of the principal's leadership and the greatest degree of teacher satisfaction.

Research employing "Leader Behavior Description" was excessively oriented to questions of principal-teacher interaction. As a result, a narrowly conceived measure of "teacher satisfaction" became the most common criterion used to judge a successful principalship. Additional analyses of intramural relationships discovered that the principal's status and authority depended on interactions that went well beyond the dyad of teacher and administrator. Relationships with parents, pupils, and higher-level administrators are now recognized as important. Additional analysis has shown that teacher job satisfaction, although desired, is not always the most appropriate measure of school effectiveness.

The most recent literature has portrayed a school's managerial setting as a "negotiated order."[7] Principals, teachers, other employees, pupils, even parents are in a web of negotiation within the school. The participants together work out a complex arrangement of responsibility and authority, of many role expectations, interests, values, group relationships, and goals.

In this perspective, school management, particularly conflict management, becomes heavily politicized. Groups within the school environment pursue different interests and influence each other. Edwin Bridges showed that the principal is both originating executive and responding pawn in the decision-making milieu of the school.[8] Both staff members and the principal have a variety of sanctions at their fingertips to control one another's behavior. The principal may threaten transfer, or the employee might request it. Teacher and staff assistants can use connections in the community "to create sentiment against the principal," or cultivate contacts elsewhere in the organizational hierarchy to circumvent the principal. Dan Lortie addressed the limits and difficulties of administrator influence over the school staff, particularly teachers. Teachers work largely alone; they depend very little on the school hierarchy for assistance. Because of this, the principal's power to influence teacher behavior diminishes. To reverse this tendency and exert a modicum of administrative control, the principal may cultivate productive relationships and create teacher dependence.[9]

Barsky showed that the principal creates bargaining chips for himself by showing interest in the staff's personal problems or lending assistance with professional matters. The principal ingratiates himself with teachers by personally handling much of the detail and paperwork of the school and assuming responsibility for pupil discipline and control.[10] Hanson reported in his case study of the "Silverwood" schools that:

> Students negotiated with teachers for less homework; teachers negotiated with janitors for repairing the light fixture now instead of later in the day; teachers negotiated with administrators for more instructional materials, different room assignments, or new committee assignments; administrators negotiated with teachers for increased vigilance in the halls; administrators negotiated with parents for increased participation in school affairs or more patience and understanding with the school reading program. The end product of the ongoing negotiation process is to bring order and stability to the potentially disruptive contested zone.[11]

The Principal as Instructional Leader

Observation and supervision The conventional wisdom assigns the principal a major role in overseeing the quality of instruction in the school. It is widely accepted that the most important task of the principal is to directly supervise classroom instruction, and evaluate and improve teacher performance. Courses on the supervision of teaching are required by nearly every state administrator certification program. The universality of such requirements reveals the general feeling that the principal should devote much time to improving curriculum, developing staff through in-service programs, coordinating student reassignments, innovating instruction, and introducing new learning technology.

However, studies on what administrators actually do have discovered that principals spend relatively little time directly attending to teaching and learning. Peterson observed elementary principals who spent less than 5 percent of their time in classrooms, and no more than 6 percent of the day planning and coordinating the school program, the curriculum, or the deployment of instructional materials. Martin and Willower discovered that high school principals spend just 17.4 percent of their time on teacher supervision and curriculum development.[12] In our own study of work patterns (See Chapter 3), we found that principals spend an average of just 7 to 9 percent of their time observing teachers. Consequently, some scholars conclude that classroom instruction appears to be "virtually unaffected" by organizational and administrative forces; there is little evidence of administrator influence on the core teaching and learning technology.[13]

School climate Nevertheless, interest in the possibility of an instructional leadership role for the principal has persisted. By the late 1970s developing literature on school effectiveness[14] suggested that the building principal can influence learning in the school. The principal's influence, though, may be more indirect, creating a favorable climate for learning; the most effective role may be supportive rather than supervisory or evaluative.[15]

For example, research by Rutter et al. on secondary schooling in inner city London discovered that aspects of the school as a social organization—its morale, climate, and atmosphere—can influence its effectiveness.

> Clearly what children learn will be determined by the nature and quality of the teaching they receive. However, . . . what can be achieved by classroom teaching may be greatly influenced by the overall characteristics of the school itself as an organization.[16]

In most research of this type, effectiveness is determined by measures of students' attendance, success on examinations, behavior, delinquency, and post-school employment rates. Starting with these measures, the following phenomena as reported by Rutter are found to bear directly on the effectiveness of a school:

1. Academic emphasis, including policies regarding homework, display of student work, and a high ratio of teaching to non-teaching time per week
2. A regular, rigorous and consistent student reward and punishment structure
3. A clean and tidy physical environment
4. Policies emphasizing student responsibility and participation
5. Staff cooperation in planning courses jointly or departmentally

Additional investigations of links between the site administrator and school outcomes have explored further the impact of school climate.[17] Noblit conducted comparative ethnographic case studies of principals' administrative styles, school climates, and youth crimes in the high school. Rist examined the role of a principal as a "cultural maximizer" in a single all-black ghetto school. In both investigations, the principal was found to be the creator of the school's atmosphere of ideas, values, and acceptable standards of behavior.

Stoll analyzed differences in reading test results between overachieving and underachieving schools in Florida. The researcher found that the more effective schools were more likely to have administrators who communicated the importance of reading, worked toward a coordinated reading program, and provided adequate instructional materials. Similarly, Edmonds investigated the correlates of instructionally effective and ineffective inner city schools in New York and Michigan, finding that effective schools are characterized by "strong administrative leadership," an emphasis on basic school skills, "a climate of expectation," and a regimen that is "orderly without being rigid." Vallina compared principals' behavior and reading achievement scores in Title I-ESEA schools in a school system in a large city. The principals of successful schools were more likely to maintain high standards, were more apt to concentrate their time on faculty evaluation and improvement than on "administrivia," were more concerned about the physical appearance of the school, and made greater effort to enhance community relations. Venezky and Winfield reported that the "achievement orientation" of the principal, rather than a human relations orientation, was a significant factor in successful reading instruction in poverty-area elementary schools.[18]

Finally, Clark, Lotto and McCarthy aggregated some 97 studies of urban school achievement, concluding that site leadership is crucial in determining school success and that this leadership is typically attitudinal and motivational, and capable of engendering an achievement climate. They further found that successful schools engage in staff development and establish clear goals and objectives. They concluded that successful urban schools also have high levels of parent contact and involvement.[19]

The principal as socializing agent A final, and infrequently investigated, aspect of the principal's instructional leadership role was clearly recognized by Wolcott in his ethnographic study of a single elementary principal in Oregon. He devoted a chapter of his book to the principal as a socializer of teachers into the norms, values and standard operating procedures of the school. Although the cycle of classroom observation and evaluation used by Wolcott's subject involved genuine appraisals of teacher performance, it also involved an important ritual function of affirming the principal's status within the organizational hierarchy and communicating to teachers about their conduct within the school. For example, the principal communicated his notions of acceptable dress standards and use of the school telephone, as well as how long he expected teachers to remain in the school building following afternoon dismissal of pupils.[20]

Teaching other adults how to function effectively in the school community should come naturally to principals; their professional training and experience are firmly based on teaching. But many seem to leave behind the sense of responsibility to teach, a function that is often considered a cornerstone of administration.[21]

The literature generally acknowledges that a major share of principaling activity concerns events taking place within the school building. This activity, as noted by scholars, features the principal as both a coordinating manager of a complex organization and a pedagogical expert continuously attempting to improve instruction.

In the following sections we present our own findings on the micro-society inside the school building. The two expectations of the principalship discussed in this chapter become in real life a dialectical tension between a desire to control the unpredictability of the school environment and the desire to improve and invigorate the learning environment through deliberate change. We describe it as a tension between *stabilization and enhancement.* As it turns out, the behavior of the principal also affects the school community in subtler ways. One of these is the *transformation of attitudes,* an obligation of leadership not fully appreciated in discourses on administration. Finally, we turn to the phenomenon of *climate control,* and the ways principals unobtrusively inject their own values into the teaching-learning nexus.

WHAT WE SEE

It is difficult to convey in print the charged atmosphere of a city school.[22] There are daily routines, long periods of uneventfulness, and much procedural repetition. But the management of a city elementary or secondary school occurs in an environment of considerable tension and anticipation. Many events are unpredictable and can easily drift out of control. Things happen fast, without warning: a near-drowning in the swimming pool; a stabbing in a stairwell; a school assembly that becomes a mini "riot"; two children lost on a field trip to the zoo; a student, or a teacher, "gone berserk"; and the usual rash of fights, cuts and bruises. These are worries on even the most placid days.

Stabilization and Enhancement: A Manager's Balancing Act

The building principal's first responsibility is to harness the unpredictability of the school community. As the one most often in contact with the school's pupil, parent and neighborhood clientele, the principal must maintain an orderly learning environment. The principal is also in charge of the teaching and learning activity; he or she is expected to be the "instructional leader," to encourage new curricula and experimentation, upgrade staff quality, add programs, and alter attitudes. The principal must constantly search for additional school resources, rearrange personnel and institutionalized structures, improve the image of the school, and encourage parent involvement.

Both stabilization and enhancement activities are essential elements of the principalship role—and they must be pursued simultaneously. Much tension exists between them. Too much stabilization could deaden the enterprise; too much enhancement could be disorienting and counterproductive. How does the principal find the right balance? Three key areas in which the principal seeks to balance improvement and enhancement and stability and control are: school discipline and control; parent and community involvement; and teacher and staff performance.

Discipline and Behavior Management

Every principal supervises school decorum and order. Styles vary. Some principals give much personal effort to the strict control of pupil behavior, the cleanliness of the school, etc. Others are willing to accept a bit of noise, confusion, and untidiness while maintaining control. Although disciplinary structure can be maintained for its own sake, and certainly is necessary to pupil safety and classroom efficiency, many principals extend the maintenance of control to enhance the school's learning atmosphere. In this strategy they concentrate on the anticipation of likely problems, the quick control of events and crises that do occur, and the development and enforcement of school rules as guides to proper institutional behavior.

Problem anticipation For much of each day, principals are on the go—touring the corridors; monitoring the cafeteria during lunch periods; checking on classes in session, assemblies in progress, library noise, or physical education activity in the gymnasium; helping a clerk fill out a form; making sure that aides, hall monitors, playground supervisors, and street crossing guards are on duty; and generally being available to both staff and students who have questions, comments, or problems.

Much of the principal's movement around the school is a "search routine," maintaining a physical presence in the school and trying to anticipate trouble. A common observation by the principals is that this activity helps them gauge the school climate. A halls tour of just a few minutes, spending a few seconds listening to the sounds coming from each classroom, gives a quick reading of "what's going on," of how well the school has "settled down to its business," and of what the "mood of the student body seems to be today."

Most principals quickly develop a sixth sense about possible trouble. As Principal Decks explained in detaining some students in the halls while allowing others to pass undisturbed, "Some kids you don't need to ask. You know they're okay." Elementary and high school principals alike commonly position themselves near a main entrance and walk the halls at various passing periods. Frequently at these moments a fight is stopped, excess noise quelled, the disciplinary rules enforced, and potential incidents spotted and averted.

The principal who is visibly in charge at times of potential disorder creates an impression of purposefulness in an uncertain environment. Many occurrences demand adroit handling by a principal who is on the scene and ready to act decisively and immediately. Similarly, heading off confrontations before they develop is a critical element of the job. For one principal, recent racial incidents at a neighboring high school demanded tightened security in planning a dance. Rumors of a gang battle at a local park led two elementary principals to warn students away from the park over the weekend. A field trip planned and conducted by an irresponsible teacher prompted efforts to insure that several conscientious parents and school aides went along. A very busy intersection near the school was checked each day to make sure an adult crossing guard with a poor attendance record was actually in place.

Event management Faced with the threat of unforeseen and potentially disruptive events, principals commonly seek to control unintended activity. One strategy is to try to minimize the fallout from any unusual event. For example, Principal Smith learned that a rock had been thrown through a second floor window, spraying the room with glass. His initial response, after making sure there were no injuries, was not to send people to look for those who threw the rock. Instead, he sent staff to the second floor to enter classrooms and explain the incident, quiet things down, return pupils in the halls to class, and enforce order. "They'll all be excited and keyed up on the second floor now, and that tension will build and build if we don't quiet everything down right away," he explained. Principal Gordon stressed to his teachers the importance of not referring to the previous day's student outburst in the auditorium as a riot. "If we use the term 'riot,' then we've created it," he said. The teachers were urged to drop all further discussion of the incident: "It's over! You can't run this thing into the ground. Shift your talk to the students who performed well all day long at the festival, not to the problems that lasted just a few seconds at the end," he counseled.

Rule enforcement Despite the availability of security aides, assistant principals for discipline, teachers on hall duty or cafeteria duty, and even police on full duty in some schools, principals spend a good deal of time each day personally enforcing school rules and maintaining an orderly school environment. Elementary Principal Aschner spends an average of 75 minutes in his working day supervising the movement of pupils into and out of the school building, overseeing behavior in the cafeteria and halls during the lunch hour, and touring the school corridors during passing periods. Elementary Principal Bukto spends less time policing the school during the day but eats lunch with the students in the cafeteria and leaves the building with the pupils at afternoon dismissal. Through such strategems, he can stop fights and shoo pupils off the school grounds toward home; this takes an average of 25 minutes in his day. High School principals Cohan and Daminsky spend an average of 30 minutes of their working day supervising student behavior ("Hats off please"; "Hurry or you'll be late to class"; "Where's your ID badge?") as pupils enter and leave the building, eat lunch, change classes, and gather for special events such as an after-school dance.

A common problem for high school principals is school security vis-à-vis the community. It is difficult to keep outsiders out of the school and to force legitimate insiders to wear their ID tags. Both elementary and high school principals usually do a bit of housecleaning while patrolling the halls. More than simply a concern for cleanliness, this activity, along with the effort to enforce rules, communicates an important message of environmental quality; this can be critical when the physical plant needs repair or rehabilitation.

The need to balance orderliness and stability against institutional development and improvement creates tension. As the school attempts to control the behavior of students, it also must be sure that rule enforcement is responsible and consistent; if inconsistency in rule enforcement develops, that can produce as much chaos as the original disorderly behavior.

For additional episodes raising questions of discipline strategy, see Case Two, page 274, Case Three, page 288, and Case Seven, page 298.

Fostering Parent and Community Involvement While Controlling Outside Influences

School administrators have traditionally been wary of establishing too open a relationship with their surrounding communities.[23] Nevertheless parent and neighborhood involvement has now become a major focus of the school principalship. Parents are now used as aides and volunteers in instructional work. It is well understood, however, that parent involvement and outside influences upon the school are to be kept in balance. Principals are expected by the school system to establish friendly and useful relationships with their neighborhoods, but are also expected to protect the larger organization from the pressures of community groups. Principals come to value both the political power and the extra help that a supportive neighborhood can provide. But they also understand the need to maintain a distance between the school and its community in critical staffing, resource allocation, pupil control policy, and school curriculum decisions. Parent involvement is a destabilizing influence on the school; however, parents who share the institution's goals can also add much to the program.

Principals employ three strategies to balance constituent interests and parental involvement against the stability demanded by the school's values: (a) the use of the community to protect areas of principalship authority and/or resource control; (b) the discretionary use of the principal's office to build community support; and (c) the orchestration of community involvement to engender interest in the school without generating school-community conflict.

Using the community to protect the school's work. Occasionally, with the principal's tacit consent, parents will pack a school board meeting, flood headquarters with mail, or picket the school board offices, expressing concerns about a school's program, staffing, or resource allocation. The principals of schools where these drastic actions occur are not highly regarded, however, by their superiors and peers. The overt use of community support to pressure a school board is frowned on. When Principal Carter encouraged, as a last resort, a letter writing campaign and articles in the community newspaper to acquire some critically needed textbook funds, the funds were accompanied by direct criticism. "You shouldn't have done that, you embarrassed us," commented his immediate superior.

Generally, school protection tactics are much more subtle. Principals involve parents in fund-raising bazaars, bake sales, Christmas pageants, science and art fairs, and field trips to the state capital, museum or zoo. The school channels parent energy into supportive activities and projects that increase, sometimes considerably, the staff resources available to the principal.

Some principals cultivate area residents, even grandparents, as spotters for the school—people who know the community well and can warn the school of unusual developments: there's a rumor of drug dealing at a corner grocery; two gangs had a fight over the weekend at a nearby park; Mrs. Tolan's husband was arrested last night and their four children are very much on edge. Occasionally principals politicize a few parents, keeping them informed of board of education actions, letting them in on rumors of policy change, and providing them with inside information about the larger bureaucracy. These parents are frequently active on school advisory committees that serve higher levels of the organizational hierarchy; the parents are a political force of some potential, one that can help protect the school from harassment originating elsewhere in the school system.

Building community support Many principals devote a substantial amount of time to the cultivation of the surrounding community in support of school goals. Principal Masters schedules a series of coffees in the homes of parents, inviting a few parents to the home of another, to discuss the work of the school and become better acquainted. Principals Harper and Cory devote attention to outreach efforts, organizing visits to nearby senior citizens' homes and clubs, and arranging food baskets for needy families at Christmas. Principal Johnson is active in a local businessman's organization and has persuaded a neighborhood bank to sponsor savings bonds and cash awards as prizes for academic excellence in his school.

One of the most effective means for solidifying community support, however, is the principal's discretionary response to requests for special consideration. Most often, such discretion involves providing access to the school and its programs through unusual channels or procedures. A father, an influential community leader, requests that his son be admitted to the school's special education program, even though the district's testing procedures have failed to indicate the need for special education. Principal Roberts tells the father he'll go ahead and start the boy in special education anyway, if the father can secure a letter from the family's doctor requesting the placement. In such an action, the principal obtains a valuable political friend in the student's father.

Similarly, discretionary authority may frequently be used to enhance school enrollments, despite district rules on attendance area boundaries. When there is space available, a previous relationship between a family and the school (a relative attends or has attended), and some legitimacy to the parental request (e.g., the family lives fairly close to the school but is just beyond the attendance boundary), the principal will usually be flexible in admissions decisions.

Orchestrating community involvement Parental participation in the life of city schools appears to be greater than ever before. The "four walls" interpretation of the school as a bastion of professional activity closed to all outside influence has been replaced by a new attitude of local involvement and community responsiveness. Parents are now playing important, formal roles in the instructional program, often as paid aides to teachers and staff, or as volunteer tutors, teacher aides, library assistants, and sponsors of special programs in reading, art, or computer technology.

In other roles, parents are increasingly involved in school fund raising, pageants and school assemblies, field trips, and the sponsorship of extracurricular activities. Parent advisory councils are now concerned with an increasing range of resource allocation and program decisions that were previously considered the responsibility of professionals. The schools are also reaching out to parents through newsletters, home visits, recreation nights, and open houses.

The school's stability however, depends on the combination of community involvement with very little real parental power in school policymaking. As we have observed earlier, the school principal is expected by the larger organization to be responsive to, *but also protect the school system from,* community interests and demands. The principal must balance parental involvement against the need for authoritative control over the school. Principal Russell explains that he has a very active cadre of parent volunteers and that many people from the neighborhood are involved in the school's work. He mentions, however, that the school's formal parent advisory council hasn't met much over the last few years—ever since the council began demanding a voice in teacher evaluation. Principal Harper, in another example, complained about his difficulty in getting parents active in school affairs, mentioning that few people attended parent advisory council meetings and that it had been unable to elect a council president for two years. Harper indicated he was quite concerned, though, because a number of parents were dissatisfied with one of the school's teachers and had threatened to bring their grievance to the attention of a higher-level administrator. Harper said, "I don't want them washing our linen in public like that."

For a dramatic example of parent involvement in school policy, see Case Eight, page 304.

Upgrading Staff Quality While Preventing Staff Conflict

The faculty expects the principal to support them and respect their professional independence. But the larger organization expects the principal to supervise and evaluate the teaching staff—to upgrade the quality of instruction and exercise overall instructional leadership. Efforts to enhance the quality of teaching and the task performance of the school staff must be balanced against the need to stabilize the principal-staff relationship. Principal Greene attempted a serious and tough reevaluation of her teachers; in her annual evaluation notices to teachers, she lowered many ratings. Many responded by applying immediately for transfer to other schools.

Constraints of legal and organizational authority complicate the balancing act. The teacher's union contract limits class size, on-duty and off-duty hours, and the amount of extra work such as curriculum committees and lunchroom supervision. Procedures for the evaluation and dismissal of teachers are elaborate, time-consuming, and filled with organizational pitfalls. Moreover, in some school systems, many employees—maintenance and cafeteria personnel, itinerant teachers, testing specialists—are not directly responsible to the building principal.

Despite these constraints, the principal must be responsive to and have sufficient flexibility to handle the demands that surface. Despite full classes, new arrivals must be accommodated. Despite an agreement on unassigned teacher time for "preparation periods," the personnel available to the school must be used fully to insure that the children are always supervised. Despite the assistance of clerks, assistant principals, aides, and others, the administrative work of the school demands that classroom teachers take on committee assignments and curriculum development tasks. They must be available for club or activity sponsorship, for the flood of paperwork, and for pupil supervision at sporting events, dances, festivals, and club meetings both before and after school hours.

In sustaining a balanced relationship with the school staff, principals concentrate on: (a) the communication of role performance expectations, (b) the fulfillment of teacher expectations regarding professional autonomy, and (c) the development and maintenance of a reward system for cooperative behavior.

Communicating principal expectations In efforts to enhance the quality of instruction, principals spend little time in in-service training or curriculum development. Although periods of in-service training are built into the calendar, both principals and teachers generally go through the motions of planning and carrying out teacher in-service—using the time for sales pitches from textbook publishers, for a talk by someone from central headquarters, or for some administrative announcement and procedural explanations (e.g., an explanation of the special education provisions of P.L. 94-142). Similarly, classroom visitation and the supervision of instruction are not stressed by most principals. It is common to hear principals mention that they feel guilty about the little time given to teacher observation; a typical excuse is that one really doesn't accomplish much by "sitting in classrooms all day."

Principals do, however, try to communicate to faculty and staff that they are present, are aware of events in the school, and that their expectations of staff performance are being checked. On their tours through their buildings, principals constantly duck in and out of classes in session, briefly glance through the classroom door at activities inside, occasionally stop in the back of a room for a few minutes to watch a teacher. Principal Bachman notes that it takes just a few seconds for him to gauge a classroom. Is the teacher standing or sitting? Are the pupils at their desks working, or is there too much movement around the room? Are there books, papers or worksheets in evidence? With the weaker teachers, says Bachman, he'll spend extra time making sure they know his expectations and are managing their work well.

Many high school and elementary principals also collect weekly lesson plans from their teachers. Although the plans may not be checked very carefully, the activity communicates the message that the principal is interested in their work. When teachers and staff perform extra duties, most principals spot check to insure they are on station as scheduled and performing correctly.

Fulfilling expectation of teacher autonomy Respect for the professional autonomy of the classroom teacher is fundamental in teacher-principal interaction. The principal protects the teacher from outside interference and supports him or her in problematic situations.

Much professional autonomy is, of course, structured into the procedures and contractual obligations of the administrative setting. The union contract places strict limits on the principal in teacher evaluation, dismissal, and in the allocation of work assignments. Other school system guidelines restrict the demands that can be made upon the teacher. Beyond these contractual and procedural guarantees, however, the classroom teacher often needs the additional protection that the school principal can provide. Principal Andrews visited all ten of his school's new teachers just before the end of the first marking period in the fall, warning them to be sure they had lots of evidence to support each grade. He cautioned each teacher that the pupils and their parents in this school were not reluctant to question a grade, and the teacher "had better make sure he's covered." Principal Robinson encountered an angry parent who claimed her son's teacher had hit him across the nose with a ruler. After discussion of the incident, the parent and principal went to see the teacher. As they left the office, Robinson remarked in an aside, "I've told her before to put that ruler down." Robinson added, however, that she felt it was her responsibility to defend the teacher. For an account of the ruler incident, see Case Six, page 295.

Rewarding cooperative behavior Bridges has described the extent to which the building administrator is more of a pawn of organizational relationships than he is the origin of meaningful activity.[24] Constrained by professional norms, the union contract, board rules, funding formulas, and state or federal laws, the principal frequently expresses a feeling of powerlessness. In a response to a local newspaper survey, one principal in the community under study said, "The principal is really no more than a toothless tiger. Every conceivable responsibility is placed on his shoulders, but he is not given sufficient authority to do the job."

Despite some severe restraints upon his capacities for rewarding and punishing, the principal does have some hard currency to distribute to those who are most cooperative. In spite of resource allocation by formula and job placement by central office directive, principals make decisions about the distribution of money and jobs that add significantly to their authority. Principals Banks, Crowder, and Donnelly illustrate three key mechanisms that can be used.

1. Banks receives a call from the district office, informing him that six teaching positions for the summer will be available for the faculty from his school. Now off the phone, he explains that a large number of his teachers have requested summer contracts and this

in one area where he has an opportunity to "acquire a hold" over his faculty. Banks says it is totally his decision; the teachers know this and it makes a difference—especially to those who need the money. In a few minutes, Banks leaves his office and begins a tour of classrooms to check with a number of teachers he is identifying for summer school, some of whom hadn't even applied. Returning to the office, he says, "They were all excited."

2. Crowder mentions that he has finally received approval to firm up the school's assistant principal position. Mrs. Stallings, the acting assistant, can now become a full-time assistant principal, freed from all classroom duties. What he has to do now, says Crowder, is go through all of the motions of opening the job up to everyone and interviewing all of the eligible candidates. All last week he interviewed people in his office. Twenty-three people applied and he gave them each about fifteen to twenty minutes, asking all applicants the same set of six questions. He remarks, "It was rather funny, of course, because I had to give Mrs. Stallings an interview too, and she and I had earlier put together the six questions." Crowder goes on to mention that he would have had to interview more people, but some who called bowed out when they found out there was an inside candidate. Now, he explains, he has to write up his evaluations and send his request for appointment of Stallings in to personnel. As soon as this goes through, he wants to move Mr. Wilson out of the classroom part-time to the counselor position that will become available. Wilson is a very sharp and hard-working young man who should be guided into administration.

3. Donnelly is roaming from one committee meeting to another, as his teachers meet in groups after school to develop and improve curricula. He explains that the faculty meet once each week after school for forty-five minutes. Participation is totally "voluntary." However, says Donnelly, he does consider attendance and involvement in committee work in staff ratings for the year. He remarks that the teacher chairing one group received only a "satisfactory" rating last year. (Only the two highest ratings, superior and excellent, qualify a teacher for career advance-

ment within the system.) "She came weeping into the office, asking what she could do to raise her rating. We had a talk, and she apparently got the message; in her group she's doing a topnotch job, really enthusiastic."

THE TRANSFORMATION OF ATTITUDES: EMOTIONAL CHANGES IN A MINI-BUREAUCRACY

The principal receives many directives from the central office. Although each directive can be understood as a specific instruction with a limited purpose, it is also a part of the conceptual framework of school policy. For an instruction to be effective at the site level, it may be necessary for the faculty and staff to comprehend the purpose and policy behind the directive. The principal is often the person who can place a specific directive within the larger framework of school policy. To do so, the principal must introduce new ideas about schools and their purpose to the staff. Specific changes at the unit level that reflect these ideas can then be interpreted to the staff within this framework. Underlying this function is the belief that directives, even when carried out to the letter, may not have the intended effect if school staff do not interpret them within the spirit of the policies they reflect.

The Context of Attitudes: A Case Study

Principal Anderson called her assistant principal in charge of scheduling into her office, instructing him to bring along his schedule for the teacher aides. When he arrived, she told him that the district coordinator for bilingual teacher aides had visited the building the previous day. The coordinator had complained that Mrs. Garcia had too much hall duty in her schedule. Anderson said that Garcia's schedule must be changed so that "the amount of time she'll spend in the corridor is minimal." The coordinator "really harped on that," she emphasized.

Anderson invited her assistant to sit down, saying that they would go over the aide program schedule together. This included bilingual aides financed with money from the state, aides-in-training financed through government CETA funds, and regular aides who were part of the budgeted school program of the Board of Education. After studying the schedule, Anderson concluded, "We can't use Garcia this way. We'll put her on phones calling bilingual youngsters who are not in school. We'll put her to work getting students into those programs."

It became clear, however, that there was a good deal more that was wrong with the aides' schedule. The two regular aides who had been with the school for many years were assigned to office duty in the attendance and the program offices. The newer aides, who were part of the bilingual and CETA programs, spent most of the day guarding halls and securing exits. When questioned about these assignments, her assistant's reasoning was simple. The regular aides had worked in offices for years, knew the ropes and could be counted on to do their jobs. The newer aides were assigned to fill a need for greater security in the halls. The assistant principal pointed out that the teachers had refused to sit at the exits and guard the halls, and the student monitors could not be given that responsibility. That left the aides. "How could we cover our exits without the aides?" he asked, and added, "We do need security in this building."

Anderson responded by pointing out, "We depend too much on the veterans." The new aides wanted a chance to prove themselves, too. That way, "they can get some of the arrangements that the old-timers have been able to get for themselves." She told him, "Frankly, you wouldn't want to be in the halls all day and neither would I." The aides who were in the halls all day resented those who never had hall duty. Furthermore, if these assignments were not balanced better, she warned, "We are going to have a grievance, because that's what it's boiling up to." She suggested that they revise the schedules by assigning the experienced aides some hall duty, putting the CETA aides in the office where they could be trained, and placing the bilingual aides under the supervision of the bilingual department chairman for more periods during the day. They agreed to meet as soon as possible with the experienced aides to explain the change in schedule. They also reviewed the schedules to find the lighter periods in each office, when the experienced aides could be absent and it would be safe to leave a trainee in charge. Finally they began to identify specific office tasks that would be appropriate for a trainee.

The aides had different backgrounds and experiences. The two office aides were white women; one was a former teacher. Their skills were well developed and they were needed in the offices where they worked. The other aides were mostly black and Latin. They did not have office skills or experience, but were eager to learn. In fact, the guidelines for the CETA program stressed that these jobs were supposed to be training positions that could move unskilled workers, like corridor guards, into more skilled positions, like office work.

Later in the day the assistant principal returned to Anderson's office with one of the experienced aides, Mrs. Bocca. They sat at the conference table, which was in an alcove of the principal's office. Anderson wanted to know whether her assistant had filled Bocca in on the situation. Bocca nodded yes. Anderson then said to Bocca, "What the whole thing boils down to is that you and Marie Johnson (the other old-timer) are burrs in everyone's side." She complimented Bocca, "The skills are obviously not comparable, the things you are able to do are far greater than what the other aides are able to do." Furthermore, she let Bocca know that her work was appreciated by the administrative staff. "We, as administrators of the school, look upon you as staff that we can count on." "But," she said, "look at this, I want to show you something." Anderson then placed the aides' schedule on the table before Bocca, so that Bocca could see the different assignments of all the aides. The principal pointed out that some aides were scheduled for hall duty period after period. "You know," she said, "having three periods in a row at an exit is really a bore."

Bocca responded by explaining how hard she worked, that even though she spent the day in the program office, she still brought work home every night. She indicated that if she were given hall duty to satisfy the other aides, she would fall even further behind in her work. Once again Anderson assured Bocca that the change in schedule in no way reflected a lack of appreciation for her hard work. The reason they had to make changes was that the other aides had complained that assignments were not distributed in an equitable manner. "The animosity is now building toward a grievance on behalf of the other aides," she explained. Anderson pointed to the schedule and said bluntly, "Anybody from the outside who would take a look at the program schedule for the aides would say it's not fair." She said that the schedule should be re-written so that it was "more presentable." Anderson told Bocca, "The problem is that your assignment on this program sheet simply does not reflect the hard work that you do. You need to be assigned to a corridor in order to make this more equitable."

Anderson then turned the discussion to how they might make these changes with the least possible disturbance to Bocca's office duties. They discussed periods of the day when the office duties were lightest, and talked about tasks that a trainee might be able to learn. In this context, Bocca volunteered that she spend a couple of periods a day delivering materials to various rooms; this activity might be combined with hall duty. Following this suggestion, her first period assignment was changed from "program office," to "corridor duty on the first floor." Bocca was pleased and said, "Sure, I'm doing that anyway. There's no change; we're just calling it something else."

A few minutes later the assistant principal told Bocca that one aide was complaining that she was at exit five for three consecutive periods. This prompted Bocca to say, "Since Dora is complaining so much, give me exit five and then put her some place else during third period." They decided to put Dora in the library third period where she could help catalogue new books. Bocca cheerfully added that exit five was near the program office. "That way, if something comes up in the office and I'm needed, I can run over to the office."

When the schedule changes were settled, Anderson moved to the training issue. She told Bocca, "You know, we rely on you very heavily. We need you to train somebody who will be your back up." And then she added, "If you try and train somebody and they don't make it, then it's up to me to talk to them and tell them that they haven't made it."

Bocca was unhappy. She told Anderson that last year she tried to work with Garcia, but Garcia "couldn't alphabetize anything." Furthermore, when the other aides came into the office, complained Bocca, "they just sit and wait until you tell them exactly what to do." She said they had "no initiative for getting work done."

Anderson explained that that may be, but that the purpose of the CETA program was to train people. She said, "The way to train people is to show them how to do the things that you want them to do. First you show them. Then you let them try to do it two or three times, and you watch them and see how they do. Then, if they can't do it after a while, you let me know that they're not capable of learning that skill." She explained that Bocca could not expect trainees to be able to do the office skills, but they needed to determine which aides would be able to learn office skills. Anderson stressed that the idea behind the CETA training program was to provide the opportunity to learn. "We have to try people," she said.

Bocca said that she had tried before. She brought up Natalie, who was supposed to help in the library, but "couldn't even read." Anderson countered by stressing that their responsibility was to offer the chance for the aides to get the new skills. Bocca was not won over. "I know what the problem is," she responded, "they feel it's discriminatory." "Well," Anderson sighed, "it *is* discriminatory, in a way."

Anderson continued to reinforce her position on this problem. "Now this aide that will be assigned to your office, if she isn't capable, then that's one thing. But we really have to ask ourselves whether or not we're currently using her effectively. The changes we will make will be tentative. If somebody is not working out in a new assignment, then they won't stay there." Bocca was still unhappy. She complained, "The trouble with all these other aides is they think that working in an office is easy. They don't really know what goes into this."

Later in the day the other experienced aide met with

Anderson on the same issue. Anderson asked her to sit down at the conference table and introduced the problem by saying to Mrs. Johnson, "As you know, we've had a problem, and you and Bocca are the targets." She added, "It's going to be a hassle unless I do something." She explained that the current programs did not look fair or equitable because it looked as though some people had better schedules than others. Bocca's schedule had already been changed. She would be at exit five during fifth period and in the corridors during the first period. Anderson then told Johnson that she wanted her out of the attendance office during fifth and sixth period. Also, Derek would be taking her place during fourth period.

Johnson explained that she had been working on student registration all week. She said of Derek, "If you put her in the attendance office, be sure that I'm in there at the same time." She felt that Derek could not be left alone because, "she can't even answer the phone to talk to anyone." Anderson said that they must give Derek a chance. She emphasized that either Derek would make the grade or she would lose the job. The principal explained that she thought fourth period was a light time in the attendance office, which is why she chose that period to assign Derek. Johnson softened, telling Anderson that "Derek can handle the tardies." Anderson pressed for more responsibility for Derek. She told Johnson, "Well, maybe she can handle the transfers out too." Anderson added, "Teach her how to do it. Spell it out to her in words of one syllable."

Johnson replied, "Well, yeah, but she messes it up and that's why I get upset."

Anderson told Johnson, "Well then you tell me when she messes it up. That's for me to deal with."

Anderson said Johnson had to be willing to be out of the attendance office during fifth and sixth period to cover hall duty when it was needed. Johnson said that she didn't mind the idea of hall duty. Then she added, "I wouldn't care if you put someone in there (the office) with some intelligence, but Derek doesn't have it."

Anderson told her, "Listen, if you give somebody a job and they do it wrong, then show them how to do it right. And watch them try to do it right. Then come to me. You've got to realize that it takes time to learn everything involved in working in an office."

Johnson replied, "I know, but they make mistakes and then the teachers come down yelling at me."

Anderson switched the subject, inquiring after Johnson's family. They talked briefly about recent weddings, births, etc. Then Johnson wanted to know if the changes were going to start the next day. Anderson said, "Yes," and concluded the meeting by saying, "I want you at exit one during fourth and fifth periods."

Comment

Prior to the visit of the district bilingual coordinator, the school's inexperienced aides were scheduled to guard halls and maintain security at building exits for most of the school day. Although this filled a gap in manpower at the school, it ignored the purpose behind the aide programs. The CETA aides were supposed to learn new skills, so that they could upgrade themselves and find office jobs elsewhere. The bilingual aides were supposed to directly assist students in bilingual classes. When it came to assigning work to these aides, these purposes were overlooked in favor of the need to guard hallways and provide security at the school's ten exits.

At the same time, two experienced aides were assigned to clerical duties in the school's attendance and program offices. In order to meet the demands of the aide coordinator, and head off a grievance by the CETA and bilingual aides, the principal changed the scheduling patterns for every school aide. Instead of assigning aides to either hall duty or office-classroom duty on the basis of experience, each aide was reassigned a balance of hall duty and office-classroom duty. The reassignment was more equitable to the new aides and provided them training opportunities.

Of course, principal Anderson had every right to reassign the aides. But she recognized that there were elements of danger in the change. To satisfy the CETA and bilingual aides, and help them refocus on their duties instead of their shared complaints, it was necessary to reassign the experienced aides to some hall duty as well as to reduce the hall duty of the newer aides. By treating the old-timers the same as the newer aides, Anderson reduced the appearance of hierarchy, an important consideration since the hierarchy in this case also followed racial lines.

While it was more fair to remove the special privilege enjoyed by the old-timers, Anderson could not ignore the fact that the school's administrators counted on them to carry out the office work. To maintain the productivity of the experienced aides, Anderson took several steps to placate their feelings. They were invited to meet with Anderson to discuss the changes; their work was praised. Also, the changes were minimized. The administrators were careful to reassign the aides during the light periods of the day. Hall duties were selected that overlapped with the old-timers' current schedules. Both aides were unhappy about the changes, but were willing to cooperate because the conference informally reaffirmed their sense of being special.

It is to Anderson's credit that she did not limit these changes to mere alterations in assignment that reduced the appearance of favoritism. She went further, attempting to win over the experienced aides and obtain their help in establishing a valid training program for the CETA aides. She established two ground rules to win the old-timers to the spirit of the training objective. The assignment of new aides to office work would be tentative. Furthermore, Anderson promised that if an aide failed to learn new skills after a reasonable training opportunity, the aide would be removed. It was more difficult to win them over on the training issue. They were afraid that productivity would suffer, things would be messed up by the new aides, and their time would be wasted. Yet, Anderson stood her ground. At the conclusion of each conference, it was clear to both aides that the reassignment was not merely superficial. Both experienced aides would be expected to carry out the spirit of the training programs by helping the new aides learn office skills.

Probably the most significant policy issue in this example is the question of whether the inequitable distribution of assignments was motivated by racial discrimination. This question is appropriate because a hierarchy of assignment was evident, with the high status office positions distributed to the white aides and the low status guard duties assigned to the black and Latin aides. From this example, it is clear that the administrative team distributed assignments according to skill, and possibly according to seniority. Bocca realized however, that since the distribution of assignments also corresponded to race, "they feel it's discriminatory." It is not unusual to find policy on racial discrimination in conflict with the seniority guidelines in a school system. The white staff tend to argue for privilege on the basis of seniority; the newer black and Latin staff argue on the basis of equality.

Anderson was aware of the role of seniority assignments in perpetuating the distribution of privilege along racial lines. This is evident in her observation that the assignment process for aides "is discriminatory, in a way." By pressing for opportunities that would teach office skills to aides of all races, she attacked the status quo of keeping some aides in the office and others guarding the halls. Once the newer aides had office skills, they could be assigned a balanced schedule on the basis of those skills. Once this was possible, the skill distribution that made inequitable schedules rational would disappear. Finally, she was affirming the essential rationale for equality in all organizations—when given the opportunity, people of all races will demonstrate their ability.

We see from these episodes what might be called imaginative management: using the prosaic occasion of reassigning duties as a medium for changing two employees' attitudes toward their work, their colleagues, and their organization. Seniority has its privileges, but a larger purpose is served if other criteria are admitted. The women accepted the changes and made adjustments in their own work patterns. But in doing so, they were assisted by the principal in transforming their attitudes toward their fellow workers and the needs of the organization.

CLIMATE CONTROL: INSTRUCTIONAL LEADERSHIP BY INDIRECTION

The acid test of any school is whether its students master appropriate coursework within a reasonable period of time. Principals have the responsibility of judging whether teachers teach well. Much literature in education administration is devoted to the selection, evaluation and improvement of a school's faculty. The principals in this study did not devote much time to these supervising activities. Much more time was spent on student discipline, parent contact, and general monitoring of the school building.

Principals seemed to believe that these non-supervisory activities were important supports for student achievement. An implicit division of labor was in effect: teachers were responsible for presenting lessons and getting students to pay attention and participate in learning activities. The principal supervised the teachers, but was also responsible for establishing and maintaining in the school building a tone that was supportive of the learning activity. The two case studies in this chapter exemplify two principals' understanding of this widely accepted responsibility. The studies also indicate some specific efforts they made to improve and maintain a climate they believed to be supportive of instruction.

Prototype A—Hutchens Takes Charge

When Lila Hutchens became principal at Grove Elementary School, things had been out of control for some time. The last permanently assigned principal had been removed from his position by the Board of Education. He took every school record and administrative document with him. During the intervening two years, the vacancy was filled with interim principals, and none established an administrative presence. Those curious about what a school might be like if there were no principal might look at Grove School before Hutchens.

The teachers took responsibility only for their own classroom and students. They sat in the faculty lounge until the class bell, and then went to their classrooms, where some students waited and others straggled inside. Misbehaving pupils were shooed from class and wandered in the halls where there was no supervision. At recess, students rushed unescorted from their classes to the playground, and teachers went to the lounge. The same pattern was followed at lunchtime when students either left for home or ate in the cafeteria. As far as Hutchens could tell, no textbook had been ordered for the school in two years. The building, built in a classical style at the turn of the century, was in disrepair. Many windows were broken. Walls and floors in one hallway were grime-covered and water stained. The desks and chairs, which were permanently bolted to the floor, were badly broken and marred. One of Hutchens' first acts as principal was to stop random student movement in the halls and restore order to the school's gathering areas.

Hutchens established rules to regulate student movement to and from classrooms. No student could leave a class without the teacher's permission; students with permission would carry a pass. Students would remain on the playground before school, at recess and after lunch until their teachers joined them there and escorted them into the building. Students could only use the door and play areas to which they were assigned. Students would gather in class groups on the playground to wait for their teachers. After class, teachers would escort their students through the halls and out of the building for recess, lunch or to go home after the school day.

To enforce these rules, Hutchens roamed the school reminding students and teachers of their duties. She greeted students and teachers each morning on the playground before they entered the building. She stood in hallways and at the exits, making sure students did not enter the building early and that they used the correct door when they came inside with their teachers. She asked to see passes of students walking in the halls during class time. She frequently met with students who broke the new rules, explaining the rules to them and letting them know that she would enforce the rules. When students repeatedly broke the rules, she met with their parents and explained the rules to them. Repeat offenses were punished with suspension and additional parent conferences. No outsider could enter the school without first securing a permit in the central office. No permits were issued to former students or students who did not attend the school. Hutchens stood in the hallway and near the exits at recess, lunch and after school. She also toured the school at least once a day during class time.

At Hutchens' invitation, social work majors from a nearby university and a social service agency visited the school. As part of their training, they initiated a counseling program for children who were constantly breaking school rules. Hutchens also took steps to remove the most troublesome students from regular classrooms. They and their parents were encouraged to apply for special programs at other campuses. She requested that a school psychologist test them in preparation for removing them from regular classes and placing them in special classes for disorderly students.

Although Hutchens handled the discipline problems herself, she trained the school clerks to handle some of the frequent, routine student problems. For example, when a student fell and skinned her knee during recess, the clerks were directed to look up the child's emergency phone number and to notify her parents.

Hutchens also tackled the rundown, neglected appearance of the school. After much complaining to the district office, a new engineer was assigned to the building. With his arrival, windows were replaced and the building scrubbed. Hutchens instructed teachers to work with students to plan bulletin boards for the hallways. She encouraged a group of parents and teachers to buy paint and work after hours to paint the more unsightly areas.

She began to build a curriculum resource area in one corner of her large office. Here she stored catalogues and samples of textbooks and teaching materials. She formed teachers' curriculum groups which invited publisher representatives to make presentations at faculty meetings. She also discovered that the teachers who had been at Grove for years did not follow the Board of Education curriculum guidebook or use the criterion-referenced tests in reading that had been developed for system-wide use. To introduce the official materials to these teachers, Hutchens enlisted the help of two newly-assigned teachers. These newcomers were familiar with the materials, learning objectives and tests used throughout the system. They shared their knowledge and experience with the other teachers informally in the lounge and in scheduled workshops.

Hutchens explained that it was her philosophy to be available to teachers and children. She wanted them to feel that "someone cares." Although this approach allowed students and teachers to disrupt her continually during the school day, she felt that it was the only way to make the changes she had introduced the normal routine in the school. The paperwork she was expected to complete, especially that which required concentrated periods of time and much care, could not be done during school hours. So, she stayed at her desk into the late afternoon, and spent many evenings and weekend hours at home working on these tasks. These were the two sides of her principalship: while school was in session, she was constantly on the move seeing that her routines were followed. When the school had quieted down in the afternoon after dismissal, she turned her attention to reports and other paperwork.

Hutchens' administrative style concentrated on the relationship between students and the school as a whole. When students do not feel they are a part of the school, and do not follow school routines, their entire sense of membership is confined to their own class and teacher. When the authority relationship with the classroom teacher is broken, students are likely to be uncontrolled. Even when a teacher has an excellent rapport with the students in class, the students may experience the teacher's absence as a lifting of limits unless more general limits are part of the building routines. The authority to enforce more general limits rests with the principal, who must extend it effectively to the faculty and staff. The following example illustrates this.

One afternoon, three girls burst into Hutchens' office. They told her that a high school boy had entered a classroom where there was a substitute teacher. They said he was sitting in class, throwing things at people; the substitute had lost control.

Hutchens rushed to the classroom. A woman teacher was standing helpless in front of the class. Students were walking and running about at will, talking and shouting. When Hutchens entered the room she told the students, "Get into your own seats!" Immediately, she approached the teacher's desk and looked for the seating chart. It was not there, so she asked the children to give their names. After completing a new seating chart, she asked the class, "Where is your work?"

Hutchens told the students to pay attention. Even though their regular teacher was absent, they still had to behave in a proper manner with the substitute. She checked the classroom and the cloakroom for the high school student but he was not there. Before leaving the room, she told the substitute to use the seating chart to be sure that no other students came into the room. The substitute complained that the students were throwing paper clips. Hutchens told them to pick up any paper clips that were on the floor near their seat. Then she left and returned to her office.

A half hour later, Hutchens noticed that two boys from the class were running down the hall. She asked them why they were not in class. They said they were just now returning from the bathroom. She reminded them that they were supposed to have a pass if they were in the halls. Suspecting that students were walking out of class and roaming the building, she went back to the room. Once again, the students were out of their seats. The moment they saw Hutchens, however, they returned to their seats. She told two boys to pick up some paper that was scattered around their desks on the floor and checked the seating chart to learn who was missing. She arbitrated a fight between a girl and a boy.

She checked the halls outside the classroom, then returned to verify that the students were still quiet inside. She walked up and down the rows of desks. She told the substitute that she wanted the names of students who did not complete the day's assignment.

She reminded the substitute that no more students should leave the classroom. On the way back to her office, Hutchens spotted several more students from the class and told them to return.

Hutchens remarked, "If I were younger, I could not do this job." She felt that it took her combined experience from on-the-job training at other schools to know what to do in a school where she was starting from scratch administratively. It was with great pride, therefore, that Hutchens announced at the end of the first year that reading scores in her school were up 35 percent from the previous year's. She felt that her relentless efforts to establish school-wide order had begun to pay off.

Prototype B—Lopez, a Visible Presence

Spring Elementary School was built about 1900. A complete rehabilitation within the past five years gave the building a bright, friendly atmosphere. The addition of modern lighting, fresh paint and numerous repairs improved the classrooms and hallways. Many bulletin boards and display areas now decorate the public areas.

In the main hall where volunteer tutors meet with students before school, welcome signs greet visitors in Spanish and English. Spring is a large school, serving nearly 1000 students from kindergarten through eighth grade.

It is also a strictly neighborhood school. The houses and apartments of white working and middle class families make up most of the neighborhood. Although many Asian, Middle Eastern and Hispanic children attend the school, the parent council and PTA leadership is firmly controlled by the white group. This group is against busing students in and out of the neighborhood to achieve integration. When Jose Lopez was assigned as principal, he met several times with these parents. They made it clear that they expected their principal to be a strong disciplinarian. He was to suspend any student who caused trouble, even those guilty of minor infractions. They spoke glowingly of his predecessor; he supervised the playground, shouting to students who played too roughly or trespassed into the wrong play area. Lopez realized that many parents watched the playground from their windows, looking to see whether he was there enforcing the rules. They liked to see the principal on the job.

Another group that greeted Lopez when he became principal was his administrative team which consisted of three white women: the assistant principal (who doubled as the learning disabilities teacher), the reading teacher, and the school counselor. Generally referred to by Lopez as "the girls in 101," they kept a pot of hot coffee and a generous supply of fresh rolls in their busy, friendly office. All had been at Spring school for many years. They functioned as his brain trust during his first year as principal. They offered advice, let him know when he was stepping on someone's toes, and filled him in on school gossip. He respected their abilities in their specialized areas and trusted them. Also, his experienced clerk knew the ropes and could handle the paperwork. The faculty was experienced and, he felt, generally competent; he knew the students' reading scores placed the school's academic record well above average, though not at the very top.

As principal, Lopez spent most of his time looking for trouble. He knew that most principals let their freed assistant principal handle discipline matters; his assistant principal however, was a teaching specialist who was needed in that area. Lopez preferred to leave curriculum and instructional matters to the brain trust, while he handled the discipline. He personally handled any disciplinary referral made by teachers or other staff, arbitrated problems between teachers and parents, and frequently roamed the building and playgrounds.

Lopez conducted three or four tours of the school each day, which took him by every classroom on every floor. He also checked washrooms and the cafeteria-auditorium areas. Before school started, he verified that students who had been admitted early to see their teachers had gone to their classrooms and that the teachers were with them. He also checked in on the "breakfast gang" in the cafeteria. He spoke with the cafeteria worker and the small group of children who participated in the free breakfast program. He returned to his office and checked with the clerk that there was a teacher in each class, but he left the securing and assigning of substitute teachers to her discretion. When classes started, he looked in on all classrooms where there were substitutes.

When parents entered the school, he spoke with them about the reason for their visit. Spanish-speaking parents looked to him to translate bureaucratic matters for them. When parents telephoned the school, he took the call. One parent told him at an open house that his daughter was receiving obscene phone calls because someone had written her name and phone number on one of the tables in the school's library. The next morning Lopez went to the library and scraped out the offending words. When children were ill or injured, Lopez telephoned the parents. At recess, Lopez followed his predecessor's example and patrolled the playground, stopping fights and enforcing order.

At lunchtime, Lopez sat on the stage above the students, supervising them with a microphone connected to the stage sound system. Students waited until he told them to get in line to buy milk.

When students misbehaved, he called them by name and they had to finish eating their lunch at the base of the stage. After lunch the misbehavers went to the principal's office instead of the playground. When the students finished eating, he dismissed one class at a time to go to the playground. On rainy days, he led a bingo game. After the play period, he allowed the misbehavers who were waiting in his office to go to class.

Lopez announced any departure from the usual school routine. When an indoor recess was necessary because of bad weather, he announced the fact himself over the P.A. system. He made other announcements and organized all special events. When some classes were invited to attend a film because their students had the best attendance records, he ordered the film, notified the teachers and ran the movie projector himself.

In addition to these daily routines, Lopez met with students who had been referred for discipline. His most consistent strategies during these conferences were the threat of suspension and the threat that their parents would be notified of their misbehavior. Thus he was able to gain the cooperation of most students. During his first year at Spring, in fact, he suspended only one. These conferences eventually convinced both parents and teachers that he was a strong disciplinarian. The following examples illustrate his methods with students from several age levels.

Playing with fire A teacher aide who was supervising students during recess sent Tom to the office for playing with matches. After learning from the aide what had happened, Lopez invited Tom into his office. He took a blank index card from his file and wrote down Tom's name, telephone number and address. Then he looked up from the card and said, "Tell me how it happened."

Tom explained that he saw a book of matches on the playground and picked it up. He lit them and dropped them. Then his friend hit him, so he threw the matches at his friend. Unfortunately, they hit a girl instead. "But," he added, "the pack was already out," when he threw it.

After a few minutes of silence Lopez said, "You know, even though the matches are out, they're still hot."

Tom tried to defend by saying, "But I didn't mean for them to land on her."

Lopez told him, "Well, I know. But, one thing led to another which led to another. If you hadn't lit the matches, you wouldn't have thrown them at your friend and they wouldn't have hit the girl. It's lucky for you that the girl was not burned." Then he added, "Maybe tomorrow a parent will come and complain that a boy burned their daughter. I'll have your name here and that way I won't have to come looking all over the school for you." Lopez handed Tom a pass to return to his class. As Tom left Lopez added, "We'll call you if we have any reports."

Crayons or erasers? Lopez read a note that a boy brought to the office from his teacher. The note explained that Roger was throwing crayons. Lopez invited Roger, a second-grader, into his office and completed an index card as Roger answered the routine questions. Then Lopez turned to Roger and said, "I understand that you were throwing crayons in your class."

Roger denied it, "I was throwing an eraser."

"Was it a pencil eraser or a blackboard eraser?"

Roger held up his thumb and forefinger, indicating a small eraser.

"Well, why were you throwing it?"

Roger said that a girl was putting paper by his desk.

"So, this girl was putting papers on your desk?"

"Yes," Roger said.

Lopez was silent for a moment. Then he asked Roger, "Your mother, did she say to throw erasers at this girl?"

"No," Roger answered.

Lopez continued sarcastically, "Oh, then your father was the one who said to throw erasers?"

"No," Roger answered.

"Well, then who did say it?"

"No one."

"Well," said Lopez, "then you must have told yourself to throw them. Why did you tell yourself to throw them? Don't you have any control? Who should be punished for your throwing them?"

"Me," Roger said. "I should be punished."

"Not your mother or your father, but you." He then asked when Roger had gym class.

Roger did not know, so Lopez asked for Roger's room number and went to check his schedule. Meanwhile, Lopez explained that he would write a note to Roger's teacher saying Roger was not to have gym class this week.

As Lopez finished writing the note he asked Roger, "Now *who* is supposed to be punished for the erasers?"

"Me," Roger replied.

Lopez handed Roger the note and sent him back to class.

Pushes in the bushes When Martin came into the principal's office with the playground supervisor, the skin beneath his right eye was already beginning to darken. Lopez questioned Martin about what had happened. Martin explained that Jerry had pushed him into some bushes. As he got up Jerry hit him in the face. Lopez motioned for Martin to sit in the outer office as Jerry entered from the hallway. Lopez invited Jerry into the principal's office, closed the door, and completed the index card.

Jerry said that several other boys were there and they were all pushing one another into the bushes. It was a joke and everyone was laughing. But when Martin was pushed into the bushes he got mad. Seeing that Martin was mad, Jerry pushed him into the bushes again, and then hit him.

Lopez asked Jerry, "So how do you feel?"

Jerry was silent.

"You must feel something. You know, this is not an everyday occurrence with you."

"Well, we did it for a joke," Jerry answered.

"What happened to your good nature, if it was a joke?" Lopez wanted to know.

Jerry began to cry. "I didn't do nothing," he whined.

"You know," Lopez said, "sometimes the neighbors call about boys being in their bushes. You weren't satisfied to simply push him into the bushes. Do you see what you did to his eye?"

"Yes," Jerry replied.

"How do you feel about that? How would your mother feel?" asked Lopez.

Jerry was silent.

"Are you proud?" Lopez asked.

"No," Jerry answered.

"I could call your mother. I could suspend you," Lopez explained. "What should we do about it? Do you have any suggestions? You could apologize, but will Martin accept it? I don't know how angry Martin is with you. Shall we try an apology?"

Jerry, who had been looking down at his hands and crying, answered, "Yes."

Lopez went to the door and asked Martin to join them in the office. He asked Martin, "What should we do? Should we call his mother?"

"Yes," Martin said.

"Should I suspend him?" Lopez asked.

Martin said nothing.

"Will you accept an apology?" asked the principal.

"Yes," Martin said.

"Well, what's it going to be?" Lopez asked seriously.

"You could suspend him," Martin replied.

"Would it make you feel better?" Lopez inquired.

"Yes," answered Martin.

Then Lopez asked Martin how Jerry might feel about

being suspended. "Would it make Jerry happy? Would it make his parents happy? What if, after the suspension, he tried to get you again?"

"Then I'll get somebody to get him," Martin said.

"Well, we'll have a small war. Do we want that?"

"No," Martin responded. He thought for a few moments and then suggested "You could keep him in from recess for a few weeks."

Lopez turned to Jerry and asked, "Would you rather stay in from recess than be suspended?"

"Yes," Jerry said.

The boys agreed on this punishment and promised to apologize. Lopez sent Jerry back to his class with a note instructing the teacher to keep him in from recess. He told Martin to sit in the principal's outer office and hold ice on his eye until the swelling was reduced.

Comment

These cases illustrate the principal's responsibility for creating a school atmosphere that will support classroom learning. Principals structure the movement of students in the halls, playground and other public areas of the school. Order is accomplished through rules that regulate behavior in these areas and through widely accepted norms for student conduct. An important norm for student behavior is the expectation that they obey directives issued by *any* adult on the faculty or staff. Students must recognize the authority of all adults, not just that of their own teacher and the principal.

Principals arrange for the maintenance of a building. They set the schedule. Any variations from the regular schedule are either initiated or approved by the principal. The principal decides when the weather is bad enough to hold recess indoors. The principal adjusts the schedule to make space for an assembly. Textbooks and other instructional materials are ordered by the principal. In this way new structure and resources are introduced into normal school patterns.

The principal's office is the traditional destination of misbehaving students. Here, the principal instructs the misbehavers to follow the rules and participate in the school's social system; he tells them they cannot make their own rules. The principal initiates steps to remove chronically disorderly students from regular classes. The principal regulates access to the school building; generally outsiders can enter the building only with his or her permission. Non-students are usually denied entry because they may unintentionally break rules and norms or intentionally undermine school order. Principals also serve as a buffer between teachers and parents; they negotiate conflicts and prohibit parents from disrupting learning activities.

The ways in which principals meet these responsibilities are varied. The school situation and the principal's own style have a great effect on the means selected. Some general guidelines from Lopez's situation merit special comment.

1. The principal was a presence within the school. This presence was a concrete representation of the authority behind rules and norms. The students knew that the principal was looking for misbehavior. They knew they would probably be seen misbehaving, and they also suspected that instilling this fear in them was the principal's way of enforcing order and routine.
2. The principal knew how to process administrative decisions in the larger school system. This process included arranging for the testing and placing of special education students, ordering textbooks and other supplies, and submitting eligibility documents for a school's athletic teams.
3. The principal built a mental image of the entire school, based on frequent exposure to the events and people in the building and on the playground. This reservoir of knowledge about the school, its customs and people helped the principal solve problems and take initiative. The principal knew, for example, the places and times when trouble was apt to break out. When possible, he was on the spot to assert the presence of order and authority. Lopez knew that when students formed lines during recess they often shoved as they jockeyed for position in line. He stood guard and stopped fights by discouraging rowdy outbursts.
4. The principal established a system for administering discipline in the school. Lopez's index cards are a good example of such a system: Students learned that there would be a written record of their misbehavior. This record would also be used administratively if decisions were appealed at a higher level. His system also included a method to inform teachers and staff how he planned to respond to a referral.

THINGS TO DO AND THINK ABOUT

1. Principal Carter used a letter writing and newspaper campaign to persuade the board of the need for new textbooks at his school. How might he have accomplished the same goal with fewer consequences? Develop an alternative approach to this situation.
2. Building community support for the school has changed over the years. Principals today do it differently than did principals in the 1960s and 1970s. What are the differences? Describe the issues confronted by principals during the two different periods of time. The controversy surrounding the Ocean Hill-Brownsville situation in New York City pointed up some of the problems faced by principals; it may be a good starting point for comparison purposes.
3. This chapter is based on two expectations of the conventional wisdom as discussed in Chapter 1. The first is that the principal is the manager of the local school environment. Second, the principal is the instructional leader of the school. Concerning these two tasks, how have the expectations of the conventional wisdom changed over the last decade? What do you predict will be the changes in these tasks over the next ten years?
4. Analyze the performance of your own principal as instructional leader. How much administrative time does he or she allocate to this activity? Although the evidence supports the view that principals typically do not spend much time in classroom supervision, many persons still claim that instructional leadership is the most important responsibility of the principal. What do you think? How can this task be performed within the mix of other pressing time demands?
5. Regarding instructional leadership, one scholar puts it this way: "The improvement of instruction embraces a wide range of activities that good principals engage in if they are worth their salt, and many of these activities are not direct supervision of instruction or staff development." What are some of these activities, and how best can a principal perform them?
6. An unspoken norm of the principalship is "Always back the teacher up when dealing with students, parents, and outsiders." An incident is described in this chapter (page 85) and in Case Six (page 295) that illustrates this norm in action. What would you do as principal in this situation?
7. Review the case study in this chapter involving Principal Anderson (pages 87–91). Some scholars claim that the socialization of employees is one of the principal's most important responsibilities. Describe your first job experience. What role did the principal play in your socialization?
8. In the case described on pages 94–98, Principal Hutchens took charge of a chaotic situation by establishing strict rules for student conduct and personally enforcing them. Are there other ways a principal could restore order to a school out of control?

NOTES

1. Charles E. Bidwell, "The School as a Formal Organization," in James E. March, ed., *Handbook of Organizations* (Chicago: Rand McNally, 1965), pp. 972–1022.
2. Willard Waller, *The Sociology of Teaching* (New York: John Wiley and Sons, Inc., 1965), pp. 1–14.
3. Arthur Blumberg and William Greenfield, *The Effective Principal: Perspectives on School Leadership* (Boston: Allyn and Bacon, Inc., 1980), pp. 19–22.
4. Howard S. Becker, "The Teacher in the Authority System of the Public School," in Amitai Etzioni, ed., *Complex Organizations: A Sociological Reader* (New York: Holt, Rinehart and Winston, 1961), pp. 243–251; also, Dan C. Lortie, "The Balance of Control and Autonomy in Elementary School Teaching," in Amitai Etzioni, ed., *The Semi-Professions and Their Organization: Teachers, Nurses, Social Workers* (New York: Free Press, 1969), pp. 1–53.
5. Becker, "The Teacher in the Authority System," pp. 248–249.
6. See, John K. Hemphill and Alvin E. Coons, *Leader Behavior Description* (Columbus: Ohio State University, 1950); also, Ralph M. Stogdill and Alvin E. Coons, eds., *Leader Behavior: Its Description and Measurement* (Columbus: College of Education, Ohio State University, 1957); and, Andrew W. Halpin, *Theory and Research in Administration* (New York: Macmillan, 1966).
7. Peter M. Hall and Dee Ann Spencer-Hall, "School System as Negotiated Order?: A Comparative Analysis of Two Medium-Sized Public School Districts," Paper presented at the annual meeting of the American Educational Research Association, Los Angeles, April, 1981; also, Anselm Strauss, *Negotiations: Varieties, Contexts, Processes and Social Order* (San Francisco: Jossey-Bass, 1978); and, E. Mark Hanson, *Educational Administration and Organizational Behavior* (Boston: Allyn and Bacon, Inc., 1979), pp. 124–126.
8. Edwin M. Bridges, "Administrative Man: Origin or Pawn in Decision-Making?" *Educational Administration Quarterly* 6 (1970), pp. 7–25.
9. Dan C. Lortie, *Schoolteacher* (Chicago: The University of Chicago Press, 1975), pp. 55–81. See also, Charles W. Guditis and Perry A. Zirkel, "Bases of Supervisory Power Among Public School Principals," *Administrator's Notebook,* Vol. 28, No. 4 (1979–80), pp. 1–4.
10. Henry Barsky, "The Political Style of an Urban Principal: A Case Study," Unpublished Ph.D dissertation, University of Pennsylvania, 1975.
11. Hanson, *Educational Administration and Organizational Behavior,* p. 125.
12. See Kent Peterson, "The Principal's Tasks," *Administrator's Notebook,* Vol. 26, no. 8 (1977–78), pp. 1–4; also, William J. Martin and Donald J.

Willower, "The Managerial Behavior of High School principals," *Educational Administration Quarterly,* Vol. 17, No. 1 (Winter 1981), pp. 69–90.

13. Terrence E. Deal and Lynn D. Celotti, "Loose Coupling and School Administrators: Some Recent Research Findings," Center for Educational Research, Stanford University, 1977; also, Terrence E. Deal and Lynn D. Celotti, "How Much Influence Do (and Can) Educational Administrators Have on Classrooms?" *Phi Delta Kappan,* 61 (7), 1980, pp. 471–473. See also K. A. Leithwood and D. T. Montgomery, "The Role of the Elementary School Principal in Program Improvement," *Review of Educational Research,* Vol. 52, No. 3 (Fall 1982), pp. 309–339.

14. For reviews see G. F. Madaus, P. W. Airasian, and T. Kellaghan, *School Effectiveness: A Reassessment of the Evidence* (New York: McGraw-Hill, 1980); also, J. M. McPartland and N. Karweit, "Research on Educational Effects," in H. J. Walberg, ed., *Educational Environments and Effects* (Berkeley, Calif.: McCutchan, 1979); and Naftaly S. Glasman and Israel Biniaminov, "Input-Output Analyses of Schools," *Review of Educational Research,* Vol. 51, No. 4 (Winter 1981), pp. 509–539; Steven Bossert, David C. Dwyer, Brian Rowan, and Ginny V. Lee, "The Instructional Management Role of the Principal," *Educational Administration Quarterly,* Vol. 18, No. 3 (Summer 1982), pp. 34–64; and Carolyn S. Anderson, "The Search for School Climate: A Review of the Research," *Review of Educational Research,* Vol. 52, No. 3 (Fall 1982), pp. 368–420.

15. See Deal and Celotti, "How Much Influence Do (and Can) Educational Administrators Have on Classrooms?"; also, Chad D. Ellett and Herbert J. Walberg, "Principals' Competency, Environment, and Outcomes," in H. J. Walberg, ed., *Educational Environments and Effects,* pp. 140–164.

16. M. Rutter, B. Maughan, P. Mortimer, J. Ouston, *Fifteen Thousand Hours* (Cambridge, Mass.: Harvard University Press, 1979), p. 54.

17. See, for example, Wilbur Brookover, et al., *Schools Can Make a Difference* (East Lansing, Michigan: Michigan State University, 1977); also, Gerald Grant, "What Makes a Good School? The New Policy in Education," Paper presented at the annual meeting of the American Educational Research Association, Boston, April, 1980.

18. George W. Noblit, "The Control of Schools: Principals, Climates, and Crime," Paper presented at the annual meeting of the American Educational Research Association, San Francisco, April, 1979; Ray C. Rist, "On the Role of Principal as 'Cultural Maximizer' in an Urban Black School," ERIC, 1972; Ronald Edmonds, "Effective Schools for the Urban Poor," *Educational Leadership,* Vol. 37 (October 1979), pp. 15–24; L. S. Stoll, "Reading Program Administration: Does it Make a Difference?" *Administrator's Notebook,* vol. 27. no. 3 (1978–79), pp. 1–4; Salvatore Vallina, "Analysis of Observed Critical Task Performance of Title I-ESEA Principals, State of Illinois," Unpublished Ph.D dissertation, Loyola University, 1978; and, R. L. Venezky and L. F. Winfield, "Schools that Succeed Beyond Expectations in Teaching Reading," Technical Re-

port #1, University of Delaware Studies on Education, Dept. of Educational Studies, August, 1979.

19. David L. Clark, Linda S. Lotto, and Martha M. McCarthy, "Factors Associated with Success in Urban Elementary Schools," *Phi Delta Kappan,* vol. 61, no. 7 (March 1980), pp. 467–470.

20. Harry F. Wolcott, *The Man in the Principal's Office: An Ethnography* (New York: Holt, Rinehart and Winston, Inc., 1973), pp. 227–274.

21. R. Bruce McPherson and Robert L. Crowson, "Sources of Constraint and Opportunities for Discretion in the Principalship," in Jack Lane and Herbert J. Walberg, eds., *Educational Administration and School Effectiveness,* (Lexington, Mass.: Lexington Books, 1983).

22. We emphasize once again that we do not condone, let alone recommend, some of the practices set down in this book. We report them; you are invited to evaluate them.

23. D. Mann, *The Politics of Administrative Representation* (Lexington, Mass: Lexington Books, 1976).

24. E. M. Bridges, "Administrative Man: Origin or Pawn in Decision Making?" *Educational Administration Quarterly* 9 (1980), pp. 7–25.

5

Principaling and its Effects on the Community

Principals are wary of parents. Amid the hectic pace of a working day with its many short bursts of activity principals are sometimes required to downshift to a slower pace to engage a parent in a twenty minute conversation. But principals make the effort because they know that the parent is a primary constituency that must be cultivated. Thus, while secretaries, students, and faculty wait outside the door the principal responds to a parent's concerns, trying to smooth ruffled feathers.

WHAT WE KNOW FROM THE LITERATURE

Traditionally, the principal's view of community relations has been territorial and protective. The principal sees himself as the one who keeps the gate and turns aside incursions into the school's work. Principals and teachers, as trained professionals, establish and enforce a protective shield that will allow the school staff to work freely without the interference of special privilege or politics. This view maintains that teachers teach best when not intimidated by parents, schools work best when upgrading community life rather than pandering to it, and the school shapes values most successfully when it is able to demand certain standards, not only of school work, but also of proper dress, speech habits and general decorum.

This is changing. Although principals are still wary of parents and are still expected by their faculties to keep outsiders out, the traditional closed-system isolationism is no longer possible. It is yielding gradually to a more open-systems view of site-level administration. Battles over community control of schools in the 1960s signaled the end of school separationism. In the 1970s, federal programs routinely required parental advisory committees. In the late 1970s and 1980s, the struggle to maintain enrollments pushed the school into the political arena.

As a consequence, the scope of the principalship has been broadened well beyond the school's walls. The school administrator is now thrust into the turbulence of community life—including its pressures, prejudices and power plays. The role of the newer, open-systems principal may range from merely identifying community needs, to a more wide-ranging effort at home-school communication to a full-scale development of the so-called community school. The latter serves its neighborhood as recreation center, adult learning center, meeting house and library, as well as a site for the instruction of children.

Despite the changing conventional wisdom, there has been little research on the dynamics of the school-community relationship from a managerial perspective. Although the local school is now recognized as the key point of contact between the school system and its surrounding environment, evidence of important interaction between the principal and the local school clientele is in short supply. By the beginning of the 1980s, some research was finding that successful schools are characterized by relatively high levels of parental involvement.[1] However, exactly what principals do, and with what effect upon the community, has never been clearly articulated. Two dimensions of principaling and its effects on the community *have* been

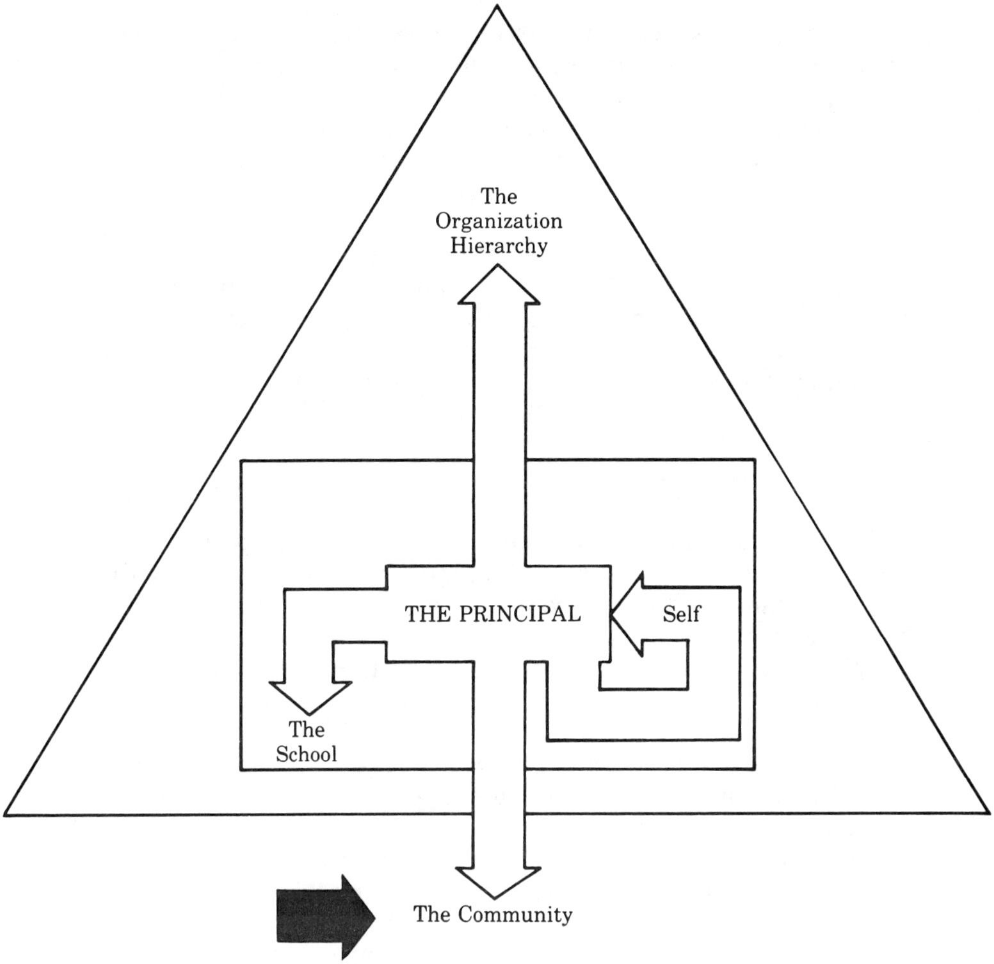

Figure 5.1 Principaling and its Four Sectors of Effect

explored, and provide insights into the findings reported later in this chapter: (1) the neighborhood-based politics of education, and (2) the conception of the neighborhood school as the inculcator of a sense of community among the residents.

The Neighborhood-based Politics of Education

Although keeping the schools out of politics is deeply ingrained in the administrative tradition, the building principal's job is now increasingly recognized as an important political position. In their book, *Practical Politics for School Administrators,* Wiles, Wiles, and Bondi define the local school as "a socio-political arena" where administrative decisions are subject to the use of power, negotiation and compromise, and the interplay of many competing values and interests. In contrast with the traditional bureaucratic model of hierarchical control, and its claim of predictability and homogeneity of principals' action, the arena perspective suggests that in reality administrative choice is often messy, confusing and contradictory. The successful principal may be like a competent poker player who tries to come out ahead in the long haul, winning some and losing some, while seldom holding a sure hand.[2]

The Principal's Political Role

One line of investigation from this perspective has explored the "representational role" of the principal in contact with the local community.[3] Specifically, who do principals represent? On whose behalf do they act? Do they bring the interests of parents into the decision-making network of the school system? Or do they believe it is the principal's job to act first on behalf of the school system bureaucracy?

In surveying the representational behaviors of principals, Dale Mann identified three paradigms: the trustee, the delegate, and the politico. The dominant style was that of the trustees, the administrators deeply imbued with the long tradition of professional autonomy and authority and committed to doing what is best for children and the community as they, the professional experts, see it. In contrast, few principals were found to be delegates, those who chose as first priority to reflect the needs and wishes of the local constituencies. Still fewer were politicos, those rare tacticians capable of balancing the requirements of both the hierarchy and the community as the situation warranted.[4]

Both Mann and another investigator, Summerfield, discovered that the principal's representational style is not embedded in a concrete set of administrative values, and can be changed by neighborhood involvement. Neighborhoods that became involved in their schools and learned to interact positively were able to cultivate in their principals a more delegate-oriented representational style.[5]

Although principals do tend to assimilate the trustee role, protecting the school's autonomy, the more open environment of today's communities forces principals to learn the politico's art of brokering between headquarters and the community. Peterson, for example, has suggested that the building principal is more affected by community interests and expectations than his superiors. As one moves up the organizational hierarchy, resistance to sharing power with outsiders grows.[6] The principal is expected to be most responsive to the organization's clientele, to be open to the community, and to implement guidelines specifying the boundaries of parental advisement. Although community involvement is highly valued by the bureaucracy, the principal who fails to shield the larger organization from client demands or who uses parental assistance in direct confrontation with headquarters is not well regarded by hierarchical superiors.[7]

In this balancing role, the principal often plays one constituency against the other. Principals protect the school from parental pressure by citing system rules and policies; they channel parent demands into non-threatening areas of involvement, and resist community access to the more sensitive and critical activities such as teacher evaluation. However, principals are always tempted to collaborate with parents to obtain from superiors extra resources or special favors. They sometimes use parent groups to intimidate the school's teachers, or encourage members of their P.T.A. to serve on headquarters' advisory committees, where the school's direct representation at the system-level can help control the agenda.

The Principal's Adaptive Role

A second line of investigation into the neighborhood-based politics of education has explored the principalship as a position that assists the school system in adapting to its parent and community clientele, and conversely in adapting the clientele to the organization. Whether or not they are involved in overt political behavior, principals serve in a "boundary-spanning" position in education.[8] This context of involvement at the friction point of school and community life creates an interactive atmosphere which is unlike that of other managerial echelons. As boundary-spanner, the principal is in a position to sense unrest in the outside environment. He or she is the early warning radar for the system and can pass on important information to senior officials. This allows headquarters to capitalize on supportive conduct or prepare to neutralize hostile maneuvers in the community. The principal is also able to assist the community in dealing with the bureaucracy, understanding its procedures, and using its services most effectively.

One of the first to discuss the principal's important position at the interface of the school system bureaucracy and its client community was Harry F. Wolcott. He suggested that the principal frequently acts to smooth out and humanize the actions of the educational organization. The universal policy is localized and particularized at the school site. What can appear to the layman as organizational insensitivity is filtered through the human sensitivity of the principal, as a rule or procedure is eased into actual use.[9]

Conversely, the principal may adapt the particular to the general by bending the client to fit the bureaucracy. Several studies in the late 1970s and early 1980s were guided by Michael Lipsky's "theory of street-level bureaucracy."[10] These investigations explored the ways in which persons at the point of contact with an organization's clientele will seek to facilitate client compliance with bureaucratic procedures. Weatherley, for example, studied principals' implementation of special education policy in Massachusetts, finding that in the face of state law requirements and insufficient time and money to apply the law, many principals routinized and rationed the provision of services to eligible children, short-circuited child review requirements, and concocted procedural tricks to facilitate parental compliance with special education placement schedules for their children.[11]

Creating Community through the School

With a breakdown of the older, protectionist philosophy, the newer conventions have assigned the principal the job of creating a community dimension for education.[12] The effective school provides an open environment where parental involvement can produce a cross-fertilization of educational program and parental expectation.

Ideally the community relations initiative leads to the Community School.[13] Such a school serves as a learning resource for the entire population, adults as well as children. Moreover, it serves as a focal point for neighborhood participation in non-school areas—recreation, housing quality, zoning ordinances, safety and security, job availability, drug abuse control, and other civic interests. Roe and Drake suggest that the community school should be a catalytic agent, providing means

> . . . for people in the community to assess their needs and existing resources, and meet those needs by sharing those resources in an efficient and effective manner to build a better school and a better community.[14]

The most important agent in this broadened educational process is the building principal, who

> ... is not only responsible for the instructional program for the usual school-age students in the attendance area, but also must encourage and facilitate educational growth and service opportunities for all residents in the community.[15]

Short of the ideal of the community school, the conventional wisdom holds that the principal should at least seek the establishment of "enlightened school-community relations."[16] A community relations program should be more than a selling job. It should include steps to identify community needs, respond to community norms and values, elicit lay participation in the school, commit the school's time and resources to the community relations effort, and change or remedy school programs as warranted.[17] Lipham and Hoeh write

> Regardless of organizational level (elementary or secondary), parents should be invited to participate frequently in school activities. Contacts with teachers, counselors, and administrators must be encouraged so that parents will feel comfortable about initiating communication with the school whenever they have questions. Only in an environment of openness and trust can parents fully comprehend the school's mission and the means by which the school is attempting to fulfill that mission.[18]

A long tradition of separating school from community has been replaced by a recognition that the local school *is* wrapped in politics and *is* intimately tied to the welfare of its environment. Yet serious strains remain between the older and newer traditions. Principals do play a political role, but their constituencies are in tension. The pressures that the principal experiences inside the building are magnified in the socio-political pressures in the wider community.

In the following sections we present our findings on the effects of the principal on the community. The dialectic between answering to the bureaucracy and answering to the public is a continuing feature of administrative life in today's schools. This is described in Socializing the Clients.[19]

Other strategies are available. Almost every principal is confronted by the dilemma posed in Crazy Mother as Mascot. She (or he) can be a nuisance, but is nevertheless an individual the principal would do well to befriend as a valuable link to the community. We also witness how principals exploit community characteristics in Holding the Customers, and how the public relations problem is solved through Image Building.

WHAT WE SEE

Socializing the Clients

The principals observed in this study spend approximately five percent of their time interacting with people from the immediate community, usually the parents of youngsters in their schools. Although this percentage is not a major allotment of time, this sector of the principal's administrative life is one of the most critical. The parent is the primary client, and parents must be considered the preeminent judges of a principal's success or failure. Accordingly, while parent contact may be of low frequency, it is almost always of high intensity. The minutes spent with parents are typically among the most decisive of the principal's interpersonal encounters.

Often these contacts are initiated by the parent, and the principal reacts. It may be a request for information or assistance, a complaint about a teacher or other pupils, or a complication developing out of the school's program and student activity. Many contacts, however, are initiated by the principal and are part of a formal structure established by the school system to insure community involvement. These interactions are usually required for pupil placement in special education under the provisions of P.L. 94–142, or grow out of parental advisement within the framework of advisory council provisions of federally-funded programs. They may originate because of using parent volunteers in some areas such as reading, math or science. Other, more informal, contacts initiated by the principal most often involve episodic matters of pupil behavior, achievement, or illness, or they may result from special requests from the principal for parental assistance in field trip chaperoning or playground supervision.

Throughout the range of parent and community interactions, the principal is actively engaged in shaping and guiding community expectations. The layman has tended to exaggerate the power of the public school, and most of these expectations could never be satisfied, even under the best of circumstances. The principal's managerial work includes *de-educating* the public about the school's capabilities, and *re-educating* it about what it can reasonably expect from the school.

Molding parental expectations Few public service organizations attract the active attention of their key clientele as much as the public school. In the eyes of most parents, the lives of children are significantly affected by the nature of the elementary and secondary school experiences. The school's response to the needs and personalities of their children is central to both the responsibilities and rewards of parents. Unchecked, however, parental concern could inundate the teaching and administrative staff in a deluge of special appeals, explanations of action, and unusual cases. One key activity of the building principal is to mold expectation and guide parental interest so that client behavior is acceptable and manageable.

A central focus of the principalship is to screen parental demands from the teaching staff while simultaneously responding to parental concerns. Teachers also expect principals to respect and assist their autonomy. An example: Mrs. Jenkins is concerned about her son's declining grades, and asks her son's teacher to send home a weekly report on his progress. Principal Richards explains to the mother that the union contract only requires teachers to report on each child's progress every ten weeks. So, he cannot ask for weekly summaries. He tells the mother, however, that he will personally check on the boy's progress from time to time and give the mother an occasional call.

Principals similarly cool off parental demands in areas such as disciplinary action, homework or grading policy, teaching style, and curriculum emphasis—areas in which organizational norms expect the principal to support the teacher. Such calming procedures require principals' undivided attention, as they provide a sympathetic ear to upset parents without compromising organizational or professional values. An example of the failure, in the eyes of his staff, of one principal to perform this role satisfactorily was observed at Rockland School. Mrs. Arnold, having just learned that her son has been consistently truant from school, angrily asks the principal why parents are not informed when youngsters have been absent several days in a row. Principal Rokach placates her; he will ask the classroom teacher to do this. Later the teacher consents grudgingly to the request, and asks why a truant officer or the school administration cannot provide this service. She expresses her resentment at the extra duty that Rokach has unthinkingly assigned to her.

A second tactic for shaping the expectations of clients is to establish limits to school responsiveness. These limits are often interpreted and applied to model proper parental and pupil behavior toward the school. At an open house, for example, a student in trouble asks Principal Moore to meet that evening with him and his father. Moore refuses; he doesn't have time and, besides, open houses are not for this purpose. The father must come in on Monday as planned. The student complains that his father will have to give up a day of work to come to the school and is very displeased. Moore responds, "You should have thought of that before getting into trouble."

Principal Rutledge responds similarly to a parent who is complaining that a gym teacher has refused to accept her request to excuse her daughter from gym. According to the mother, the teacher claims the required physician's statement must be written on a proper Board of Education form rather than on a separate prescription note. Rutledge mumbles that the prescription note could probably be stapled to the form, but checks with the gym teacher before adopting that solution. The gym teacher explains that the family has been a problem for him and that the girl has been bragging to her friends that she is about to be exempted from P.E. Rutledge returns to the waiting parent and says that there is nothing the school can do—the physician's statement must appear on the proper form.

Helping parents with non-school problems A significant aspect of principaling, especially in poor neighborhoods, is the helping relationship that principals establish with parents and pupils in dealing with welfare needs. The areas of involvement are wide-ranging, and exceed what might be considered the responsibility of the local school official. Principals give much attention to adequate clothing and good health. They help youngsters obtain special clothing necessary to school participation, such as tennis shoes or warm jackets, or they help parents obtain medical and psychiatric services. The helping principal also extends educational opportunity to particular families. A gifted child is assisted in gaining admission to a special math program at another school. Summer school programs are located for pupils who are short of credits for graduation, or who need extra tutorials in reading.

Principals often exceed these simple school-related welfare services. They help parents interpret and fill out an insurance form for reimbursement for doctor's expenses, assist parents with legal and police problems, intervene and assist in marital disputes and child custody battles, and offer help in coping with language problems. They sometimes become deeply involved in the special crises faced by some children and their families, perhaps a child repeatedly threatening suicide, a youngster who is a habitual runaway, or a "good kid" who has been stealing. Occasionally a principal may regret involvement in a matter that later gets out of hand, but the assistance is usually valued and appreciated.

Many principals go beyond helping actions to provide outright protection for parents and pupils. A football player, for example, fails to return home all night after a school dance, and the principal telephones, including the student's girl friend, to locate him. A principal in a Hispanic community turns down a request from a television producer for two Latino boys to act in a film. He has discovered that the story involves the shakedown of a white youngster by

Latinos, and he doesn't like it. An elementary principal takes popcorn and candy away from a fat boy in the school.

Guiding parental involvement Opportunities for parental access to schools have expanded. Formal structures of parent involvement, in an advisory capacity, are now part of the procedural requirements of many state, federal, and even local programs. Employment initiatives, particularly CETA,[20] have expanded the roles of community residents as aides or paraprofessionals. Increased use of parent volunteers and expanded opportunities for classroom observation mean more informal access.

In spite of enhanced opportunities for parental access, building principals still find that they must encourage greater parental interest and participation. Schools vary widely in the extent of parental concern and involvement. When they are attempting to increase involvement, principals schedule frequent festivals and PTA meetings with some form of pupil performance to get parents to show up. Common also are informal coffees with parents in their homes, efforts to enlist parents as sponsors of field trips, and encouragement of active fundraising efforts like candy sales, bakery goods exchanges, and holiday bazaars. In schools with effective interaction with the surrounding community, parents volunteer as teacher aides, neighborhood lookouts and spotters, and even as carpenters or painters.

To mold parental expections, principals also communicate a participatory protocol for parental involvement. Principal Simpson of Fostoria School, for example, encouraged parental participation but was upset when a group of parents threatened to go over his head to a districtwide advisory council with a complaint about teachers. "I don't like them washing our dirty linen in public like that," he said. Another principal, noticing that several parents escorted their youngsters to and from the building each day, asked them to stay until all the children had filed into the school; this increased the community's responsibility for order on the playgound.

Parental involvement can become disruptive. Principal Evans, newly assigned to Tucker School, has to tread very carefully. A few parents, in control of the school's PTA and allied with a number of the teachers, forced the former principal out. And, in the following example, Principal Brazelton of Eisenhower High School is embroiled in a take-over effort by a militant community group and works to deflect the pressure into acceptable channels.

Eisenhower High School has recently suffered an auditorium fire, causing much damage but no injuries. It appears the fire was set by some arsonists over the past weekend. The school's parent council has distributed a flyer asking for help in identifying the culprits, and is now meeting at the school to discuss the matter.

There is concern about whether the auditorium can be repaired in time for graduation, and there is a motion to be considered—a reward for the capture of the arsonist.

The turnout is fairly large. The president, Mrs. Conroy, opens the meeting by reporting she has been assured that the auditorium can be repaired in time for graduation; she is very glad to hear this because there was fear they would have to raise funds to rent a hall. She suggests that the school and the parent council each contribute a hundred dollars in reward money.

At this point a number of people begin to speak up. The discussion is directed not at Conroy but at Brazelton. One person asks how they can be so sure someone from the community set the fire, and that the community has knowledge of it. The school has been undergoing some rehabilitation lately; it might not be someone from the community, but rather someone employed by the contractor.

Other people speak. The flyer that went out said that they must "seek out the person among us who set the fire." This assumes that the guilty party is from the community, the speakers contend. It is inappropriate, some say, to blame the community for the fire. Others ask, "Do you have copies of the report from the police and fire departments? What do they say? We need the facts, not assumptions. Why would a community person just set the fire and not steal anything? It must be someone with a different motive—maybe a worker involved in the rehab who has a complaint against his employer, or somebody else who is angry at the Board of Education."

At this point Conroy asks for a vote on the reward money, but this aggravates the issue. No vote is taken, and tempers flare. The most outspoken critics are not parent council regulars; one of the regulars asks the newcomers if they are from the community. Addresses are given to show they are, but a hostile atmosphere now reigns.

At a question about why the night watchman did not guard the auditorium properly, and why the alarm system did not work, Principal Brazelton redirects the discussion to the school's security problems in general. There is constant theft from lockers, there is insufficient security staff to cover the many halls and exits, there have been recent cuts in security aide resources. The discussion does shift, and many questions are now asked about the school's security.

Soon, one person suggests that the community can get help only if residents go to the Board of Education offices as a group and demonstrate for more security for the school. Brazelton quickly intervenes and suggests that they ask Mr. Forman, the officer in charge of security for the school system, to talk with the council. Conroy jumps in to say that the parents, for one thing, must start helping with security. Another regular council member adds, "The parents can come to this school to volunteer, that's a great idea. We've got to take a first step here, pledge ourselves to assist security, not just discuss this as something somebody should be doing." Another council regular adds pointedly, "We sit and talk, but who shows up to do the work? There's a big difference in saying at a meeting that you want to be involved in something and actually showing up for work to be done. You've got to get up, put your clothes on, and get yourself going." There is no response from the previously vocal newcomers, and the principal offers to walk over to the auditorium with anyone who wishes to inspect the damage.

Crazy Mother as Mascot: Disarming the Volatile Critic

A principal's encounters with parents are usually brief and purposeful. Parents may ask the principal's assistance on procedural matters such as registering their children for school, or they may meet the principal to decide whether special education services are appropriate for the child. Parents frequently initiate meetings when they want to discuss problems with their child's schedule. Parents who come to pick up ill or injured children often say hello to the principal.

When a student chronically misbehaves, the parents usually confer with the principal several times. These conferences are designed to show the child the seriousness of school disruptions and the need to behave better in the future. The fact that parents are called to the school for a disciplinary conference may itself be a punishment for some children.

But in addition to those parents who visit for procedural or disciplinary reasons, there are always a few who repeatedly show up to participate in the school's program. They come ostensibly to lend a hand. They volunteer to tutor students or assist a teacher, participate in enrichment programs that provide special trips, materials or entertainments, or sometimes take part in fund raising projects.

Among these helpers, there is occasionally a regular volunteer whose self-appointed role goes beyond augmenting the staff. Such a parent seeks to participate in the administration of the school and the evaluation of teachers and programs. We refer to this parent as *Crazy Mother*. Although she is usually, in fact, a mother, Crazy Mother can also be a father. Mothers generally have the free time during the day to devote to school activities.

What is crazy about Crazy Mother? She approaches the school with an overriding need to explore and improve her children's instruction. She is not interested in schedules, union contracts, central office bulletins or other constraints of organizational life. Her suggestions, therefore, seem crazy, because they contradict what is possible organizationally and consistent with the school's established practices.

And yet, crazy mother is more than just a complainer or troublemaker. Because she is a volunteer, she knows more about the teachers, programs and students than most parents. Her concern for children is respected. She is closer to the staff than most outsiders. Her presence, enduring interest and generally good motives give her a position somewhat like a mascot. She is not a member of the team, but her spirit and sense of purpose have won her a place with the team.

A Prototype

John Dewey Elementary School is unusually large. Most of its 1400 students are black. While 700 students are from low income families and qualify for a free lunch program, the remaining students come from middle class families. For many years the middle class parents pressured the school's administration to establish stiff academic standards for teachers and students. In the past they organized community demonstrations and protests when they felt that teachers were poorly prepared or incompetent. The active involvement of parents in school life led to so much conflict between parents and teachers that a former principal was driven from the school.

The current principal, Celia Owens, is a black woman who lives in the neighborhood. She was offered the job repeatedly before she accepted it. Her first priority was to restore the principal's authority. Capitalizing on her popularity when selected, she established ground rules for parents' participation in academic programs. At a meeting of parents and faculty where the rules were announced, she added "Either *I* run the school or you can get somebody else."

She understood that many teachers felt threatened by the parents' constant surveillance and criticism. The new rules helped. Once she gained control of parents' access to teachers, she also became the mediator of any conflict that developed between parents and teachers. Although she allowed parents to observe classes, they were not permitted to speak with a teacher while the teacher conducted class. When a parent had a complaint about a teacher, the parent was to meet with Owens and allow her to work with the teacher to improve the situation. To keep the school out of family disputes, particularly battles over child custody, Owens refused to discuss placement, achievement or other school matters with any relative who was not a child's legal guardian.

The parents came to trust Owens. They generally felt that she tried to keep academic standards high. The students' reading test scores were above the city average but below the national norm. Many students, however, had math and reading scores far above the national norm. Owens developed an array of advanced and enrichment courses in art, film making, foreign language and black history. Original plays and musicals performed by the students in school were also presented at community meetings and religious services. She structured the special programs so that all students could sample them for one period a week; more intensive exposure was provided for the oldest and brightest students.

Since Owens became principal seven years ago, she has fired three tenured teachers. The process of dismissing a teacher is extremely complex and time-consuming. Observation in the classroom, documentation of teaching inadequacies, conferences with the teacher, visits by headquarters staff, and follow-up reports on the teacher's repeated failures to improve—these take months to complete and the paper work can fill file drawers. Owens believed that removing these poor teachers had a positive impact on the school that justified the effort. Both parents and teachers considered her as effective, and her authority in the school was strengthened by this demonstration of the grave consequence of poor teaching.

Owens communicated with parents in three ways. She attended monthly PTA meetings where parents asked questions about the school. She sent to parents each month a newsletter which contained important information about schedule changes, school routines, fund-raising events, staff changes and volunteer posts. She encouraged parents to communicate freely with her by phone and face-to-face in the neighborhood as well as the school building.

Many parents volunteered in classrooms and learning laboratories. They organized a book distribution program and raised money for cultural events. Owens set aside a social room where parent volunteers could meet, eat lunch and talk. The provision of the room was considered a courteous gesture; but it also directed parents away from the faculty lounge, where teachers wanted to relax and speak informally about the day's events.

When parents work in a school, they witness events that stray from the standard rules and procedures outlined by the Board of Education. After one such occasion, Owens informed a teacher that a parent had complained that she smoked in the classroom when the children were at gym or recess. Owens said that the parent had also informed the superintendent, and he had said that the smoking must stop. The teacher and Owens exchanged knowing looks as Owens indicated that "you know who" had turned the teacher in to the central office. A smoker herself, Owens saw nothing wrong with the teacher smoking, as long as the children were not present. Still, they had to follow the rules to the letter—especially since "you know who" would probably be watching them closely.

Mrs. Washington, the mother of two outstanding students, had volunteered at Dewey School for two and one-half years. When her family moved to the neighborhood, she felt that the school was unresponsive to her inquiries about her children's program. When she told Owens that she felt that teachers would not listen, Owens encouraged her to get involved in some of the volunteer efforts in the school and to come see her whenever she had a question. Over the years Washington had visited Owens many times to ask questions and offer opinions about how the school should be run.

A recent issue concerned the problem of children entering the school after the class bell had rung. While in the building the previous day, Washington had argued with a teacher's aide about admitting children who returned late from lunch. To resolve this dispute, Owens asked the aide and Washington to meet her. Washington requested that the meeting be held in the early morning so that her husband could attend as well.

At 9:05 the Washingtons arrived. Mr. Washington, an attorney, was well-dressed and relaxed chatting with Owens about community events. Mrs. Washington also communicated a message with her crisply tailored suit and her hair drawn neatly into a bun. She did not join in the friendly conversation, but tapped her fashionable high heels as they waited for the aide.

After a few minutes there was a knock at the door, and Owens invited the aide, Mrs. North, into the principal's office. Mrs. North, an older black woman, was overweight and had a rumpled, worn appearance. She shuffled to the far side of the office and slowly lowered herself into a chair. She smiled nervously as Owens asked her to explain what had happened the previous day.

North said that yesterday she was showing several children who had arrived late how to open the outside doors. She said the children often came to the door and did not know how to open it. Then, according to North, Washington began to interfere by opening the door for the children herself and letting the ones that were outside come in. North told her not to open the door for the children, and this led to the disagreement.

Washington then gave her side. She heard children outside and went to let them in. North stopped her, saying, "Don't open the door, the children know how to open it." She said that North did not explain that she was giving the children a lesson on the use of the door. Furthermore, on several occasions, Washington claimed to have seen children locked out at this exit. She regretted that there had been a disagreement; the real issue, she explained, was the door. The lock was temperamental, was not always open when it should be, and was hard to open even when the door was unlocked.

Owens admitted, "I know that it is a difficult lock," and promised to check it immediately. She added, however, that she was troubled that Washington was upset and that there had been an argument. Washington said, "It is upsetting not to be able to bring my child into the building when it is supposed to be open." She added that the school clocks are often off by several minutes, and children return late from lunch because of it. Then Washington asked, "Why can't Mrs. North be there to let us in? I have frequently stood out there and banged on the door," she explained.

Owens said that she had instructed North to open the door from the inside if she heard someone knocking. However, North had an assignment in the classroom after the class bell, and she was not supposed to be in the hall once the bell had rung. North admitted, however, that sometimes she was not at the door before the class bell because she had been delayed at her previous assignment. Owens instructed North to let people in until the class bell rang, and also promised to fix the lock. Then she asked Mr. Washington if he had any suggestions.

He suggested that the children be called from the playground into the building just before the class bell. In the past the assistant principal called the children in from the playground every day, but recently no one had done it. This left many children on the playground after the class bell rang.

Owens agreed. She told him, "In fact, the same issue was raised at last night's PTA meeting." She scheduled a meeting with the security guards and promised to instruct them to call the children in from the playground. Also, teachers would be instructed to remind children of playground procedures. Washington agreed, saying "Children don't think very far ahead. Some children will just stand there and cry if they see that the door is locked. They won't know or think of how else to enter the building." Owens then asked whether there were any more issues. The Washingtons said there were none, so Owens sent North to her assignment.

Once North had left, however, Washington had a great deal to say. "Mrs. Owens, this has been going on all year, it is extremely irritating, and it forces me to come to the school and let my child in that door." Owens promised to take immediate action on the lock. Washington then concluded "I don't think Mrs. North understands the problem. . . .she just refused to listen! She didn't tell me that she was teaching the children to open the lock."

Mr. Washington said, "This whole thing is not a physical problem with the lock. It has to do with something else . . . someone should be there at the door, supervising that entrance as the kids come in. She or someone should be there *in fact.* For the first three weeks of the school year, I made a habit of walking my children to school myself. Things worked out very well with Mrs. North. The assistant principal also was often there to help get the kids into the building. Then, after about three weeks, I decided to send the children by themselves. But after I stopped going and helping Mrs. North and the assistant principal, I discovered that the assistant principal stopped helping. Then Mrs. North didn't show up. Now, the children stay on the playground, and when the class bell rings, there's no one to bring them in. Furthermore, because there is no one letting the children in the door, the children bunch around the door and cause a disturbance. Sometimes a group of children at the door keep other children out in the cold. Several times, I have brought my own children to the school and found this situation. I have beaten on the door until my knuckles were red, waiting for someone to open the door from the inside to let us in. I've seen children on the playground a full ten minutes after the class bell—and nobody there to let them in. You know, Mrs. Owens, children around here are treated as non-people. Something has got to be done about this situation."

Owens thanked him for bringing this to her attention. She promised "to definitely work on this." After the Washingtons left, she immediately asked the school engineer to her office and explained that the door must be repaired so that it could be opened easily. "I want that done immediately, if not sooner," she ordered. He replied that he would call the carpenter.

Then Owens muttered wryly to herself, "I was surprised to see Mrs. Washington in her high heels and blue eye shadow. Ordinarily she doesn't wear make up."

Comment

This account tells how a principal handles parents who take an overactive interest in the school's affairs. The smoking incident shows the impact of parental criticism on school personnel. Such criticism can strengthen positive bonds between teachers and the principal. Owens indicated that the teacher should follow the no-smoking rule; but she urged this, not because it was a good rule, but to smooth over potential conflict with a parent. The crazy mothers, who continually complain about school personnel and procedures, contribute to solidarity and a sense of belonging among the staff and administrators.

The incident involving the Washingtons illustrates

strategies that this principal used when responding to parents. An important first task was to reduce the interpersonal conflict between Washington and North so that the issue itself could be confronted. It appears that Washington had felt for some time that North was not doing her job. Seeing children trying to get into the door, Washington had assumed the duty of bringing children into the building. She was outraged when North told her not to open the door for the children. If North was too slow and lazy to stand her post, reasoned Washington, she should not have rebuffed her assistance.

Owens reduced the interpersonal conflict by having North and Washington confront each other in her office. Although Washington was skeptical of North's explanation that she was teaching the children to open the door for themselves, she accepted it. Washington responded by redefining the problem as the faulty lock. Owens picked up this "depersonalization" of the problem and promised to fix the lock.

Then Owens began repairing the relationship between the two women. She made it clear that North could not "be everywhere," and that she had given her instructions to be at her classroom assignment on time. Mr. Washington suggested that the problem was one of playground supervision and the assignment of staff. He then went further, claiming that the problem was not "a physical problem with the lock." As a parent, he wanted someone at the exit to bring children in from the playground and open the door. He was humiliated by standing in the snow and beating on the door. To him, the insensitivity to this frustration amounted to treating children and parents as "non-people." The message was clear: somebody had better start to care about managing that exit more fully, or there would be trouble.

Aside from offering some support for North, the principal did not defend the situation at the exit. She did not offer any of the possible reasons why it was difficult to cover all exits or adequately supervise the playgrounds. Instead, she promised to "definitely work on this," keeping a free hand to determine how to allocate her staff. Solving the situation was her problem, and by accepting the responsibility for it she left her authority intact. Her plan was to get the lock fixed so that children could let themselves in when they arrived late and to assign the security guard to the troublesome exit.

It is interesting to note Washington's appearance. By dressing up she emphasized her social status. This, and bringing her husband along, emphasized that the problem was important and that her concern should be taken seriously. Yet, the Washingtons did not really want to make trouble for Owens. They were interested and involved parents who wanted to affect their children's school. But they did not want to be destructive.

Holding the Customers: Headhunting in Scholastica

One of the manager's imperatives is to protect resource allocations. In any organization unit administrators strive to hold the line on staffing levels, budgetary allotments, and overall resource capabilities. A manager's standing with subordinates and peers, the manager's right to the allegiance of employees, and a manager's capacity for creating good morale and high productivity depend on both the image and evidence of resource stability that he or she communicates. Organizations that are losing budgetary resources usually suffer a decline in purposefulness, security, and confidence that goes beyond the loss of operating funds.

A common criterion for resource allocation in education is student enrollment. Levels of professional and non-professional staffing, distributions of instructional materials and office supplies, allocations of furniture and equipment, and even salary levels of principals are frequently keyed to enrollment. Accordingly, it is advantageous for each principal to maintain enrollment; a lower headcount is quickly translated into loss of instructional resources.

One of the principal's key tasks, then, is to monitor, protect, and stimulate school attendance. The task calls for frequent, sensitive interaction with the community, involves occasional competition with other principals, and contains some elements of conflict with superiors.

Methods of Enrollment Control

Increasing the attractiveness of the school District enrollment policies provide clear-cut attendance boundaries and pupil identification and specify enrollment procedures for each of the city's schools. Nevertheless, principals of both elementary and high schools have discovered that programmatic and curricular changes can affect their school's appeal. A first strategy is to differentiate or expand the program in some attractive fashion, revising the curriculum so that it better holds the interest of pupils enrolled in the school, promotes better pupil attendance, and guards against dropouts. Principal Walters of Westmont High School met throughout the school year with faculty members in the science, history, and foreign languages departments. He pointed out that the school had severe difficulties with pupil attendance and enrollment, and some curriculum changes to modernize the school's offerings had to be made. "We may have to cut physics, for instance, and add environmental science. It's in," he explained. Later, after a meeting with his faculty, Walters said, "I've got to get my faculty to see that they have to re-shape the traditional curriculum of the school. Their jobs are at stake."

Principals also try to make their programs attractive to students entering school. The idea, as one principal expressed it, is to develop "a hook to get kids into this school." Principal Jennings of Wilson High School worked carefully with her faculty to inaugurate "early involvement classes" for academically gifted seventh and eighth grade pupils in a number of nearby junior high schools. The younger students would travel to the high school for part of each day to take advanced classes in selected subject areas.

In an elementary school setting, Principal Farnsley, newly appointed to Larson School, devoted considerable attention in his first year to the school's kindergarten program. He worked with the teachers to make kindergarten a more rigorously structured learning experience, less of a loosely organized socialization-into-school experience. Farnsley learned that in the heavily Catholic neighborhood surrounding his school nearly every five-year-old attended the public school kindergarten because no parochial school program was offered in the area. However, only about half the youngsters continued into first grade in the public school. By re-shaping and emphasizing the academic side of kindergarten, he hoped to increase the appeal of the public school to area families.

Additional strategies for attracting students commonly involve manipulating the pupil reward system to sharpen the school's image. The school district under study kept a record of, and partially evaluated principal performance in terms of, monthly reports of student attendance. Consequently, principals often devised special means, such as popular movies, to reward pupils for good attendance. In considering the image of the school, principals were well attuned to events and opportunities that offered a chance to communicate their school's message. Principal Leavitt, for example, was very upset when he learned that only two pupils from Greenbriar High School would be participating in the city-wide science fair. The fair, like success in sports, draws media attention to individual schools, and he took steps the following year to encourage more entries.

Bending the rules Clear procedural guidelines govern the allocation of students to schools, and documentation such as inoculation records, and evidence of age and residence must be provided. Under pressure of enrollment and resource need, however, principals become flexible and responsive in special situations. They bend the rules for student admissions, and take liberties with enrollment reporting and district instructions on attendance rosters.

When there is space, and particularly when there is some prior tie to the school (perhaps a sibling had attended), principals freely interpret attendance-area boundaries. Elementary Principal Foster indicated that this approach gave her a hold over some of her pupils: "In general, I'm not picky about where the students in the school live." However, she added that if a youngster became a behavioral problem, she always checked the home address. If it was outside the school's attendance boundary, she would insist on a transfer.

Principal Martinson commented after a parent conference that he was aware the father actually lived in a nearby suburb and drove his children to and from Froebel School every day. Martinson said he looked the other way since the children were extremely bright. High School Principal Greer commented after an incident in the hall that many students were nervous about getting caught and were reluctant to give their home addresses, for fear they would be forced to transfer to their rightful school. He said he always had to reassure them that he did not really care where they lived.

On an individual basis, principals are as willing to overlook many prohibitions governing school admissions documention as they are flexible about school attendance boundaries. Some of the restrictions, such as a proper inoculation record or a birth certificate, are occasionally waived; sometimes a long extension for compliance is given. Occasionally, the procedures and paper work necessary to a special enrollment situation are simply bypassed. Principal Bachman, for example, told his secretary to enroll a number of students without proper records and papers whom he was convinced were illegal immigrants. He mentioned that district policy required him to direct the problem to the central office if there was a question of illegality, but that this would have created more trouble than he cared to deal with.

The illegal immigrant case also shows how information control can be useful to principals in bending enrollment rules. The bureaucracy depends on data supplied by the principals to formulate resource allocation plans. Because of this, the principal communicates carefully with headquarters. Principal Marks of Neeley School mentioned one day that final enrollment figures for the fall were due. She planned to gamble and over-report her actual enrollment because new children were still coming in every day. She was sure her enrollment would reach her reported figure. She wanted to avoid losing a position; once cut, they were difficult to regain.

In a similar situation, but with a reverse twist, Principal Martin remarked that headquarters figures for the enrollment in his bilingual classes were badly inflated. He had decided not to say anything, though, because corrected data would probably have cost him a position. In another example of information manipulation, Elementary Principal Bowker decided to hold the files of eight new kindergartners. The pupils' parents brought them to the wrong school, thinking Bowker's school served their portion of the neighborhood, rather than the next school over. He decided to wait to see if his own attendance area produced enough kindergarten children to fill the two classes before directing the parents to the proper school.

Retaining, courting, and counseling clients Principals spend a considerable amount of their own time talking with pupils and parents about enrollment. At the elementary level, parents frequently shop for a school with a reputation for either quality or disciplinary control. They might also seek to send their children to a familiar school, perhaps one attended by older siblings.

Principals are lenient in enforcing attendance boundaries. Generally, however, they are selective in filling available classroom space with out-of-district applicants. Principals stress the favors they are doing and communicate standards of behavior and achievement the children will have to meet. Parents who appear serious and concerned are more likely to win admission for their children.

Improving the caliber of the student body is also a key priority of the high school principal. In a telephone conversation with Principal Tayton of Hannaway High School, Mrs. Williams threatened to withdraw her daughter and send her to another school. Tayton urged the family not to take that action, pointing out that the daughter was the top student in the junior class, a leader in the school, and important to the school program. Principal Hampton said to a counselor who had informed him that a student was asking for a transfer, "Let him go, that guy's been nothing but trouble for us." Just a few minutes earlier, Hampton had urged an especially talented pupil to wait until summer before transferring.

Principal Arneson agreed to see a parent and a prospective student who had arrived, without appointment, early in the school year to ask for a transfer into Coolidge High School. Arneson explored the reasons for transfer with the family, then went to the outer office to call the former school to check on the student's school record. He discovered that the pupil had a record of chronic truancy. Arneson returned to his office and denied the transfer request. He explained he would not consider a transfer at this time and that the student should wait until the beginning of next semester, at the earliest.

In some districts, a voluntary pupil transfer approach to school desegregation is discussed. Most principals attempt to conscientiously carry out desegregation initiatives. As middle managers they are in a conflict situation. One Board of Education policy encouraging the transfer of pupils into desegregated schools where space is available contradicts another policy awarding building resources on the basis of pupil retention.

Most principals encourage the transfer of their pupils to

the special schools and facilities that form the crux of the desegregation effort—traditional schools, magnet schools, career development centers. But they do so in such a manner as to hold intact their present levels of staffing and other resources. While selected pupils can be assisted in transferring, a large outflow of students would dangerously upset pupil-teacher ratios.

Occasionally, principals caution their colleagues on established norms of polite behavior in raiding one another's schools. One principal kiddingly remarked, in response to another principal's sales pitch for a new program, "Oh, you want to drain me of my white kids." They also find that a full disclosure of information about an innovative program might prevent a student from participating. One mother decided not to enroll her daughter in a new program when she discovered it meant spending all day in another school, with busing back and forth. In this case, information overload saved another student for the headcount.

For an examination of other strategies to improve attendance see Case One, page 258, and Case Seven, page 298.

Image Building: Non-Educational Factors at Work

Building a school's image is of prime importance to principals. Much of their energy is devoted to it and much of their behavior can be interpreted in relation to it. There is no agreement among principals about what the proper school image should be. But there is consensus that only two groups of people matter to the principal: the external clients, the parents or the community at large; and the internal school bureaucracy, including the central office administrators.

Building the external image The principal is responsible for how the school looks to the public. How does he help the school enhance its status in the community? We illustrate with Miller Fine Arts Academy. It is a special unit in the magnet plan of the school district, with a unique curriculum for children interested in the fine arts. Even though the school has a fine educational program which contributes to its community image, it is the non-educational factors which have brought it wide acclaim and increased community support. The principal is a master at gaining visibility for the school.

Miller Academy was converted from a regular elementary school to a magnet school as a part of the district-wide program. It was a school of decreasing enrollment in a rapidly changing neighborhood. But an active integrated community group, led by some determined young parents, was struggling to keep the school open. They were convinced that, with the proper leadership and a committed faculty, the school could become a model for the entire district. The principal, Silas Herbert, was brought in to convert the school to an academy, and it reopened with a district-wide attendance area.

Herbert's first act was to meet with the community people who had urged conversion of the school to an academy. He was convinced that its image could not be maintained solely on its academy status, and he recognized the political vulnerability of the magnet program and the program's ties to the district's controversial desegregation policy. For this reason, he began immediately to build a political foundation for the school in the neighborhood. He met with the people who had been the prime movers in the conversion of the school, and allied himself with the community leader who was soon to become president of the school parent council. Along with this alliance came access to the local press and visibility within the community.

Because Herbert had demonstrated his ability to get a good press, he was continually approached by people with ideas for the school. For example, several community leaders wanted the school to sponsor an exchange program with a school in Italy. Through an international organization specializing in such exchanges, forty children from Italy came to Miller Academy for three weeks. Each child lived in the home of a Miller student and even the Italian teacher, counselor, and administrators stayed in the neighborhood. The exchange was widely covered in the press, and a photo of the principal greeting the Italian children was published in the newspaper.

Another example of the school's ability to attract press coverage was the presence of reporters and photographers at most routine school functions. A call from the principal resulted in coverage of a Halloween party or a Miller Science Fair. This influence with the press was the result not only of Herbert's persuasive abilities, but also of the support of the influential citizens with whom he cooperated.

A more typical example of external image building is Principal Barber of Langford Elementary School, which had a predominantly black and Hispanic student population. Barber also served as principal of the nearby federally-funded Marks Child-Parent Center for pre-school children. This center was designed to involve low-income parents in the early phases of school. Langford School had no glamorous educational program and Marks Center, while addressing a critical community need, was undistinguished in its academic and parental involvement activities.

So what did Barber do to enhance the status of his two institutions? First, he recognized the parents' determination to see the school establish a model for discipline; the absence of good home models made this critical. Thus, Barber let the parents see how seriously the school took discipline. During the lunch hour, for example, he conspicuously stood in the schoolyard with a bullhorn, shouting orders to children at the top of his lungs. What was important about this exercise was not whether he had any effect on the children but whether he was heard by parents in nearby apartment buildings. Barber so valued this form of image building that he pointed his bullhorn toward the apartment buildings rather than toward the children!

Another resource available to Barber was parental involvement in decision making. He was constantly seeking ways to promote parental participation. It is available to all principals to help build an image, but it is seldom used. Barber used it extensively. He knew that a local hospital had a federally-funded program in postpartum care, and that a small portion of the money was earmarked for a sex education program for children 12–14 years old. Barber invited the director of the program to meet with him and his PTA president, Martha Gosage. The PTA had expressed concern about the problem of teenage pregnancy for several months. Barber saw this program as a way to respond to a critical community need.

Barber asked Gosage to introduce the sex education program at a PTA meeting. For the program to succeed as an image-building activity, he felt it necessary to have parents directly involved. He asked the program director to develop a one-session program, in addition to the five classes for children, which would require parents to be present with their children. The hospital sex education program director was enthusiastic and was willing to devote her time to run this session herself; she also promised to bring along a doctor to answer questions. The PTA president also became enthusiastic about the program and promised to call a special meeting of the PTA to discuss it. Barber had found a vehicle for improving the image of the school in the community. Seeking permission from the PTA to pursue the program guaranteed the necessary parent involvement and effectively brought the PTA into partnership with the school.

The sex education program was a great success. Barber received much appreciation from parents and was commended by the PTA for providing a good educational experience for children and parents. By involving the parents, he was able to build the image of a school that addressed real social problems. Although not all principals would accept addressing social issues as a responsiblity of the schools, Barber was committed to the idea. He was able to demonstrate his and the school's willingness to work with community problems.

Parental involvement, particularly through the PTA, is not considered necessarily desirable by all principals. The PTA, and parental involvement generally, ranged in popularity as a tool for image building from one extreme to the other. Barber at Langford School and Herbert at Miller Academy were among those principals most willing to work with parents to enhance the status of the school in the community. In contrast, several principals felt that parent groups were either conspiring to have them removed from office or simply unreliable in helping the school solve a problem. Few principals, however, were willing to ignore their parent groups, even if they found them useless. During an hour-long PTA breakfast meeting and social gathering, one principal avoided speaking to a single parent; he spoke only to teachers. When asked why, he said, "I never talk to parents. There's something wrong with people who meddle so closely in school affairs. I don't trust most of them." This attitude is certainly unusual but it reveals the lack of communication and general distrust in some communities between local school administrators and the public.

Other practices are used to improve the school's image. Here are a few examples:

1. At one high school the principal has encouraged an elaborate farm system at feeder elementary schools for the recruitment of athletes. The system is complex, employing a network of alumni groups and coaches to visit each elementary school. The farm system also cleverly involves the administrators and the PTAs of the feeder elementary schools in the recruitment process. The overall result of this effort, as stated by the principal, is improved athletic teams and a greatly enhanced status for the high school in the community.

2. Another image-building technique used by many high schools is the freshmen orientation to familiarize eighth graders from feeder schools with the programs and activities they will experience the following year. This type of orientation program is aimed as much at the parents as at the children themselves. The overall goal is to show the parents that the school cares about each child.

3. Principals typically favor carefully organized benefits to build an image. For example, the principal of one school personally organizes a Christmas pageant for senior citizens in the neighborhood. This is a major musical production featuring students and parents, and coordinated by the Mayor's office. It usu-

ally attracts press coverage and draws positive attention to the school.

4. In recent years, the public has become increasingly interested in schools' standardized reading test scores. Principals recognize that schools showing great improvement in test scores look good to the public. Our research data indicate that some principals place considerable pressure on teachers to improve the scores. This memorandum was sent to teachers early in the academic year by one principal and illustrates the seriousness with which the reading test scores are taken:

> As you know, 200 new students transferred into our school this year. Therefore, our school statistics do not show the movement of last year's student body adequately because one-third of our students are new.
>
> We have received many children who are several years behind in their reading skills. Our work is cut out for us.
>
> It is extremely important that each child be taught the skills at his level. *Do not wait* until the end-of-level test is given to reteach unlearned skills.
>
> Daily intervention is necessary. . . .it is crucial that classroom intervention techniques be employed by teachers prior to end-of-level testing. Our children can succeed with your help.

The school's image within the system Principals often go to great extremes to enhance the image of their school within the bureaucracy. Strategies to achieve visibility within the system are often considerably different from those discussed in the previous section and usually unknown to the general public. For example, the principal of a school recognized for its model reading program and success in the annual tests was able to parlay this success into an even better public image. He capitalized on his, and the school's, good name to obtain certain favors from the superintendent. Because of the school's reputation the superintendent was made to look good and she was more than willing to grant his special requests. For instance, the superintendent brought important guests, often top-level administrators from other systems, to the school. Thus, the good image of the school spread through the hierarchy, and even though this principal was not unusually ambitious, his own career within the system was enhanced by the attention his school received. The image-rich get richer.

To better understand the benefits to a school of a good image within the system, it is instructive to note the problems faced by a principal whose school lacked it. Ms. Enis was battling the building engineer over some repair work. The engineer suggested that the matter be taken to the deputy superintendent for adjudication. Although Enis was not on speaking terms with the deputy superintendent, she had to follow the engineer's suggestion in order to avoid an embarrassing situation. After the engineer left the office, Enis went into a tirade about the deputy: "I never talk to him! He doesn't like me! He's never supportive of what I try to do!" Enis strongly suspected the deputy was undermining her with those above him at district headquarters. As proof she mentioned that no visitors were ever brought to the school, all communication was transacted in writing, and no services were ever offered, other than those required by the central office. The situation was difficult for the teachers as well as the principal.

One upwardly mobile principal tried very hard to establish a good image within the system by being an exemplary bureaucrat. He took pride in completing all forms correctly and in doing his reports and other paper work perfectly. He spent every evening doing homework and bragged about spending every weekend on it as well. For his efforts, he was recognized within his district as the model of efficiency. He was pointed out by the superintendent as "the man to see if you need help on forms." He enjoyed the praise he received for being the best, although concrete rewards were small.

Several principals enjoy demonstrating their political influence within the system. Those who get things done have high status. In most cases, however, getting things done means manipulating the bureaucracy. A good example is the principal who enjoyed spreading rumors of his clout with superiors. He boasted to his colleagues that he had received this special favor or that special compliment from his superior. He would point to concrete acquisitions for his school—some new lunchroom equipment, a computer lab specially allocated to his school, or some fancy new office machinery he claimed he had fast-talked out of the purchasing department. He also dropped names of superiors who had commented favorably and publicly on his school, or he cited specific instances in which a deputy superintendent was more helpful than necessary in helping the principal get rid of an unwanted teacher. These anecdotes never failed to impress his fellow principals, and although they were embellishments of what actually happened, they were true enough to convince doubters.

THINGS TO DO AND THINK ABOUT

1. In this book, principals are sometimes portrayed as playing games with their teachers and others in the school hierarchy. Study the book *Games People Play* by Eric Berne and then try to create a set of psychological games, using the Berne model, called "Games Principals Play."
2. Describe a situation in which your principal was trying to mold parental expectations of the school. Was it necessary for the principal to manipulate information in order to accomplish this goal? In the example on page 117 is Principal Richards manipulating information in order to protect his teachers? How might the situation have been better handled?
3. Describe a principal you have known who considers himself or herself a community actor, i.e., a local political leader. What are the values he or she is trying to inject into the school through this behavior? Can the principal be a political leader without jeopardizing the integrity of the school system?
4. The role of volunteer parents in the school is controversial. Too much can be disruptive; too little can be a sign of apathy. How might a principal be trained to acquire the skills necessary to work with parents? Describe an exemplary program you have seen involving parents. What was the principal's role?
5. The external image of the school can be an important factor in the morale of the school faculty. Principal Herbert, described in this chapter, seemed to be a master at building the school image. What were his basic assumptions? What might you suggest to your principal to help improve the external image of your school?
6. Examples of principal behavior in this chapter (page 117 and 123) strike some people as bordering on unprofessional, perhaps even unethical, conduct. What might you have done in each situation to avoid this criticism?

NOTES

1. See, David L. Clark, Linda S. Lotto, and Martha M. McCarthy, "Factors Associated with Success in Urban Elementary Schools," *Phi Delta Kappan* vol. 61, no. 7 (March, 1980); pp. 467–470; also John E. Ingram, Jr., "School Community Relations and Student Achievement," Paper presented at the annual meeting of the American Educational Research Association, San Francisco, April 1979.
2. David K. Wiles, Jon Wiles, and Joseph Bondi, *Practical Politics for School Administrators* (Boston: Allyn and Bacon, Inc., 1981), pp. 1–17.
3. See, Dale Mann, *The Politics of Administrative Representation* (Lexington, Mass.: Lexington Books, 1976); also, Harold L. Summerfield, *The Neighborhood-Based Politics of Education* (Columbus, Ohio: Charles E. Merrill Publishing Co., 1971).

4. Mann, op. cit., pp. 15–35.
5. Ibid. p. 58; also Summerfield, *The Neighborhood-Based Politics of Education.*
6. Paul E. Peterson, *School Politics Chicago Style* (Chicago: The University of Chicago Press, 1976), p. 226.
7. See David Rogers, *110 Livingston Street* (New York: Vintage Books, 1968).
8. See, Mary T. Moore, "The Boundary-Spanning Role of the Urban School Principal," Unpublished Ph.D. dissertation, the University of California at Los Angeles, 1975.
9. Harry F. Wolcott, *The Man in the Principal's Office: An Ethnography* (New York: Holt, Rinehart and Winston, Inc., 1973), p. 320.
10. See, Michael Lipsky, *Street-Level Bureaucracy: Dilemmas of the Individual in Public Services* (New York: Basic Books, Inc., 1980).
11. Richard A. Weatherley, *Reforming Special Education: Policy Implementation from State Level to Street Level* (Cambridge, Mass.: The MIT Press, 1979).
12. See James G. Cibulka, "Creating a New Era for Schools and Communities," in Donald A. Erickson and Theodore L. Reller, eds., *The Principal in Metropolitan Schools* (Berkeley, Calif.: McCutchan Publishing Corporation, 1979), pp. 78–105.
13. See William H. Roe and Thelbert L. Drake, *The Principalship,* 2nd edition (New York: Macmillan Publishing Co., Inc., 1974), pp. 48–51.
14. Ibid. p. 49.
15. Ibid. p. 50.
16. Larry W. Hughes and Gerald C. Ubben, *The Elementary Principal's Handbook: A Guide to Effective Action* (Boston: Allyn and Bacon, Inc., 1978), pp. 282–283.
17. See Charles L. Wood, Everett W. Nicholson, and Dale G. Findley, *The Secondary School Principal: Manager and Supervisor* (Boston: Allyn and Bacon, Inc. 1979), pp. 72–75.
18. James M. Lipham and James A. Hoeh, Jr., *The Principalship: Foundations and Functions* (New York: Harper & Row, 1974), p. 335.
19. Some classic studies of the socialization of a clientele, in the early 1960s, were Blau's research into bureacrat-client interaction in an employment office and Skolnick's study of the decisions of patrolmen on-the-beat. In the early 1970s, Katz and Eisenstadt provided a fascinating account of how new immigrants to Israel were socialized by persons in client-service roles. Israeli bus drivers, for example, would step down from their buses to teach new arrivals how to queue and would carefully explain that the bus cannot transport each individual to the door of his or her destination, but must operate only between designated bus stopping points.

See Peter Blau, *The Dynamics of Bureaucracy* (Chicago: The University of Chicago Press, 1963); also Jerome Skolnick, *Justice Without Trial* (New York: John Wiley and Sons, 1960); and Elihu Katz and S. N. Eisenstadt, "The Response of Israeli Organizations to New Immigrants," in Elihu Katz and Brenda Danet, eds., *Bureaucracy and the Public* (New York: Basic Books, Inc., 1973), pp. 73–87.

20. Comprehensive Education and Training Act, a job-making initiative of the Federal Government during the 1970s.

6

Principaling and its Effects on the Hierarchy

The building principal is the executive of the local school. Yet the principal is not an autonomous professional, like the family physician or lawyer, but is embedded within and necessarily responsive to a hierarchical organization. To teachers and other staff members at the school site, the principal is the boss. To the superintendent, the central office staff, and the school board, the principal is just another employee occupying one of the lower rungs on the managerial ladder.

WHAT WE KNOW FROM THE LITERATURE

The traditional and still most commonly held notion of the educational organization is a hierarchical pyramid: authority radiates downward from a centralized apex of power to a distributed base of responsibility in the neighborhood schools. Figure 6.2 represents the conventional notion of downward and outward flowing management typically represented in a school district's organization chart. At the top, community preferences become school district policy when legislated by the Board of Education. These policies are then executed by the superintendent. The superintendent's orders flow through the next echelon of staff specialists—curriculum, business affairs, personnel—who help form detailed rules and procedures. These instructions are then passed to building principals for implementation and transmittal to teachers and pupils.

As this hierarchical model of organization life has gained general acceptance in the public mind, there has grown up around it an accompanying set of assumptions, almost a mythology, about how things work in such an environment. One of these assumptions is that interaction between different levels is regulated and rationalized through the careful structuring of offices, titles, and explicit fixing of responsibility at each echelon. Another assumption is that such a tight structure binds together the various elements in the organization on behalf of a set of shared goals and values. The objectives of the school system are honored by all individuals and are progressively translated from policy into practice, level by level, by persons performing separate organizational roles devoted to a common end. A third notion is that a tight hierarchy guarantees rationality in decision making. With the free flow of information, carefully delineated areas of responsibility, unimpeded channeling of commands downward, and wide and unequivocal sharing of corporate objectives, managers at each position can plan and implement administrative decisions effectively.

In the 1970s and early 1980s, this model of school system organization received close, critical attention. Coming under particular scrutiny was the pyramidal model as a point of departure in university programs for the training of school administrators. Revisionist scholars began to argue that assumptions of hierarchical symmetry of communication and command, of shared goals and values, and of rationally distributed responsibility and authority did not accurately portray the circumstances within which school administrators actually function. In particular, the revisionists asserted that the prototypi-

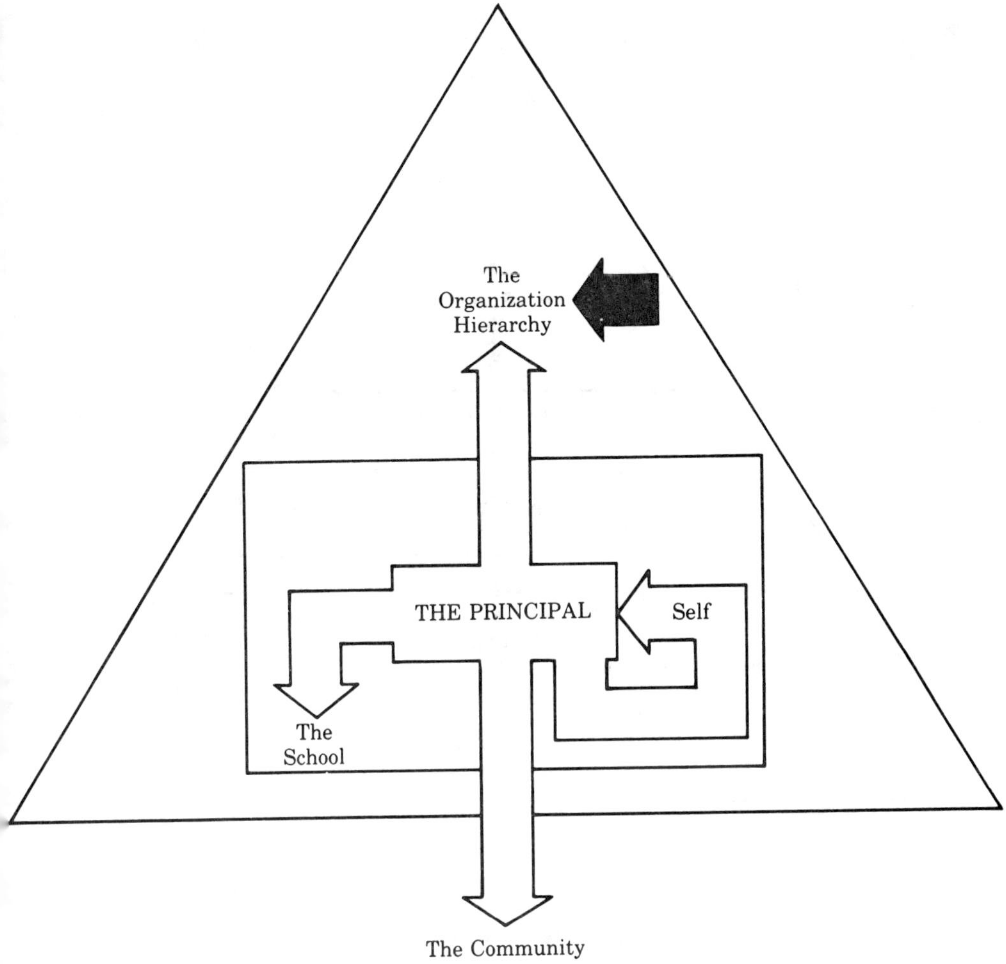

Figure 6.1 Principaling and its Four Sectors of Effect

cal school system is, in reality, a collection of loosely coupled units, that it harbors within it and is forced to tolerate many competing goals and value orientations, and that ambiguity and irrationality characterize its decision making.[1]

Hannaway and Sproull, for example, studied school district bureaucracies and found that among administrators at all echelons only small portions of the working day are devoted to interactions with individuals at other levels. Furthermore, administrators at the school site, as well as those at upper levels, devote little of their time to coordinating and controlling the core tasks of the organization, cur-

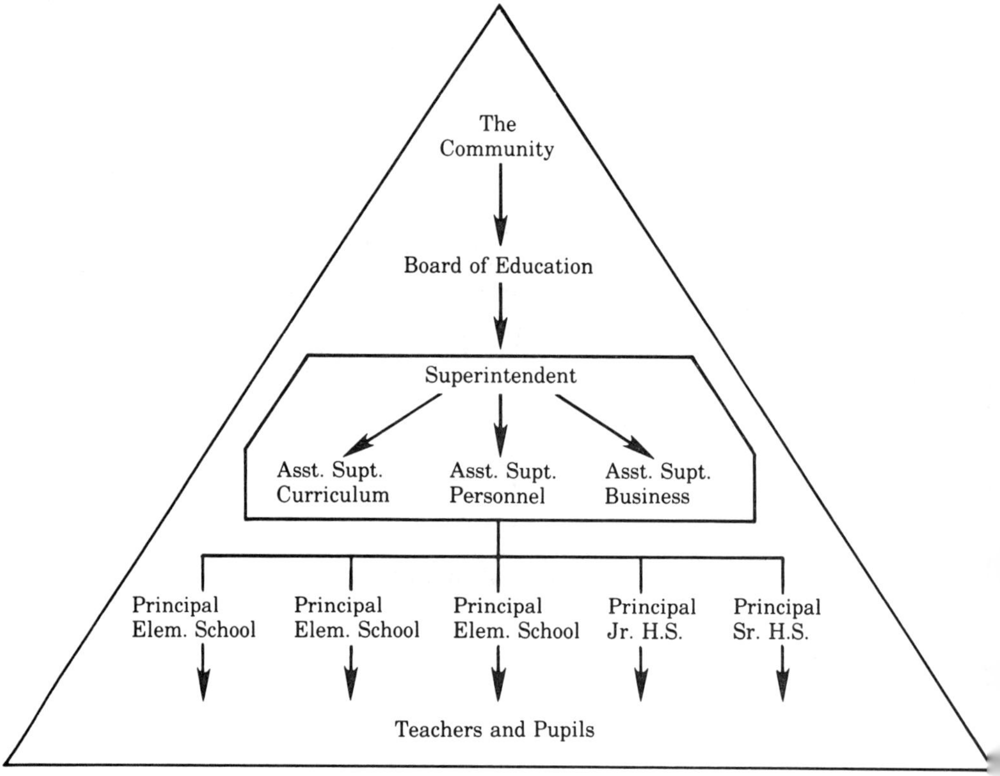

Figure 6.2 Education's Administrative Pyramid

riculum and instruction. The researchers concluded that within the loosely structured environment of educational organizations, ". . . the activities of management seem to be only marginally related to the production (e.g., student learning) activities of school."[2]

In the face of this lack of fit between traditional and emergent views on how educational organizations actually function, it is instructive to examine two key dimensions of the principal's organizational role. The principal is the quintessential middle manager in the hierarchy. On one hand, he or she is an employee subject to the orders and instructions of higher officers. On the other hand, the principal is executive decision maker at the school site, serving as boss over a semi-autonomous unit, with operational jurisdiction over as many as several hundred people.

The Principal as Middle Manager

The building principal functions in education's critical middle territory between thought and action, between policy and execution. At the principal's managerial level, directives and procedures are translated into the day-by-day activity of teaching and managing children. School district rules for student discipline are applied to actual cases of classroom misbehavior. A curriculum guide becomes an operational lesson plan and then emerges as an hour of instruction in science class. A line in the school district budget becomes reality with the delivery of fifty new math textbooks.

The job of translating policy into practice is essentially judgmental. At the policy level, the rules and procedures handed down by the larger bureaucracy are generic and universal, necessarily couched in terminology that reduces events to standardized and interchangeable elements. At the practice level, the problems are individual and idiosyncratic. In site-specific situations, management "by the book" is not always possible or even desirable; flexibility, consideration of unique circumstances, and sometimes a sense of compassion are often called for.

For example, Kerchner and his research colleagues found principals caught between the superintendent and the teaching faculty when implementing the teachers' union contract. Understandably, top level administrators are wary of the mischief created when contract rules are applied differently from situation to situation. They often stress to their principals the importance of system-wide conformity in contract interpretation. But building principals, forced to treat individual cases as they arise and to apply contract provisions selectively, find flexibility critical in maintaining close relations with their faculty. Without superintendent support, principals often feel out on a limb in dealing with contract demands.[3]

Analyses of the middle manager's organizational milieu have stressed the congeries of constraints that surround principaling. One group of researchers argues that the organizational hierarchy in education has lost effective control over its own managerial apparatus because the bureaucratic constraints on administrative behavior have simply become overwhelming. David Rogers has suggested that school systems are more encumbered than most organizations with fixed rules and standardized procedures. He has described the effects of overcentralized decision making and the "proliferation of specialized administrative units" on the managerial flexibility of local school staffs. Over-reliance on procedural guidelines and outdated Standard Operating Procedures (S.O.P.'s) results in long delays in securing needed school services. The preoccupation with standardized regulations frustrates the development of new or unusual school programs and widens the gap between headquarters' understandings and local school demands.[4]

Rogers portrays school systems as moribund, sometimes even pathological, organizations beset by political infighting and inertia. Other scholars, although offering more positive views, nevertheless characterize school organizations as amalgamations of jealous interest groups who represent constraining influences that confound the best intentions of a conscientious manager.

Gross and Herriott found that the local principal's ability to provide leadership in the school is constrained by such organizationally-related factors as the following:

1. the strength of the principal's immediate superior, as measured by the superior's willingness to go to bat for the principal
2. the degree to which the principal is personally able to select his school's staff
3. the nature of the school system's reward structure, and specifically whether managerial initiative is really valued and rewarded by the larger organization

Similarly, in a national study of what principals do, McPherson, Salley, and Baehr noted that there are varying institutional, collegial, and community factors, as well as differing conditions of operation to which principals need to adapt. Organizational variables such as the size of the school system, the size of each school, or the number of grade levels in a school, were found to be particularly important in constraining and influencing the work of the principal. In very large high schools, for example, principals have little direct interaction with teachers; by the scope of their responsibilities, they are forced to yield to intermediaries—department heads and assistants—the critical task of teacher evaluation.[6]

A third recent research initiative has suggested that what appears to be organizational constraint can also be interpreted as administrative opportunity. Although principals are affected by the nature of the system in which they work, the more successful administrators are able to adapt their own administrative behavior to varying conditions of employment and circumstance.[7] They rise above the many barriers to managerial directiveness and take charge of their bureaucratic lives. In his case study of a single high school principal, Henry Barsky found that knowledge of how the system functions provides the astute principal with a critical edge in performance. The principal who is acquainted with the informal organization, who knows headquarters secretaries and assistants on a first-name basis, and who understands the unwritten reward system implied by the superintendent's pet projects or special dislikes is in a position to adroitly manipulate the system for personal or professional advantage.[8]

The Principal as Decision Maker

The conventional wisdom holds that the principal's key relationship with the remainder of the hierarchy is his obligation to execute system policy through site-level decision making. As noted in Chapter 1, the decision making function has been studied originally under rubrics of scientific efficiency, later according to the canons of participatory or democratic management, and still later according to both closed- and open-system analytics. The process of decision making has been broadly interpreted over the years as an activity that encompasses policy implementation, systematic planning, school-site evaluation, innovation, and most recently "problem finding."[9]

Under the traditional notion of tightly hierarchical bureaucracy, it was assumed that decision making at the school-site would be closely controlled by the local board of education and the superintendency. It was the principal's job to implement school district policy and follow the organizational chain of command to accomplish the shared goals of the educational enterprise. Directives were to pass through the bureaucracy to be placed in operation at the school-site, as specified by board and central office. Overseeing all and governing with a tight rein, the school district superintendent was in charge of and responsible for the organization and its administrative behavior.

Recent evidence, however, reveals a looser structure. Links between site-level administrators and hierarchical superiors are not close, and headquarters has less day-by-day control over the work of individuals at each level of the hierarchy than was once thought. Meyer et al. conducted research in several school systems and discovered very low agreement between schools and district offices on what constitutes the acceptable rules and practices of the organization.[10] Although policies and rules abound, the people who are supposed to carry them out, from the top of the school system to the bottom, are not in close consensus. Consequently, school board and superintendent may be in charge of the organization in a titular sense, but significant administrative direction comes from somewhere else—the principal's office.

This new notion of the organization has at least three implications for the principal's role as decision maker in the school system environment: First, the principal as decision maker learns what to do managerially as much by "reading" the upper bureaucracy as by following its direct orders. Peterson studied principals' decisions in allocating resources within their schools. He found that the principals' allocative decisions were often affected by their "decoding" of the hierarchy's unwritten incentive system and the expectations of higher level managers.

> If central office administrators gather information about reading scores, principals can reasonably interpret this to mean that reading is important and, thus, they should allocate more resources to this area. Similarly, if superintendents are particularly quick in responding to parent complaints about a school, this tells principals that these are central contingencies to which they must attend.[11]

As indicated in a later section in this chapter, the principal may interpret school system direction more through its subtle nuances than its hierarchically-driven rules and procedures. The organization is viewed by the principal as a "shifting chessboard," calling for quick counter moves amid an almost infinite variety of problems. It is worth noting that under the conventional wisdom of a tight hierarchy, it was assumed that the building principal would respond quickly and precisely to all upper-level directives; under the loosely-coupled rubric it is understood that the principal may manage more selectively, determining on his own which moves on the bureaucratic chessboard to attend to, and when.

Second, these new perspectives further reveal that the emergent, loosely-coupled notion of organizational structure turns the bureaucratic hierarchy concept on its head. Whereas tradition assumes policy-making authority to be positioned at the top of the hierarchy, the emergent wisdom recognizes that the principal's selective choice of what to attend to, and when, in effect *makes* school district policy. Robert Lineberry has suggested that key decisions continue to be made at the apex of the bureaucracy, but the many little decisions made elsewhere throughout an organization are cumulatively just as significant.[12] Nowhere is the importance of these little decisions more evident than in the critical task of collecting and using information. As a later section indicates, the principal's ability to manipulate information requested by the bureaucracy can enhance considerably his or her strategic position within the managerial milieu.

Third, the newer understandings of organizational structure imply a heavy additional burden that is increasingly placed on the school-site administrator—the responsibility to serve as a *moral agent*. In this role, the principal must consider "the welfare and interests of all who stand to be affected" by his decisions, to be conscientious, to do "the right thing."[13] In a previous era, moral leadership was assumed to be the special province of the superintendent, with the principal not expected to assume responsibility for the impact, good or bad, of system directives. Now, the relative autonomy of the building principal is more clearly recognized, and the superintendent is willing, sometimes eager, to let the principal take the heat when events flame up.

The burden of this new responsibility is symbolized in McCullogh's finding that school principals seem unusually prone to insert naval metaphors into their conversation.[14] "Riding the waves," "sailing through troubled waters," "staying on an even keel," "keeping the ship afloat," and "running a happy ship" are commonly heard expressions.[15] Like the captain of a ship, the principal must set a course and function as the final arbiter in a mini-world on its own. But the principal plays a lonely and burdened role, with growing responsibility for moral authority. In one of our sections to follow, we show how the "creative insubordination" of the principal is closely tied to the moral dimension of school district decision making.

WHAT WE SEE

Creative Insubordination: Civilized Disobedience

One of the articles of faith in American institutional life is the chain of command. Every organization, because it involves by definition a group of people collected together for a supposedly common purpose, must be united by some apparatus designed to make all individuals move, more or less, in the same direction. We call this the chain of command, a generic phrase that implies a link between individuals (the chain), and an order to the individuals that specifies who can tell whom what to do (the command). It is conventional wisdom that organizations work because individuals voluntarily submit their actions to the discipline of this network, that the chain is what holds people together, and that the command structure is legitimate and necessary.

In an educational bureaucracy, as in any bureaucracy, the need for the chain of command apparatus is directly proportional to the size of the undertaking. The more remote and impersonal decision making becomes, the more reliance must be put on organization-oriented, as against person-oriented, considerations. Hence, the larger the educational system becomes, the more it resembles a military table of organization in which orders are handed down from a central headquarters through various echelons of administrators, finally reaching the operating unit where the clients are served.

The need for the manager to be bound by the command chain is the conventional wisdom. What is not so commonly understood in organization theory is the companion contradictory idea that the need to *ignore* the chain of command also increases as the bureaucracy grows. Precisely because decision making in large organizations relies on impersonal expectations, the need to *disobey* orders to counter their dehumanizing effects becomes more compatible with principles of good management. Knowing where and how to disobey is central to discretionary decision making among school principals.

Among sophisticated administrators, particularly those who are sensitive to the human needs of their surroundings, such disobedience to the chain of command has developed into an art form. The skillful practitioner tries to be subtle and unobtrusive. The object is for the disobedience to produce the maximum effect locally (within the school) but have the minimum impact on superiors. It must serve its basic purpose, for example, the maintenance of good morale, but do so with the least flurry of feathers among superiors. If this ratio is reversed, the principal is in trouble.

It is important to remember that this form of disobedience does not grow out of mere personal pique. The principal may or may not be comfortable with some instruction from the superintendent, but what makes disobedience a workable option is the perception of that instruction, if carried out, as inimical to the welfare of the school. If assessment of an order's impact reveals potentially significant damage to the organization, then the principal begins the review of how to disobey the order in the most artistic (least obtrusive) manner.

The ploy that failed Principals disobey in several ways, many of which are understandably mild and benign in their overall impact on the hierarchy. These forms are tentative because perhaps (1) the principal lacks standing with his immediate superiors and is timid about reaching too far, (2) the principal is unwilling to take the punishment if caught and therefore defies only half-heartedly, (3) the issue is trivial and not worth spending "credibility chips" on.

In one instance, a high school principal made an exploratory move in an attempt to test the waters. Dissembling he well knew, could be dangerous, and he was not certain how much to risk. In the end, though, he decided to venture forth because the issue was serious: getting rid of an incompetent assistant.

This principal was ordered by his superintendent to reduce his cadre of assistant principals from four to three to save money, the reduction in force (RIF) to be accomplished within thirty days. Of the four APs, two were well matched to their jobs and their removal would have been disruptive. He turned to the other two.

Assistant Principal McNerney was the least competent and, in fact, a hindrance to the principal in running the school. However, he was senior to all the APs and held a valid Principal's Certificate. He was waiting for an assignment, but because of the glacial rate of turnover the principal expected it could be months or even years before McNerney got a school of his own. AP Norton, on the other hand, was next to the most junior of the four. Although relatively new to administration, he was extremely effective, very valuable to the principal as a deputy principal and obviously on his way up in the system. Norton, therefore, was clearly the principal's choice for retention, and he chose McNerney to be "riffed."

Realizing that seniority would play some role in the system-wide riffing process, the principal nevertheless sent McNerney's name to the superintendent. Not surprisingly, the superintendent gently blew the whistle, inquiring about the rationale for the recommendation. Without mentioning the real hidden agenda—*Here's my chance to unload that deadbeat McNerney. Now, if I can just get the boss to go along . . .*—the principal spoke firmly into the telephone and made his case. "Yes, Charlie," he explained, "I know McNerney is senior, but he's the only one of the APs with a Principal's Certificate. He'd be the easiest to transfer to a principalship, or at least an assistant principalship, in another school. For all the other three, and particularly for AP Norton, being let go would mean being demoted to classroom-teacher status. I'm thinking of the people here, what's going to happen to them. I want to be humanitarian in all this. For morale over here, and for the welfare of the school, it would be better to cut McNerney than Norton."

It was clear that the superintendent did not know the four APs well enough to see through this subterfuge. Nevertheless, the superintendent ruled against the principal. The seniority criterion, although not hard and fast, must be the primary guideline, unless extraordinary reasons, not visible to him here, were offered.

In one sense, the test was successful; the principal found where the line was to be drawn. The attempted insubordination failed, and he let the axe fall on Norton. But in spite of the dissembling, the principal was looking out for the welfare of his school and for his own welfare as a principal in need of quality assistants. The system followed its rules, but the principal, the school, and even the system itself lost a little in the process. McNerney's incompetence continued as a hobbling drag on the school. Did this principal stop too soon? Was there a more clever angle of attack, a more sophisticated approach, that may have succeeded?

The numbers game Exercises in disobedience are sometime adventures in roulette, initiated by a principal who knows there is only a 5 percent chance of winning. Enrollment figures are sometimes manipulated to protect a school's head-count compared with other buildings. When a high school opens in September, the number of students who show up usually represents about 80 percent of the peak enrollment. As the weather cools and youngsters quit their summer jobs to return to school, attendance gradually builds to its maximum around 1 November, when the official headcount for the year is taken. From this point to the end of school in June, the attendance curve slowly falls to about 70 percent of the November peak. The principal is concerned about the reading of 1 November since that provides the baseline data for allocation of teachers.

Like ratings week in the television business, the principal pulls out all the stops to "score" well in the period before 1 November. One of the most reliable of these strategems is to manipulate suspension policy. If a student misbehaves during this interval, the chances of suspension from school are small. The principal will take extraordinary measures to keep the youth in the school, perhaps in a detention center (called the "Bar Room" in one school) where miscreants barred from attending class but officially still members of the student body remain through the school day.

By union contract and, therefore, Board policy, the working ratio in the district studied calls for one teacher for each 28 students. As a result the principal counts students like gold pieces, and uses his or her discretionary power to pad the numbers when possible.

The gentleman's agreement Principals are sometimes put off by Board of Education directives. In the late 1970s, principals throughout one system were instructed to provide permissive transfers of their students to other schools to enable them to take advantage of special programs there. Dubbed "Access to Excellence,"[16] the program's advertised objective was to enhance educational opportunity,[17] but its primary purpose was to increase the voluntary movement of races throughout the system to foreclose the possiblity of desegregation ordered by the Justice Department or, worse, the courts. However, those transfers were to be for only part of a school day; the students were to be bussed to and from the receiving schools within the normal schedule.

Two principals in neighboring schools, each with a receiving "Access" program, recognized immediately that full compliance would markedly affect their schools. Since one school was predominantly black and the other predominantly white, heavy transfer traffic between the two would help desegregate them. However, the part-day arrangement meant that the participating students would lose the equivalent of a class period getting to the alternate school and another class period returning, thus canceling approximately 20 percent of their instructional day. Recognizing this as an unconscionable price to pay for even so laudable an objective as racial integration, the two principals quietly decided between themselves that they would discourage transfers between their two schools. By this action, the two principals were, of course, frustrating Board of Education policy, but in so doing they were also protecting the educational instruction time of their own students, a bargain they both felt worth the risk of defiance.

Planned delinquency on deadlines Our observations of school principals also reveal a more substantial form of counter-bureaucratic behavior: the deliberate refusal to meet deadlines set by superiors. School principals are inundated with paper work. Some of it, to be sure, is vital and important such as requisitions for supplies or equipment, vouchers for reimbursement of expenditures, paysheets authorizing the issuing of checks to subordinates, etc. Certainly the board of education and the administrative staff should control organizational behavior. But at the other end of the spectrum are the endless memoranda from superiors or their staff people requesting a hundred kinds of information about the school. To the working principal, concerned with students, faculty and the vitality of the educational program, these requests have no relationship to teaching and learning. They seem to have come from another planet and, as the principal sees it, represent make-work for "the bureaucrats at HQ." An analysis of the paper flow of a school system does indeed suggest that a major part of the motivation for requesting information is simply the realization that it can be collected. A Parkinson's Law operates in which the mere obtainability of information becomes a major criterion for its necessity.

In the chain of command, the principal is expected to mobilize the resources in the school to gather the information requested. In some cases the effort required is considerable and is not confined to clerks and stenographers (for whom information retrieval is part of the job). It spills over into the routines of busy staff and faculty personnel. Can the principal afford to divert the energies of highly paid professionals to this kind of labor? If the information asked for is perceived to be merely raw material for the make-work staffers at central headquarters who look for something to do and generate their own work, the answer is clearly *no*. So, the principal must devise some method for protecting his staff from such trivial intrusions and subtly defy the system.

Some principals do not provide the information at the appointed deadline. In the abstract, this may sound risky. But the principal knows from experience that some deadlines are firm and others are soft, that some information requesters are conscientious while others are nine-to-five time-servers. The principal therefore cocks an ear to await the first call from the central office staffer asking, "Where is the information?" The promptness of this call following the deadline is the key signal. If it takes days or weeks, the principal can be reasonably certain that the delinquency has paid off—the system does not really need this information. If the call comes quickly and the voice on the other end has a tone of urgency, then the principal gathers the data.

Sometimes principals can learn to manipulate the deadlines on their own behalf. The refusal to meet a deadline, if practiced by enough principals simultaneously on the same piece of business, can effectively render the deadline meaningless. Thus, principals in league with one another and sensing the pointlessness of the information, can agree to drag their feet in hopes that a more reasonable deadline can be set, or that the request can be abandoned altogether.

Finally, the astute principal can sometimes forecast a postponement ordered by the staffer, thus negating the original deadline. On one occasion, a principal was asked to submit in forty-eight hours the names of teachers designated for summer school service. Through other channels, the principal already knew that such a request had no purpose since the summer school curriculum program had not yet been set. Since staffing always follows program decisions, the principal ignored the deadline and quietly waited for the staffer to announce that the information would be collected at a later date. Once again, the routines of a busy school had been shielded from the invasions of the bureaucratic mentality.

The literal response Principals are sometimes prepared to play "hard ball." Perhaps the most artistic and foolproof mode of this more strenuous form of insubordination is disobeying an instruction by following it literally. The principal, on receiving an order from a superior, understands full well what information is really wanted. However, a close reading of the detailed instructions reveals that if they are followed to the letter, the desired information will not be forthcoming. Thus, instead of informing the superior of this flaw in the instructions or unilaterally correcting the instructions and responding to them in their new form, the shrewd principal will inform the assistants to put together a report following the guidelines precisely. What is eventually forwarded to the superior is useless, and the principal knows it. But he or she also knows that the problem will be spotted eventually and that a more carefully written instruction will soon be promulgated.

The value of this strategem is double: As a defensive tactic, it protects the school's staff from unnecessary hours spent on gathering the more sophisticated information (what the superior *really* wants). As an offensive weapon, it embarrasses the superior's staffers, puts them on the defensive, and temporarily neutralizes their enthusiasm for thinking up new "studies" and "reports" requiring more exasperating effort.

During the late 1970s, school systems throughout the nation, especially those in large, urban centers, were required to file periodic racial composition reports with the U.S. Department of Health, Education and Welfare. These reports were ostensibly designed to provide baseline data to develop desegregation programs.

On the occasion of one of these requests, the Superintendent's headquarters personnel in one system, customarily referred to as "Downtown," issued a command to the city's twenty-seven school districts. Each principal was to conduct a census of the student body to identify the race of each student. The forms for the census employed the standard categories of the U.S. Census Bureau, and in other ways resembled government questionnaires.

The Superintendent's staff further instructed that the forms were to be filled out by the high school students themselves; this specification betrayed the staff's extreme concern in dealing with such sensitive information as race identity. As the principal had half-expected, when the students got the forms they began to make a game out of the question asking them about their race. Seeing in small print some of the sub-headings under the major categories, many students, intrigued with the sound of "Samoan," "Eskimo," and "Aleut," identified themselves as members of one of these groups. As word got around the school, the practice of mis-identifying oneself became a badge of mild protest against this kind of intrusion into their lives.

The results, of course, were chaotic. In a large high school with approximately 60 percent white, 30 percent black and 10 percent Hispanic, the principal's cursory inspection of the questionnaires revealed that in "actual fact" over one-sixth of the students were Aleuts or Eskimos! Without comment, the principal returned the questionnaires to the superintendent's office.

Creative insubordination and administrative theory

In the work of principals as with other managers, there is considerable room for maneuver for which the table of organization does not provide. Discretionary behavior becomes both more possible and more visible. One principal commented directly about her own style, "I don't break any rules, I just *bend* a few now and then."

For the conscientious principal, the objective is to use the organizational apparatus so that the ultimate client, the student, is best served. This may mean that the organizational apparatus, and the chain of command in particular, must be used *against itself* to make the institution humane as well as efficient. What is referred to as counter-bureaucratic behavior is not only a survival mechanism for beleaguered principals, but also a balance weight to the seemingly anti-educational forces constantly at work in large school systems today.

Short-Circuiting the Labyrinth: To Hell with the S.O.P.

The conventional view of the modern school system conjures up an image of a vast labyrinth, an intricate rat's maze containing complex sub-units awkwardly inter-related and difficult to manage. Finding one's way through this labyrinth has been a perennial preoccupation of administrators. When patience flags, the typical administrator will attempt to speed up the routine processes of the bureaucracy by finding spur-of-the-moment shortcuts.

In today's understanding of organizational dynamics, this practice of short-circuiting the bureaucracy may not be all bad. In fact, school bureaucracies survive partly because good administrators are not afraid to use their discretionary decision-making powers to speed up turtle-paced procedures. Such actions help school systems reach their goals in spite of the difficult bureaucratic structure. Thus, short-circuiting the labyrinth may be a form of anti-bureaucratic behavior that actually insures the survival of the system itself.

As noted earlier, school principals use their discretionary decision-making powers in relation to the community inside the school building, the community outside, the overall organizational hierarchy, and on behalf of their own occupational needs and career aspirations. Short-circuiting behavior may affect several of these spheres simultaneously, as we see in the following examples.

Wielding "the community" as an ad hoc weapon

The ability of principals to mobilize community support often has considerable impact on their effectiveness. The school building, a sub-unit within the system, gains power in the larger system when community support is available. A strongly supporting community is a valuable resource which the principal can use to accomplish school goals. One principal used her discretionary decision-making power to force a decision that the bureaucracy refused to make until community pressure was brought to bear.

Margaret Fane, the principal of an elementary school,

was ambitious, aggressive and definitely the boss within her building. Because of dual chains of command for educational program and building maintenance, Fane found she had no direct jurisdiction over the building custodians with whom she worked every day. Most principals are able, by using good personal relations, to work effectively within a system that separates building maintenance from the instructional activities. Fane, however, because of her idiosyncratic personality and her special style of principaling, required complete control of every activity in her building. This led to increasingly difficult confrontations with the chief custodian, Joseph Fried. Eventually, the relationship deteriorated to a point at which the everyday functions of the custodian stopped. He would not, for example, allow his men to enter and clean the school office, nor would he respond to any of Fane's requests.

As time passed, the situation grew more embarrassing, and the teachers and parents began to talk openly about the problem. Fane requested the superintendent to prevail upon the engineer supervisor to transfer Fried. But the superintendent refused, saying Fane would have to learn to get along with her custodian. As Fane was trying to resolve the problem through the bureaucratic structure, services performed by the custodial staff came to a virtual standstill. This brought parents and teachers into the controversy because snow was clogging the sidewalks and necessary classroom repairs were neglected. When there was an incident because the custodial staff failed to repair a classroom closet lock for a teacher, it became clear that the principal would have to abandon her efforts to work within the school hierarchy.

The principal had excellent community support because parents were concerned about the safety of their children. Four parents came to her and asked her to write a letter to the superintendent to solve the problem. Fane quickly suggested that such a letter would have more impact if it came from the community. Further, she offered to help them write the letter if they would agree to have it signed by as many community people as possible. The letter was written and forwarded. Within days the custodian was transferred.

Management by loophole In one system, the procedure for obtaining substitute teachers specifies that the principal must first alert the central office "Sub Center" each day, and then await the arrival of the substitutes designated by the Center. The procedure seemed to work well in some parts of the district but not in others. James Broder was principal of a large school in a neighborhood where substitutes were reluctant to come. He was fortunate if one out of five teacherless classrooms were covered on a typical day. Broder realized he would have to devise a substitute hiring procedure that would allow him to develop his own group of people to fill vacant teaching positions. After careful study of procedures, he discovered that the central office did not compare the records of the Sub Center with the pay authorization forms signed by the principal and submitted each pay period by substitute teachers. This was, of course, the loophole Broder needed to establish his own cadre of substitutes. Since the pay authorization forms were not checked, it was possible for Broder to call directly those substitutes who were willing to work in his school. Because the Sub Center had no record of his substitutes, it could not challenge his "private employment agency."

The short-circuit procedure worked because Principal Broder withheld important information needed to maintain the established procedure. By denying information to the system, the school gained the power it needed to manage its own system for insuring that classrooms were adequately staffed by substitute teachers. Again, in this example, the discretionary decision-making power of the principal allowed the instructional program to function normally even though he short-circuited the system.

Shortcuts to image building Image building is important to local school principals. Schools with a good reputation get special consideration from central headquarters. A principal's ability to advertise the special qualities of his school insures attention to requests for additional help, needed supplies or special favors. The extent to which a principal will go to short-circuit the system in order to build her school's image is illustrated in the following example.

A school in a lower middle-class, predominantly black neighborhood was assigned two additional reading teachers because of the serious need for remedial reading help. But the principal, Grace Lights, chose to put those two teachers to work in a way that was not intended. In sending out the notice concerning additional reading help, Lights instructed teachers to send for special help only those children who already were reading very nearly at grade level, rather than the really poor readers. This decision mystified the teachers. Why would the principal specify that the better students be sent to the special reading instructors? How could she justify such a decision professionally, even morally?

The answer lay in the fact that Principal Lights had personally studied what happened when far-below-grade-level readers had been provided additional tutorial help. The answer: not much. She reluctantly concluded that little reading gain could be expected from these very slow children. Instead, she calculated that she could get more measurable increase in reading scores by concentrating on the near-to-grade-level readers. Even a slight gain for these children would put them at target levels. She felt she could get more mileage out of the two reading specialists by giving them the better students. The strategy worked. Reading scores for the school were significantly improved and the daily newspapers, fond of reporting such statistics, took notice.

New wine in old bottles Principals must often modify policies and adapt them to the needs, interests and tolerance levels of local parents. The principal is in the critical position of understanding what the school system tries to accomplish through a particular directive or order; but he or she is also in the critical position of knowing what the community will accept. It is often impossible to adapt policy without either deliberately or accidentally short-circuiting the system.

For several years, one school system has conducted a reading competency program known as the Continuous Progress Program. Students are expected to master a sequence of competencies within fourteen specified competency levels (levels A–N). This program was introduced after decades of the traditional K-8 system of grade levels. The new system posed serious problems of interpretation and communication for both teachers and parents. It was unpopular with teachers because it required considerable time for recording large numbers of competencies. For parents, it caused unnecessary confusion at a time when the traditional K–8 levels were well understood. The principal's role was crucial both in helping the teachers find efficient means of keeping records and in helping parents understand the system.

When working with the Continuous Progress Program, the principal translated the curriculum into different languages depending on the audience. With teachers the principal always used the new categories—Levels A, B, C, D, etc. To make the program work the teachers had to be educated in a new terminology. But since parents were most comfortable with the traditional grade level designations—First, Second, Third, etc.—the principal often saved time and effort by showing how Continuous Progress worked within the conventional grading system, fearing that a technical explanation would only stir up trouble. In a major directive of this sort, headquarters planners expect that the principal will educate not just the teachers, but parents and interested laymen, in the new system. But short-circuiting gets the job done with the least fuss.

The spontaneous policy statement School principals can mold parental expectations of the school in a way that will enhance the school's reputation. Superiors expect principals to anticipate the problems and uncertainties surrounding the school system and to ward off potential trouble before it gets out of control.

Janet Gross, principal of a large elementary school, had left the school building one evening at 4:30 not realizing that a seven-year-old girl was still waiting to be picked up by a parent. The child had been sitting between the inner and outer doors of the main entrance so Gross did not see her as she left through a rear door. When Gross arrived at school the next morning, she was greeted by an extremely angry mother who said she was going to have her arrested for leaving her child in the doorway. The mother had already alerted the Parent Council president and the superintendent's office. Gross could see this was going to be a difficult matter to resolve. The principal apologized to the extremely agitated mother and promised that such a thing would not happen again. The parent finally left after promising not to let the matter drop.

A number of thoughts went through Gross's mind. Was it her responsibility to take care of a child at 4:30P.M.? Where was the clean-up crew? What could be done to establish a school policy to insure that an incident like this did not recur? Gross turned to the chief engineer in the building with whom she got along extremely well. In fact, he thought very highly of her and wanted to show his appreciation because she had praised him to his supervisor. When told the story, the engineer said that after 4:30 he and his staff would babysit children whose parents were delayed. Through the school newsletter, parents were to be informed that after 4:30 they could, in an emergency, pick up their child in the engineer's office.

Gross thought the engineer's procedure would solve the problem and sent out a notice to all parents that day. She acted hastily in order to prevent an uproar in the community over the incident, but also to quickly establish a school policy statement. After careful study of the Board of Education policy and consultation with the local principals association, Gross learned that, as principal, she did not bear legal responsibility for children after 4:30 P.M. She also learned that the Board frowned on such policies. But she felt, in this case, her policy was necessary; she also understood that the community demanded a response from her rather than legal opinions. She maintained and defended her policy.

Here is a case of a principal short-circuiting the hierarchy by actually acting without consulting her superiors before announcing her decision. Such action is unusual, but it demonstrates Gross's determination. In effect, Gross short-circuited the system by quickly stating policy and then publishing it before it could be questioned.

The old-crony network Principals are often frustrated by the lack of reward and absence of immediate gratification in their efforts to improve the instructional programs of their schools.

Frustration and defeat are much more common than success. For this reason principals seek tasks which will lead to an end product, a sense of closure in an otherwise open-ended routine.

In one school, the principal's image rested on the fact that she was able to get "anything she wants" for her school. She claimed that she could short-circuit the bureaucracy to accomplish even the most difficult assignment by calling upon an elaborate network of friends in the system. A bilingual teacher resigned from her school. Bilingual English/Spanish teachers are hard to find, but this principal saw the problem as a minor one. She knew that a call to the Bilingual Office of the Board of Education would be fruitless, so she put her informal network of friends into operation. With only a few telephone calls she was able to find at least three qualified bilingual teachers willing to work at her school. Because of her long experience of developing relationships and working with people in the system, she had acquired a good reputation for her school. The good reputation and her image as a "doer" made short-circuiting the system easier than it would be for other principals.

Short-circuiting from necessity Short-circuiting of the bureaucracy is often *expected,* as standard operating behavior, by both principals and superiors. Principals constantly receive instructional materials, office supplies, payroll checks, items of school equipment, and the never-ending flow of records and report forms from the district. The bureaucracy makes frequent errors in distributing all this. Principals usually sort everything out, find the materials needed by or intended for their school, and let fellow principals know when they have received something intended for them.

Ruth Donegan, the principal of an elementary school, was informed by her clerk that they were hundreds of report cards short in preparing for the first distribution of student reports "this coming Friday." The new cards had just arrived from the downtown printing office Tuesday morning, and a quick count had revealed the shortage. Donegan quickly began phoning fellow principals, asking for extra cards. She found twenty-five cards here, another fifty there, etc. After spending most of the morning to find the cards she needed, Donegan explained that this happened all the time, and that it would not help to ask for extra cards from headquarters—"It would take weeks." "Anyway, she explained, "everyone expects the principals to just handle these kinds of problems themselves."

Short-circuiting and administrative theory In all of the above examples, the mid-bureaucracy administrator wrestles with the practical realities of organizational life. The bureaucracy grinds out its directives, commands, policy initiatives and marching orders. . . . But when they arrive at the front lines where real people—students, teachers, parents, administrators—are all jockeying for position in a complicated environment, these pronouncements acquire a new meaning. In order to make them work as the hierarchy specifies, the principal must sometimes design spur-of-the-moment, ad hoc strategems of response.

It is clear that such short-circuiting can often facilitate the workings of the bureaucracy. It did the job more swiftly and expeditiously than the bureaucratic machinery would have. But it is also clear that counter-bureaucratic behavior, even that done for the best of motives, is only a marginal category of discretionary decision making. For one thing, in the hands of an inept principal, short-circuiting can create more problems than it solves. Moreover, precisely because it is ad hoc behavior, it is dangerous to generalize it to the larger sphere of management as a whole. Finally, short-circuiting, for all its benefits, does not sit well with superiors who are responsible for the working of the whole. Too many shortcuts may compromise the integrity of the larger enterprise. Short-circuiting like other discretionary gambits is an art form. The principal should practice it only with a keen eye out for *all* of its consequences in the school hurly-burly.

The Shifting Chessboard: Survival Tactics and the Scramble for Power

Many public school principals today are subjected to a steady drumbeat of official commands from central headquarters:

1. Improve student achievement
2. Desegregate faculties
3. Inaugurate bilingual education
4. Integrate student bodies in magnet schools
5. Comply with Public Law 94-142
6. Cut budgets in a financial crisis

In response to each new command, the principals of most systems have struggled to acquaint themselves with new regulations and procedures handed down through the hierarchy. They have tried to bring their schools into compliance with each new guideline, to acquaint their staffs with complicated changes in procedure, and integrate the new requirements into the ongoing instructional programs of the school. The broad scope, intensity and number of new programs have made managerial difficulties sometimes seem insurmountable.

In many schools there brews a deep anger and resentment toward the new programs. Teachers have been required to divert their energies away from regular programs to accommodate the new demands; at the same time, staff and clerical resources have been reduced. Also, the principals themselves have bridled at the seeming bureaucratic aimlessness of many of these directives, wondering, with each new onslaught of paperwork, just how many evening hours are going to be spent trying to stay on top of the task.

In this upheaval throughout education, many principals have simply been overwhelmed and rendered *hors de combat.* They have gradually lost an earlier enthusiasm for vigorous educational leadership, opting instead for a low-profile, paper-shuffling, keep-the-lid-on-and-the-boss-happy style of caretaker management. But other principals have reacted in the opposite way. These enterprising decision makers have been exhilarated by the challenge and have not only survived but have spotted special opportunities for administrative skill in organizational chaos. They have turned these opportunities to their own and their schools' advancement.

Managerial performance in any setting depends at least in part on rational predictions about the future. When bureaucratic disarray makes such predictions impossible, the rational manager is understandably thrown off stride. But our inquiries revealed a new form of entrepreneurialism: the ability to turn confusion to one's own advantage. Indeed, some principals find bureaucratic chaos the most exciting and productive state in which to practice their art; it is in that circumstance, when everybody else is in a state of semi-shock, that artful maneuvering through the hierarchical maze can yield the greatest gains.

In this segment, we explore the phenomenon of the shifting chessboard, that condition in which the organization's goals and expectations change focus and direction, sometimes almost overnight, and all of the troops and their sergeants must abruptly alter course and march off in a different direction. If instructional life resembles a game, then this condition is one in which the rules of the game change, but everyone is expected to go on playing. The aggressive and nimble-footed administrator exploits confusion and disorder to gain an edge on his peers and associates.

In the commentary and illustrations that follow, we focus on the experience in a large midwestern school district which seems to us prototypical of any school system in the country. Even if the details of these narratives are not exactly matched in other places, the general condition certainly can be identified as a common malaise of organized public education in the United States.

Mastery learning The issue of academic quality has stalked school systems for decades. In most places, the folk wisdom has always accepted the inevitability of a mixed system of some poor schools, many good schools, and a few excellent schools. Traditionally, students have been assigned to schools based on where they live; a family's selection of a neighborhood depends partly on the neighborhood's school. But why should schools vary so much in quality? Is there no way to bring the weakest schools and their student bodies level with the best, so that equal educational opportunity could be finally realized in all American communities?

In the 1980s, nationally-normed achievement tests revealed that the average public school student in the system under examination scored consistently well below the national norm. These statistics documented a conclusion, which the system's critics had reached independently, that a substantial number of public schools were inferior academically. Part of this was due to the perpetuation of outmoded practices such as the social promotion of failing students to higher grades in order to keep them with their age-mates. The situation became so bad that students who had been promoted through the grades according to this policy were graduated from high school without being able to read, even at an elementary school level. Because students were graded in comparison to the performance of their classmates, students in some schools were promoted with A and B grades, yet had learned far less than their counterparts in other schools with C and D grades.

To address this situation a system-wide instructional program was adopted for every elementary school classroom in the city. The elementary school was thoroughly restructured. Grades one through eight were abolished and replaced with age groupings. In this way, classmates could be age-mates regardless of academic achievement. Also, hundreds of individual reading skills were identified and classified at levels ranging from A to K. Criterion-referenced tests were developed for each level. It was then determined which levels corresponded to which groups in order that students be considered "on level" (the right number of skills for their age), "over age" (too few skills for their age), or "above level" (more skills than would be expected for their age).

Once this elaborate testing and classification system was developed, the problem of bringing students to their age level in reading was addressed. Teachers were instructed to test and diagnose each student's reading level, to develop a learning plan for each student outlining which skills were to be taken up next, and then to retest to learn whether the new skills had been learned. In this way, the learning program would be individualized and each student could show "continuous progress" in reading achievement.

Many found the new system to be intellectually stimulating and promising. Others criticized it. Regardless of their enthusiasm, however, every principal was soon confronted with the practical realities of testing, constructing programs, retesting, charting progress and documenting the reading levels of every student in every elementary classroom. Principals were soon asked to report to the deputy superintendent every ten weeks on their students' mastery levels. These reports included the percentage of students at each reading level, the percentage over age, on level and above age, and the number and percentage of students in each category at each level.

Since these reports were summaries of teachers' records, the principal hounded teachers to finish their reports every ten weeks. Understandably, some disenchantment with the plan developed. But not all teacher resistance was mere recalcitrance. Often the most competent teachers offered substantial critiques on the number and the timing of tests, and the validity of matching specific skills to their assigned levels. An additional ruling prohibited teachers from giving A or B grades in reading to students who were not "on level."

Later the system was expanded to mathematics instruction. Principals were issued goals for the number of students in their school who should move from "over age" to "on level," and from "on level" to "above level." Progress groups were now divided into smaller units, and the record keeping and student tracking became more intricate and tedious.

Looking at the program as a whole, it made a lot of theoretical sense. It was the brainchild of Professor Benjamin Bloom of the University of Chicago, and over the course of several years, Professor Bloom and his associates conducted workshops, gave courses, held seminars, and issued explanatory bulletins, tests and evaluation instruments in profusion. The system hierarchy exhorted the faculties throughout the district to learn the new system, to keep conscientious records, and to give their extra energies to making it work. Through this dedication, the hierarchy believed, the disgrace of below-national-norm achievement would be eradicated.

Understandably, the curricular confusion and pedagogical mayhem attending the installation of Mastery Learning were widespread. Many principals, although convinced of the necessity of the new program, despaired of ever understanding it themselves, let alone leading a resentful, recalcitrant faculty to understand and execute it on behalf of elementary school children. But other principals detected in the confusion some flickers of light. For one thing, the entire program was built on the proposition that the curriculum could effectively be taken out of the teacher's own hands and mapped out on a schedule designed by outsiders. The result: Less fighting with teachers over the poor performance of their students. If the students did not learn, it was the program's fault, not the teachers'. Principals also learned that focusing on specific mastery skills helped them explain to parents their child's progress better than the looser, more general curriculum of a particular grade level. In parent conferences, the principal could haul out the word mastery inventory for Level G, place it under the nose of Johnny's mother, and show her precisely where Johnny needed more help at home. Thus, the principal was able to turn the tables, if ever so slightly, in the direction of parental responsibility for better learning performance.

Finally, the more enterprising principals discovered that their own evaluation reports to the deputy superintendent could be more evidential and explicit. Instead of reporting vaguely on their school's progress over the preceding year, the principal could single out for special attention those mastery skills in which his students had made exemplary progress, moving up to or past national norms. This type of school-against-nation comparison was not possible with the old K-8 system. The more astute principals even figured out how to manipulate mastery learning skill groups so that teaching manpower could be concentrated on those just below national norms, leaving the poor students and the good students to fend for themselves. The maximum number of children could then be brought to national norms and be declared "on level," a statistic dear to the heart of every superintendent.

Faculty desegregation Concurrent with the introduction of the mastery learning program, the Board of Education of this system implemented a massive desegregation plan to integrate the faculties of all schools. The plan called for mass transfer of thousands of teachers and was followed up by complex regulations and guidelines for the subsequent transfer and reassignment of teachers to enhance desegregation. Every school lost some teachers who were transferred to other buildings. Many teachers transferred out filed formal grievence appeals; in each of these cases, the principals of both the losing and receiving schools found themselves entangled in the problem.

For those teachers transferred in, special orientation activities had to be designed. Often, such teachers needed help in adjusting to cultural differences in parents and students in their new school. Many had to travel long distances to their new assignment and were sometimes tardy or absent. Younger teachers were often transferred from a school where they were comfortable, enjoyed good peer relationships, and had found their niche. For them a new assignment represented starting over with a new group, where many old-timers had established peer norms and were anxious to protect their turf. To re-establish a cooperative spirit within the faculty and reinforce the norms of behavior that prevailed in the school, many principals took special steps to socialize new teachers. They also were forced to arrange reassignments for new teachers who could not, or would not, fit in.

Seen from a distance, this massive transfer project was another jolt of the chessboard, upsetting old patterns, destroying alliances, disturbing loyalties, and dismantling teaching teams in hundreds of schools. Since the transfer plan was essentially involuntary and moved thousands of highly skilled professionals across hundreds of square miles and across sometimes hostile racial boundaries, it is no wonder that the entire system was in an uproar for several months. When the dust finally settled, it was clear that some principals had taken the easy, but ultimately less productive, way out. Since they had no say in the transfers, they took what came, said goodbye to what departed, assigned everybody to their classrooms, and retreated to their private offices to answer the mail.

The more aggressive principals, however, used the confusion to upgrade their faculties. Position by position they manipulated the racial guidelines to obtain the best possible teachers. Some principals had already established a network of informants throughout the system and had a file of good prospects, both black and white, who would strengthen their faculties. As the year began, principals made life unpleasant for their weaker staff members, hoping to engender transfer grievances by the incompetents. These principals then accommodated the teacher by recommending a transfer to another school and going to bat for him or her to see that the transfer went through. With a position open, the principal fished around the system, card index at the ready, to find the best candidate of the right color to see if that person could be enticed to join the faculty. Since transferring from school to school was the paradigm, the personnel officer almost always approved the transfer.

Through such devices, adroit principals were able to turn the plan to their own advantage to build up the quality of their faculties. They exploited the artificially created mobility of teachers around the system, waited patiently for that moment when the right position would be open for the right person, and then set the "teacher snatching" plan into operation. Of such imaginative administrative strategems are loyal and competent faculties gradually assembled.

Special programs Bilingual programs have been legislated for many school systems through the 1970s and 1980s. In the present case, although the largest number of programs were for Spanish-speaking students, programs in other languages were also introduced. In one school, over forty languages were represented. In addition to bilingual teachers, teacher aides were assigned to these programs, and special funds were appropriated for instructional materials. To locate students for these curricula, a comprehensive testing program was developed to determine the English language proficiency of every student from a home in which a language other than English was spoken. The tests were conducted at the school and required mobilizing teachers to test and score the diagnostic instruments. Once the programs began operating, they were administered through a separate set of regulations. Hiring staff, planning curriculum, and managing progress of students was set off from the regular program so that a separate set of records was kept.

In addition to housing these programs, principals had to ease relations between the teachers in special programs and regular teachers. In one case, regular teachers demanded to know why the bilingual teachers did not take their share of supervisory duty. In another case, regular teachers felt the students were being held too long in the special program when they should be graduated into the regular program. This fight for students intensified as regular teachers were let go because of enrollment declines and bilingual teachers were added or dropped according to the number of bilingual students.

The same period saw a growth in special education programs and the passage of Public Law 94-142. In addition to housing special programs and adding non-regular teachers to the faculty, the principals were responsible for administering the programs using a complex set of regulations and procedures. Stringent documentation was required to test and evaluate students, place them in appropriate programs, involve parents, plan instructional patterns for each student, maintain achievement records, conduct yearly reviews of each student's placement and achievement, and comprehensively re-test each student every three years. In addition to maintaining the documents related to these tasks, principals were asked to coordinate the various professionals whose participation was required. These included the teacher, parents, psychologist, nurse, social worker, speech pathologist, and various coordinators.

The avalanche of paper work that accompanies a special program is a professional heartache for both teacher and principal. Everyone recognizes the need for the program, and there is a special excitement in exploring new ways to reach boys and girls in a learning environment. But principals and teachers feel that bureaucracy takes all the stimulation out of the undertaking by its incessant demand for reports, evaluations, and schedules of progress. Understandably, many principals bog down under the weight of more after-school deskwork, weekends spent over the kitchen table, and the continuing problems with their colleagues to shuffle the papers on deadline.

But other principals have found a way around and

through the paper storm to find new ways to funding the non-special segments of their school programs. Since most special programs are funded from sources outside of regular budget allotments, the clever principal can sometimes manipulate the staffing formulas to capture a larger work force than the special program itself actually can utilize. With the extra personnel, the principal can strengthen some other chronically understaffed sector of the school's program. Both bilingual education and special education are notoriously loose in their specifications on what counts as belonging specifically to them; accordingly, the alert principal is often able to piggy-back on these programs by making them available to the regular students, or pirating special program personnel for part-time work elsewhere. Once a teacher is functioning in a school, he or she is under the direction of the principal and that person's assignment can be redefined in a hundred different ways.

In the case of special education, the principal may benefit from an unexpected bonus in the form of the Individual Educational Program, known widely in the profession as the "I.E.P." This device, legislated by Public Law 94-142, is nothing more than a custom-tailored curriculum worked out for one person at a time. Originally designed for handicapped children to address each student's idiosyncratic needs, it now appears to be a pedogogical device ideally suited to the educational requirements of all children, or at least those youngsters for whom the generic curriculum does not seem to "take." Whenever non-learning rears its unfriendly head, the principal can recommend to the teacher that an I.E.P. might be a good thing to try.

Aside from mastery learning, faculty desegregation, and special programs, most crisis behavior involves money. See Case Five, page 293.

The shifting chessboard In the extant literature on school management, there is little discussion of the administrator's response to organizational disarray and chaos. Perhaps the phenomenon is of too recent origin, stemming primarily from the wider social unrest during and after the Vietnam War and the unraveling of the social fabric in the 1960s and 1970s. But perhaps the scholars' silence on this condition can also be attributed to a reluctance to admit its existence in what is ostensibly an enterprise governed by reason.

Those writers on the "loose coupling" feature of school organizations appear to have detected at least the surface symptoms of the problem, but they have not given it a name. Analyzed closely, the organization can be seen as "loose" not only structurally, but dynamically as well. The organization is in motion, and its fluidity, like that of the sea, must be constantly monitored for unexpected squalls, the big wave, a shift in prevailing winds, and half-submerged rocks.

We have remarked earlier that principals devote considerable time to maintaining the stability of their environments. The shifting chessboard idea suggests that stability itself requires change. The principal who is most adroit at keeping his mini-world together amid organizational crises is the manager most adept at innovative responses to changing conditions. Stability requires not a static managerial role, but rather a dynamic one that responds to changes in the larger enterprise.

Finally, the chessboard concept helps explain the difficulty in accomplishing any real, lasting innovation in education. Principals change and innovate constantly, but they do so mostly to return the ship to an even keel in response to some local disturbance. Hence, the familiar comment from principals, "I'm too busy surviving to think of the educational program." Or, as the Red Queen said to Alice, "Now, here, you see it takes all the running you can do, to keep in the same place. If you want to get somewhere else, you must run at least twice as fast as that."[18]

Using and Manipulating Information: "Managing the News"

As a group, school principals are generally well informed on the professional expertise of their work. But the link between the information and the use of it to make decisions is weak. Furthermore, there is evidence indicating substantial manipulation of information, especially that generated within the system, as principals make decisions.

According to Feldman and March,[19] information is valuable to an organization if it has impact on decisions, if it informs these processes and yields results. Since most modern organizations, including schools, accept the basic importance of information, some simple propositions have emerged over the years. For example, it is generally accepted that no decision should be made until relevant information is gathered and analyzed. In addition, information gathered for use in a decision is expected to be used in weighing options before the decision is made. Closely related is the principle that the need for information will be determined before it is requested and that a particular corpus of information will be analyzed and digested before more information is requested. Finally, most people accept the sensible idea that information not relevant to a decision will not be gathered.[20]

In spite of the unarguable nature of these propositions,

Feldman and March learned in their research that they do not seem to exert the same force in the activities of school organizations. Instead, they reported the following:

1. Much of the information gathered by individuals within an organization bears little relevance to decision making
2. Much of the information used to justify a decision is collected and interpreted *after* the decision is made
3. A good deal of the information is not considered in making the decisions for which it was obtained
4. Regardless of the amount of information available, more information is requested
5. Complaints that there is not enough information are voiced, while available information is ignored
6. The relevance of information to the decision being made is less conspicuous than is the insistence on procuring the information[21]

Our own studies reveal a similar pattern: School system administrators, including principals, will typically collect more information than they need or can expect to use. At the same time, administrators constantly express the need for more and complain about inadequacies in the information they already have.

Using information Gilda Hermann, the principal of an "academically advanced" model school, assumed her position with the understanding that she would have a free hand to implement some program innovations. She was especially interested in the social studies area and, using some ideas from the professional literature, she worked out a program. Since the new units required some limited training for the teachers, Hermann decided that she would personally conduct those sessions.

The first phase of the project went smoothly, and the changes were incorporated following the in-service training. In this transition period, most teachers were cooperative, although a few were not. In working through the difficulties presented by these reluctant participants, Hermann assumed the support of her superior, the deputy superintendent, who had appointed her to the position. He had implied that she had the authority to "clean house" of those teachers who would not cooperate in program changes.

Hermann's self-assurance turned out to be misguided. In her eagerness to take command of her school and engineer changes in the curriculum, she did not fully test her assumptions about the deputy superintendent. He was known for inconsistency and for playing politics. Hermann should have realized this through her own experience and through numerous incidents with other principals. In any case, she assumed that she had full control of her building and notified the uncooperative teachers that she would like them to transfer to another school. The most serious action she took was to evaluate them very low at the end of the year. But since the teachers had all been selected to work at this model school, their pride was hurt. They chose to fight rather than transfer.

Even though Hermann had the full support and understanding of the school parent council, she learned that she did not have the support of the deputy superintendent. She was not told directly, but a decision was made by the deputy to have the teachers in question evaluated officially by the school system's social studies coordinator rather than by Hermann. The rug was pulled out from under the principal after she had already notified the teachers of their low evaluations. The social studies supervisor rated all of them much higher than did Ms. Hermann, and the situation became intolerable. The entire curriculum innovation was abandoned at the end of the school year.

The political maneuvering in this episode made the principal's position untenable. For one thing, there appeared to be no precedent for a social studies coordinator being assigned the task of evaluating teachers, a prerogative historically delegated to the principal. Yet Hermann was powerless to block this out-of-channels evaluation since it was promulgated by her superior. There is no question that Hermann possessed good professional information about instructional strategies in the social studies, but it is also clear that to attempt an innovation of this magnitude required much more information than she had obtained.

Adapting the general phenomena observed by Feldman and March, Hermann's decision was ill advised for several reasons. First, she assumed a receptive environment. Although her proposal was sound educationally, other factors were involved. Also, Hermann fell into a trap by not recognizing the relevance of available information, i.e., the past behavior of the deputy. Its relevance seemed to her less important than the benefits of a nationally recognized social studies innovation. Finally, it was not until the program was adopted, the in-service carried out, and the low teacher evaluations written that Hermann took notice of the reputation of her superior. In other words, she interpreted the information after the decision was made.

Another example involves the principal of a large, crowded elementary school. The previous year, Principal Zanick had learned of a special reading program. After some study, he decided it sounded promising and encouraged Mrs. Horn, one of his more gifted teachers, to study the program materials. She implemented the ideas into her own teaching with encouraging results. About six weeks into the school year, Zanick learned of a child with a special reading problem. He recognized that the best way to help this pupil would be to place him in Horn's class. She agreed to his plan, even though there were already thirty-three children in her class, the maximum allowed by the union contract.

When the union rep heard of the impending transfer, he urged the teacher not to be a "rate breaker." The union had for several years been extremely sensitive about class size. Horn eventually withdrew her offer to take the child, because of union and peer pressure. The union rep allowed her to save face; she asserted that the original teacher was fully competent to deal with the child's special problem.

In this illustration, the principal misjudged the power of the union to pressure a union member. He apparently concluded, from the information available, that the educational soundness of the transfer would compensate for the minor, technical deviation from the letter of the union contract. But this trade-off proved unworkable primarily because Zanick had not secured a vital piece of information—the willingness of the union to acquiesce.

A final example illustrates the Feldman and March generalization that much of the information gathered by individuals within an organization has little relevance for decision making, and is sometimes even counterproductive because it points in the wrong direction. The school system's officers wished to conduct an accurate census of bilingual teachers, including those already on the rolls, others qualified but assigned to general positions, those serving as substitutes, and still others not presently employed but qualified and interested in employment. A general call went out to all principals, together with appropriate forms, for names, addresses, and phone numbers of these individuals. When the poll was completed, central headquarters produced a document reporting a severe shortage of bilingual teachers, and urging all principals to encourage interested persons to get in touch with the central bilingual office.

Of course, the principals did no such thing; they ignored the staff report for a very good reason. Because of the presumed scarcity of bilingual teachers, each principal had deliberately withheld the names of qualified persons he or she had cultivated as substitutes in this specialty. Each principal guessed that every other principal would do the same thing. So, the staff report was meaningless; it reported a severe shortage that did not exist.

This situation showcases survival tactics in the administrative suite. Principals charged with covering all classes and providing instruction to their children insured that the necessary resources would be available when needed. Protecting a "secret" list of teachers may be seen as a lack of candor, but also as a tactic of imaginative management.

Manipulating information Our studies revealed that there is a significant amount of deliberate, sometimes questionable, manipulation of information by principals to accomplish either personal or school goals. Sometimes such manipulation helps the local school, but its overall effect is to compromise system goals. Such is the case with the previous example of bilingual teachers.

But other, more site-specific illustrations also help us understand this concept. Sometimes principals manipulate information as a form of personnel management. In one instance, a principal took over a school that included a branch operation similar to that in the previous bilingual substitute illustration. But he also "inherited" the assistant principal in charge of the branch, who had developed over the years a personal following of parents and teachers, their loyalty vested in the branch building. Shortly into his new term, the principal learned that false gossip was being spread about him, mostly by individuals with close ties to the branch. The principal correctly surmised that the assistant originated much of this misinformation and was undercutting the principal's authority in branch activities.

Although the principal liked the assistant and got along amiably with him, it was clear that his own hegemony over the branch would be compromised as long as the assistant stayed in his post. The principal gradually isolated the assistant from school matters, excluded him from faculty meetings and parent get-togethers, and withheld information normally shared with an assistant. This alienation eventually made the teachers and parents of the branch more dependent on the principal, rather than the assistant, for information about the school.

The assistant's power eroded and his advice was sought less often by both teachers and parents. The principal eventually talked him into accepting a transfer to another school; he then brought in a new person loyal to him. The open flow of information was resumed and the principal was seen for the first time as the educational leader of the community.

At other times, manipulation overturns a superintendent's decisions. In one instance, a principal was assigned to a new elementary school. It was much like the one she had come from except that it was housed in two buildings, about four blocks apart. In making the appointment, the superintendent had made it clear that the two buildings constituted a single school and that the new principal would be expected to administer them as one. The principal knew that this insistence was not merely an exercise in semantics but that it had a practical effect—a limit on her school's support personnel. She knew, based on past administrative experience, that if one of the two buildings were declared a "branch" of the other, the principal would be entitled to an additional half-time clerk, a half-time physical education teacher, fractional budget lines in art and music, and, most important of all, an assistant principal to oversee the branch. It was imperative, she thought, to somehow maneuver the staff officers at central headquarters into redesignating one of the buildings as a branch.

How did she do it? She sleuthed in the minutes of the board of education meetings for the past several years and discovered an action of the board containing phraseology implying, although not specifying, that the presence of mobile units (trailers and other temporary buildings) on the school premises were to be considered "branch units" of the main building. Such units *were* in use at her new two-building school, although at the prospective "main" building. She flashed copies of the board minutes in front of her superiors, and by some lawyer-like tactics and shrewd dealing convinced them of the appropriateness of the "branch" designation. The principal received her additional staff, especially the much desired assistant principal.

In still other circumstances, information is managed to assist the superintendent's staff to make decisions they would not ordinarily make on their own. One principal often made a left-handed boast that his building was one of the oldest in the system. It was also dilapidated and in desperate need of replacement or rehabilitation. Recently, a rehab inventory had been taken and the school was indeed on the list—but in twenty-fourth place with an estimated waiting period of six years! After this discouraging discovery, the principal inquired about the criteria used for rehab priority throughout the district and learned that schools presenting a clear physical danger to boys and girls, not to mention adults, were eligible for higher ranking on the rehab list.

So the principal looked more closely at a tall brick chimney rising from an adjacent outbuilding that originally served as a heating plant for his school. Although the chimney had not been in operation for several years, it appeared to be in good condition and was in no danger of collapsing. Nevertheless, he gathered evidence from engineer friends and from sympathetic buildings and grounds people at headquarters that in very high winds the dried mortar in the chimney might give way, toppling the chimney on to the school. Did the superintendent and the school board want to take this risk? Certainly they would not want to be charged with willful negligence of the safety of little children.

The emotional appeal worked, and the rehab was started within a month. Not only was the chimney dismantled and the school refurbished, but the remodeling project captured the interest of the deputy superintendent for buildings. His notice led to some special touches, including plush seats for the auditorium. This principal's stock in the neighborhood went up markedly.

In a final illustration, we see that principals are sometimes victims rather than perpetrators of manipulated information. One principal reported receiving her new school year budget just before school opened in September. Leafing through it, she discovered a new line item for $26,000. Her superiors informed her this amount was to employ a special guidance counselor in career education, a new project funded over the summer from outside sources. She began a quick search, hired the counselor, and put him to work on the new program. Two days into the school year, the central office called to inform the principal that this new employee was being recalled for work at headquarters and that he should report there the following morning.

Although this quick transfer was a surprise, the principal began to look for a replacement, and within a week had identified a second counselor ready to take over the new job. She was asked to fill out papers needed by the payroll department. In processing these papers the principal discovered, to her astonishment, that central headquarters had not only recalled the first counselor, but also had commandeered the $26,000. She was left in the embarrassing situation of having on her staff an individual for whom there was no money.

Understandably, this slippage in the information system generated an uproar at headquarters; the principal vehemently demanded that the $26,000 be restored to her budget. In the end, an accommodation was reached, but the principal wondered what was going to happen to all those principals who had not yet bothered to read through *their* budgets to discover this Greek gift buried deep in the columns of numbers. And what was the strategy of the budget-makers downtown? Did they slip this item into individual school budgets hoping it would *not* be noticed, making it retrievable for central office use? Probably not, but the handling of this principal's line item made other principals suspicious.

Information and Administrative Theory

Transmitting and processing information is central to the administrative art. One of the manager's advantages over subordinates is having more information. But it is also true that the principal is a subordinate, and consequently has less information than his or her superiors.

This situation is what administration theory dictates. Some of a school system's information has little or nothing to do with the operation of School X. It is unnecessary to burden the principal of X with everything the top officers know. Nevertheless, the press for more information is a continuing phenomenon at all levels of any organization; there is a persistent hunger to know more than one actually needs to know in order to conduct one's own business. It is important, therefore, for managers at all levels to recognize the practical applications of the old maxim, *Knowledge is power*. In an organization it is almost literally true that decision making is more powerful (i.e., more efficient, more yielding of wanted results) if it is informed. This fact means that the control of processes is tied to the flow of information. As we have seen, if a manager wishes to weaken a subordinate, one method is to choke off the flow of information.

Information flow is a game, but the participants play it differently. Superiors withhold as much information as they can and dispense bits of information to the right people at the right time. Subordinates play the game their way, trying to acquire more information. When they cannot, they interpret the little information they do have in a manner that serves their own interests.

But, as we have seen, the information game sometimes takes on the characteristics of what contemporary politicians call "hard ball." People are motivated by self-preservation and self-advancement, and these motivations sometimes manifest themselves with a vengeance in organizational management. Most organizations expect their middle managers to be assertive and aggressive people who will look out for their own interests, as well as for those for whom they are responsible. Accordingly, a certain amount of "hard ball" is hoped for and even rewarded.

But there is a line, although hard to draw, beyond which aggressive behavior does injury to the larger organization, even though it may temporarily benefit a local school. The price of looking out for one's own bailiwick may sometimes be too high for the total organization to accept.

The task of any organization, therefore, is to search its procedures to reveal those points where devious, manipulative behavior seems most endemic, those junctures in managerial decision making where middle managers and principals most often subvert the machinery. Once those spots have been identified, the statesmanlike superintendent will redesign the procedures to make devious and manipulative behavior unnecessary.

THINGS TO DO AND THINK ABOUT

1. Examine the personnel directory for the central offices of a large school district near you. Locate the individual that you would contact if you were a principal with a question about each of the following issues:
   a. the testing and placement of special education students
   b. the permanent records of teachers
   c. copies of a curriculum guidebook
   d. achievement testing
   e. student transportation to special events
   f. athletic eligibility forms
2. Take another look at the examples of creative insubordination described in this chapter. What underlying attitudes toward the competencies and values of central administrators do they reflect?
3. The short-circuiting behavior described in this chapter represents a calculated risk on the part of the principal. Review the examples in this section and identify what is being risked for the sake of swift and expeditious action.
4. Identify a program that has been recently introduced in your school system by the central office. What are the policies that govern the administration of this program? What changes are required at the school level as a result of this innovation?
5. It is sometimes argued that the problem of manipulation of information is directly proportional to the size of the school system—the larger the system, the worse the problem. Do you think this is a defensible generalization? Why?

NOTES

1. See, Karl W. Weick, "Educational Organizations as Loosely-Coupled Systems," *Administrative Science Quarterly,* vol. 21, no. 1 (March 1976), pp. 1–19; also James G. March and Johan P. Olsen, *Ambiguity and Choice in Organizations* (Bergen, Norway: Universitetsforlaget, 1976); and Lee Sproull, Stephen Weiner, and D. Wolf, *Organizing an Anarchy: Belief, Bureaucracy and Politics in the National Institute of Education* (Chicago: The University of Chicago Press, 1978).
2. Jane Hannaway and Lee S. Sproull, "Who's Running the Show? Coordination and Control in Educational Organizations," *Administrator's Notebook,* vol. 27, no. 9 (1978–79), pp. 1–4.
3. Charles T. Kerchner, Douglas Mitchell, Wayne Erck, and Charles Pryor, *Labor Relations and the Muddling of School Governance.* A Preliminary Research Report, Labor Relations Research Project, Claremont Graduate School, February 1980.

4. David Rogers, *110 Livingston Street* (New York: Vintage Books, 1968), pp. 271–285.
5. Neal Gross and Robert E. Herriott, *Staff Leadership in Public Schools* (New York: John Wiley and Sons, Inc., 1965).
6. Bruce McPherson, Columbus Salley, and Melany E. Baehr, *A National Occupational Analysis of the School Principalship* (Chicago: Industrial Relations Center, The University of Chicago, 1975).
7. See Seymour B. Sarason, *The Culture of the School and the Problem of Change* (Boston: Allyn and Bacon, Inc., 1971); also McPherson, Salley, and Baehr, op. cit.
8. Henry Barsky, "The Political Style of an Urban Principal: A Case Study," Unpublished Ph.D. Dissertation, University of Pennsylvania, 1975, pp. 120–143.
9. Bruce McPherson and Robert L. Crowson, "Sources of Constraint and Opportunities for Discretion in the Principalship," in Jack Lane and Herbert J. Walberg, eds., *Educational Administration and School Effectiveness* (Lexington, Mass.: Lexington Books, 1983).
10. John W. Meyer, W. Richard Scott, Sally Cole, and Jo-Ann K. Intili, "Instructional Dissensus and Institutional Consensus in Schools," In Marshall W. Meyer and Associates (eds.), *Environments and Organizations* (San Francisco: Jossey-Bass Publishers, 1978), pp. 233–263.
11. Kent Peterson, "The Principal as Resource Allocator," Paper presented at the annual meeting of the American Educational Research Association, Boston, April 1980, p. 12.
12. Robert L. Lineberry, *Equality and Urban Policy: The Distribution of Municipal Public Services* (Beverly Hills, Calif.: Sage Publications, 1977), p. 160.
13. Francis Schrag, "The Principal as a Moral Actor," in Donald A. Erickson and Theodore L. Reller, eds., *The Principal in Metropolitan Schools* (Berkeley, Calif.: McCutchan Publishing Corporation, 1979), pp. 208–232.
14. Richard A. McCullogh, "The Occupational Ethos of Senior High School Principals," Paper presented at the annual meeting of the American Educational Research Association, Los Angeles, 1981.
15. The naval metaphor is probably much more common among male principals than females; it should be recognized for its sex bias as a generalizable statement about the use of language in school administration.
16. One principal, reviewing with his assistant the records of students recommended for being dropped from school, offered the aside, "This is what I call my 'Access to Exit' program."
17. The Mayor called it "a puff piece."
18. Lewis Carroll, *Through the Looking Glass* in *The Annotated Alice,* (New York: Bramhall House, 1960) p. 210.

19. Martha S. Feldman and James G. March, "Information in Organizations as Signal and Symbol," *Administrative Science Quarterly,* Vol. 26, June, 1981, pp. 171–186.
20. Ibid. p. 172.
21. Ibid. p. 174.

7

Principaling and its Effects on the Principal

So far we have seen how the principal's job affects the staff, the parents and the community, and the higher administration. In this chapter, we turn our attention to the principals themselves. How does the job affect them personally? How is the principals' behavior shaped by such elements as career planning, advancement in the profession, maintenance of self-respect, need for personal satisfaction and emotional fulfillment?

WHAT WE KNOW FROM THE LITERATURE

These questions almost never surface in the literature on school administration. Most research fails to consider the principal's own priorities, motivations, and ambitions. Nevertheless, we can gain indirect access to this information by looking closely at what the scholars have said about *job expectations* and at *work conditions,* a central focus in more recent studies.

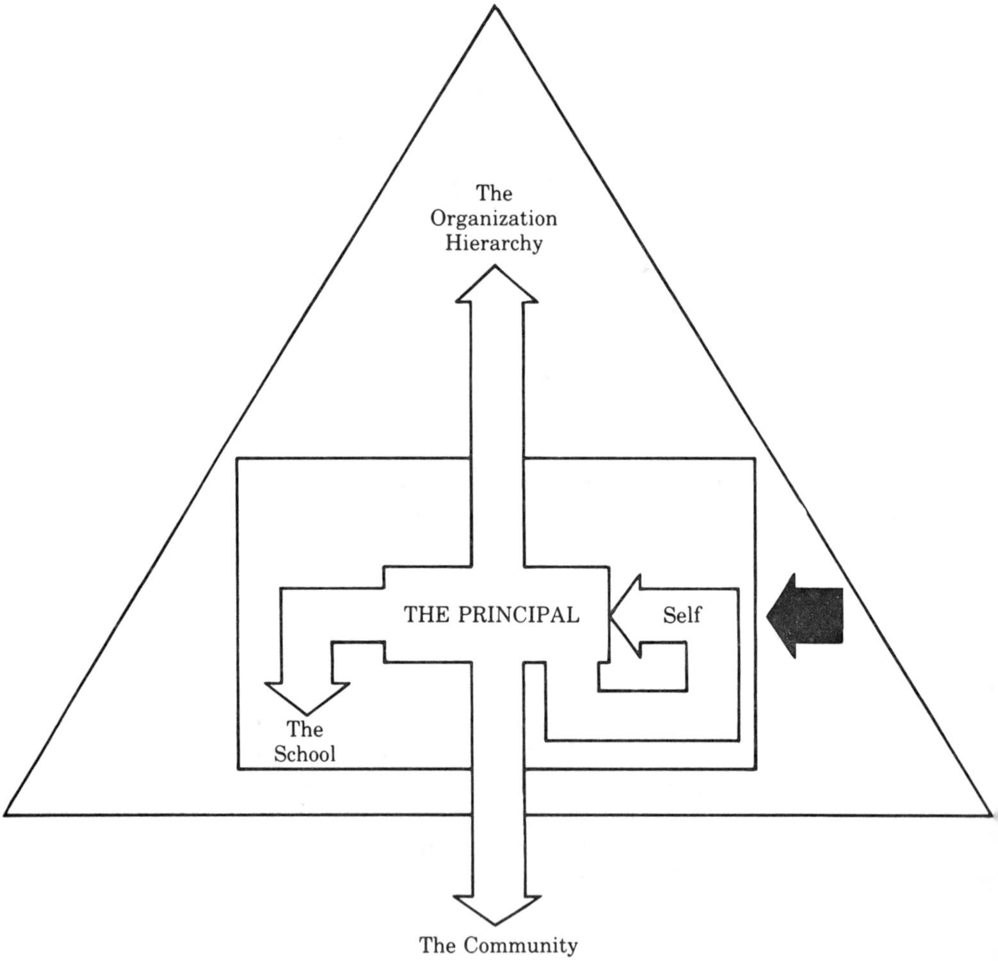

Figure 7.1 Principaling and its Four Sectors of Effect

Job Expectations

There are widely accepted norms on the proper role of the school principal. A top priority of most school systems, and one that takes a major part of the administrator's time, is providing instructional leadership. As previously noted, the improvement of learning is regarded almost universally as the primary task of the principal.[1] Additional highly visible responsibilities include program development, facility/resource planning, community relations, student services, and school site management.[2,3] These tasks require certain personal traits: long-range thinking abilities, interpersonal skills, a relaxed manner with strangers, and an approachability in public contacts. At least on paper, these are requirements of the job, and potential principals must either already possess them or learn them rapidly on the job.

Another widely accepted viewpoint is that the principal's role, in practice, is "all too often defined by people outside the principal's office."[4] Although this may be true of all occupations, principaling does seem to call for prompt and well-modulated responses to the wishes of other people. Moreover, the control that building administrators have over their own workdays has diminished considerably as a result of state and federal regulations, the increasing control from central headquarters, the growing litigiousness of students and their parents, and the intensified political environment now surrounding educational work.[5,6] The principal is in the middle, answerable to multiple constituencies—students, teachers, parents, and superiors. Each constituency has a well-developed and forcefully asserted view of how the school should be run. Everyone claims to be an expert on education and in a position to advise, or even direct, the principal. Principaling requires from its votaries a forbearing self-assurance in the face of this advice.

It is also an increasingly shared view that the role expectations of the principalship exceed by far the practical resources of time and capacity of most individuals. The principal must oversee the learning process effectively, be fully engaged in school-community relations, manage the flood of paperwork, guide staff development, meet student needs, oversee the financial and physical resources of the school, plan and innovate, manage the crises and disruptions of each day, *and* be everybody's friend. This pace surpasses the limits of good health.[7] Accordingly, some of the most successful principals are self-admitted workaholics. They love the job and are willing to put in twelve-hour days to get it done. Even then, much remains undone; thoughts about unfinished business must not invade the committed administrator's dreams.

Work Conditions

Role expectations denote the tasks to be done. But in what setting are these tasks to be performed? What are the environmental variables that help or hinder the administrator in doing the job? Contemporary scholars in school administration usually point to three conditions that make the work of the building administrator more difficult.

Tightening the law Most studies in administration sooner or later note the restrictive legal parameters governing the operation of schools. Research by Richard King shows that within the past decade, judicial decisions and restrictive legislative mandates have significantly expanded the student's constitutional rights, extended the entitlement of special treatment for handicaps or learning disabilities, and lengthened the list of requirements for equalizing male and female physical education and athletic programs. In addition, government agencies have placed formidable restrictions on teacher evaluation, the discipline of employees, and the dismissal of teachers. Weeding out incompetents is now virtually a full-time job in itself.[8]

The proliferation of separately funded programs A common complaint of today's principals is the explosion of government-financed special aid programs for elementary and secondary education. Until the mid-1960s, non-local sources of monetary support other than general state aid were typically focused upon vocational education, with some attention to curriculum development in science and mathematics. However, federal and state initiatives increased dramatically in the late-1960s with the development of grants-in-aid programs to assist such efforts as school desegregation, compensatory education, special education, early childhood education, gifted children, bilingualism, reading improvement, teacher development, and health education. At the end of the 1970s, Hill, Wuchitech, and Williams[9] surveyed the effects of federal education programs on school principals and concluded that these programs burdened principals with an overwhelming accumulation of paperwork, a confusing array of programmatic rules, and an unwelcome increase in organizational complexity.

The dispersal of authority The conditions of principaling have also been complicated by the scattering of authority over program control. New power relationships have been introduced into educational management: the growth of community involvement, government intrusion into daily operations, and the spread of collective bargaining among teaching faculties, resulting in contracts written by union and school board lawyers. Kerchner, et al. studied the impact of collective bargaining on principals and discovered that the union movement has, among other things, alienated the principal from the faculty. Ostensibly a member of "management," the principal tends now to be more cut off from his or her educational coworkers. The researchers contend that "many principals are becoming more emotionally isolated in their jobs, feeling that they are less able to bring off an effective personal relationship with teachers and also less able to feel they are really a part of the administration 'team'."[10]

We see from previous studies that the principal faces an ever-lengthening catalog of job expectations to be performed in a confining and ambiguous environment. In this context, two dimensions warrant specific attention: the career ladder, and the constant temptation to shape one's job to suit one's own needs.

Principaling as a Career

Although it is widely accepted that principals should have experience as classroom teachers, there is no universally established pattern of career development. Individual school districts differ on what kinds of training or previous professional focus are the best preparation for administrative work. Some districts are reluctant to appoint persons to high school administration who have not had extensive secondary teaching experience, even though they may have demonstrated advanced administrative skills at the elementary level. Some districts have a carefully structured, step-by-step pattern of appointment that proceeds from classroom teaching to an assistant principalship, to elementary, and finally secondary principalship. The course of progress is typically from small schools to large. Some districts select their administrators from those who have come up through the ranks within that district, and some have standardized examinations and waiting lists of qualified examinees awaiting administrative appointment. In other districts following a more ad hoc, case-by-case approach, persons are appointed to principalships directly out of the classroom, outsiders are selected in preference to insiders, prior experience at the elementary or secondary level is not a major factor in placement, and appointments are made according to whoever "catches the superintendent's eye," rather than through a formalized evaluation procedure.

With all of this variation, it is noteworthy that the career-ladder phenomenon associated with the school principalship has received relatively little research attention. However, a few recent surveys have shed some light on the characteristics of incumbent principals nationwide. In 1978, Pharis and Zakariya compared their research findings of elementary principals with the findings of similar studies conducted in earlier decades. The 1978 results showed, for example, that 59 percent of all elementary principals were under thirty-five years of age at the time of their first appointment as a principal; this percentage had increased only slightly from the 1968 figure of 57 percent.[11] The Pharis and Zakariya study also showed that three-fourths of those principals surveyed had not headed schools outside their present districts. More than half had accumulated two to nine years of elementary teaching experience before becoming principals. Five years was the median length of time spent in their present assignments.[12]

In 1958, 38 percent of elementary principals were women. By 1968, the percent had dropped to 22 percent, and by 1978, according to Pharis and Zakariya, the percentage of women in elementary principaling had dropped still further to 18 percent.[13] A similar survey among a nationwide sample of public secondary school principals in 1977 found that:

- ☐ less than 2 percent were women.
- ☐ 20 percent had been principals of their present schools for ten years or more
- ☐ the respondents averaged eight years of prior secondary teaching experience.
- ☐ about half were over forty-four years of age.[14]

A more probing analysis of career structures in public school administration has been undertaken by Karen Gaertner. Gaertner studied position changes and patterns of mobility among school administrators in a single midwestern state from 1968 to 1973. She found first that school administrators tend not to change jobs; they are, as a group, a "fairly position-stable group of people, changing positions, on the average, every fifteen years or so."[15] More important, she discovered three different common career mobility patterns. A first pattern leads through specialist careers in instruction and central office administration upwards toward the school district superintendency. A second pattern proceeds from assistant secondary principal to high school principal and then upwards to the central office and the superintendency. A third pattern leads from assistant elementary principal to the elementary principalship—and then stops. Gaertner writes, "The Elementary Principal position is a terminal position in this short career path. There are no significant connections leading out of this position to any other position in the system." Furthermore, such incumbents are "disproportionately likely to be women."[16]

At a third level of analysis, using ethnography, Harry F. Wolcott looked closely at the process of socialization surrounding the career of a school principal. Wolcott identified two important elements in this process as "sponsorship" and "GASing." Younger persons are sponsored by old hands who first recruit, then guide them through administrative careers. An influential older administrator picks a younger person with potential, helps him or her into administration, and guides the career at each step up the ladder. Furthermore, the process of "getting the attention of superiors (GASing)" adds to the young person's candidacy, through willingness to take on wider school district responsibilities, accept the authority of the organizational hierarchy, and become known outside his or her own school. But GASing is a difficult and sensitive undertaking; a person who works too hard at it or moves too fast is likely to hurt rather than help his or her candidacy.[17]

The importance of sponsorship as an element in the career development of principals is confirmed by our own data. More than just career assistance, successful sponsorship also includes an important modeling relationship. Novices learn skills from and copy the styles of their mentors; people who do not copy well are not sponsored.

Shaping the Job to Suit

As discussed in earlier chapters, there are many (often conflicting) expectations regarding what principals should do. The list includes instructional improvement, staff development, pupil control, parental involvement, curriculum innovation, crisis prevention, fund raising, and school plant maintenance.

Despite (or because of) this plethora of job expectations, many scholars claim that a basic problem of the school principalship is the lack of an adequate role definition.[18] In spite of the abundance of administrative certification standards, state school codes, local board of education policy statements, central office directives, and unwritten traditions, there are few examples of a clear delineation of the role. This vague statement of the "Duties of Principals" used by one school district is typical:

> Principals of schools are the responsible administrative heads of their respective schools and are charged with the organization, supervision and administration, and discipline thereof. They shall establish and enforce such regulations, not contrary to the rules of the Board of Education and of the General Superintendent of Schools, as in their judgment may be necessary for the successful conduct of their schools.

Harry Wolcott found principals to be preoccupied with "a search for role." The search is, at least in part, a response to the dilemma of the job as one burdened with a relatively stable set of expectations amid a continual evolution of such new and unprecedented elements as teacher militancy and judicial interpretation of students' constitutional rights. A second aspect in the search for role, noted Wolcott, is a self-consciousness about professional purposes amid the real-life indeterminacies of the job. Principals are bombarded with notions of what they are and ought to be, but are given few guidelines about how.[19]

Wolcott's observations are supported and extended in the research conducted by Arthur Blumberg and William Greenfield, who note these three problems: the need to operate under conditions of ambiguity, the organizational isolation of the principal, and a sense of powerlessness "relative to the ability to exert influence on the larger system."[20]

Blumberg and Greenfield, as well as Wolcott, document the principal's consequent tendency to retreat into a process of "surviving"[21] and/or "maintaining" (keeping things running smoothly).[22] They suggest that the better principals learn to "be in charge of the job and not let the job be in charge of them."[23] As this chapter's section on shaping the job shows, principals shape their work lives to suit their own interests and inclinations. Although the role definition is murky, the relations with hierarchical superiors loose and ambiguous, and the degree of real managerial control over the school-site problematic, the opportunity nevertheless exists to program one's own job satisfaction, and perhaps even one's success in the job, if there is a willingness to take charge.

WHAT WE SEE

Becoming a Principal

A common route to the principalship is service as an assistant principal. On occasion, other quasi-administrative jobs serve as training grounds: guidance counselor, special program director, or a temporary staff assignment at headquarters. As noted earlier, some districts administer a formal examination to screen candidates for principalship slots. Others decide on the basis of position-specific recommendations at the time of the vacancy.

As has been reported in the literature, the phenomenon of sponsorship continues to play a critical role in an individual's gradual rise in the system to positions of increasing responsibility. Of course, the encouragement of a particular candidacy involves a close match between the readiness of the candidate and the political strength of the sponsor. If these vectors coincide, appointment to the principalship is a likely outcome.

In our examination of various paths to the principalship, we noted something unique in each person's career story. So instead of plotting common elements of job advancement, we instead portray in this section two individual cases of professional movement up the career ladder.

Prior experience and the orientation of perspective

Although most principals have demonstrated administrative ability somewhere in their histories, one principal under observation brought to her job an uncommonly wide range of prior assignments. Secondary principal Marilyn Hartnett had previous experience in the central office working on curriculum development, had been both a high school counselor and an elementary school principal, and an English teacher. She also held master's degrees in counseling and in supervision. A highly verbal and self-reflective person, she often shared information about how she learned the skills she capably exhibited on the job.

During the observation, it became clear that Hartnett's experience as a high school counselor helped her conceptualize differences between an administrator's and a teacher's perspective. Her duties as a counselor forced her to become knowledgeable about all the school's courses and programs. This required her to abandon the narrow perspective of her own classroom and that of the English Department. She also began to learn the concerns of colleagues in different departments. One teacher impressed upon her the importance of vocational and home economics courses for some students. However, she discovered that teachers of these courses felt their areas were "dumping grounds" for unmanageable students. As a classroom teacher, she had had no idea that this was a problem for her colleagues. Indeed, Hartnett recognized that she may have inadvertently contributed to this feeling when she was a teacher.

Similarly, her experience in central administrative offices oriented her toward the total school system. She gained insight into how some decisions are made at lower levels within the central administration. During her years at the staff level, she visited schools throughout the system, presenting new instructional methods to teachers; from these visits she had acquired a comprehensive picture of many schools, their ambiance and organization. She had developed a mental image of system-wide administration, a working knowledge of central headquarters and the power brokers and lever pullers who operated there. When she returned to a line position as principal, she exploited this special knowledge and discovered that, through the personal contacts she had made, she was made privy to bits of vital information not available to other principals. She became, in effect, a student of central administration politics. She noted shifts in structure and personnel and speculated on their implications for system-wide policy on distribution of resources, and what they meant about the rising or declining influence of key administrators. Understandably, she tried to understand what these changes might mean for her personally in furthering her own career opportunities.

More than other building administrators, Hartnett considered herself a member of the school system's administrative team. In an interview, she described her audience as the board of education, not the local parents and school community. When asked what her main role was as principal, she replied directly, "I am here to implement board policy." She felt that the general community regarded her as "the position" of principal, not as an individual person. Then she smiled and mused aloud, "The board of education likes me." When asked what she did to win their affection, she listed three skills: First, she was good at obtaining outside funding for special programs in her school. Second, she always knew "where my staffing is," referring to the seniority status, dates of employment, and likelihood of change of status for each person under her jurisdiction. Third, she said, "I always stay within the union contract."

It would not be correct to conclude, however, that she would never rock the boat to keep her relationships with superiors tranquil. At one time, Hartnett was locked in a bitter duel with the deputy superintendent because he called frequent meetings; her attendance required too much time away from school. To register her displeasure, she customarily sent one of her assistant principals to these meetings in her place. Moreover, she objected to the clubby relationship of the deputy superintendent and other secondary principals. As a black female, she did not fit into their white, male social group.

Changes in the school system, she claimed, were slowly changing the nature of the principalship. Programs were being introduced to desegregate schools and to manage shrinking enrollments in an atmosphere of financial uncertainty. Through these programs, the system was gradually being reorganized around ad hoc, politically motivated solutions; simultaneously, students and faculty were being reassigned in the name of racial mix rather than educational criteria.

In the upheaval, some schools were closing altogether and many faculty positions were being eliminated. Historically, such moves would have aroused fierce protest from students, parents and community groups. But there were few protests, and those that were organized seemed to have little impact. "The community is losing power," Hartnett explained. "The steam is running out of their confrontational solidarity, and they just can't get the troops out like before."

As a professional, Hartnett was particularly sensitive to the fact that system-wide assignments of pupils and teachers were bound to have a negative impact on the local school. For one thing, in an era of high mobility, the principal could not remain as close to the staff, students, and community as before. The principalship itself was changing, transforming the principal into the mouthpiece of headquarters administrators. In the middle of these events, principals themselves were summarily moved from school to school to satisfy racial integration guidelines promulgated by the federal government. Such reassignments had the further effect of disrupting the continuity of a school's administrative rhythm. A principal who faces frequent reassignment is not likely to invest heavily in any assignment, looking on each post as a stopover before being moved on. In this period, many schools discovered that their greatest continuity and stability was to be found in the assistant principal ranks, where one person might be the continuing second-echelon administrator under several different principals.

She observed that the prospect of frequent transfer was emotionally wearing on the principal. It takes considerable energy to learn the personalities and attachments of everyone involved in a school's life. It is also difficult to leave behind programs that one has initiated and developed. She noted the paradox that her very desire to succeed was itself counterproductive. She wanted to succeed at each school to see it improve and respond productively to board of education policy. Yet this very success increased the likelihood that she would be reassigned to another school that desperately needed her take-charge skills.

If Hartnett's picture of the system is correct, the process of reassignment has merged into an amorphous, informal system that judges whether principals are on the way up, on the way down, or stuck on the career ladder. One's performance today is a key factor in determining one's next assignment tomorrow. Consequently, an ambitious principal's loyalties are pulled away from one specific school and community and directed instead toward system-wide loyalty.

Acquiring this view of a changing principalship had changed her own style of principaling. Hartnett described herself as less people-oriented than earlier in her career; she knew less about their personal lives. She saw herself as more formal, more distant, and more apt to retreat behind the position of principal and orient herself toward the system hierarchy rather than toward her school community.

Administrative modeling: skills and attitudes The previous case is an example of "coming up through the ranks," perhaps the most common path to the principalship. As the individual moves upward through the various echelons of school management, the scope of authority widens and, in this case at least, the identification with the total system becomes more pronounced.

More direct access to the principal's office may be provided through personal observation and a specialized form of master-student tutelage. One learns the practical aspects of school administration by watching other principals on the job. Capitalizing on this concept, the board of education launched an experimental program based on administrative modeling. Twenty-five persons were appointed to a position dubbed "associate principal." It ranked above assistant principal, commanded a higher salary, and was expected to be a short-term, interim assignment prior to formal appointment to a principalship vacancy. In the program, an associate was scheduled to work alongside a respected, veteran principal for several months and, through a form of professional apprenticeship, pick up needed administrative skills. The success of this preparation depends heavily on the teaching skills of the veteran principal and on the learning aptitude of the trainee. In the case described below, we examine the teacher-student relationship between professionals.

At one high school, an associate was appointed who the principal came to doubt would ever succeed as principal on his own. There seemed to be serious gaps in the associate's orientation to the work, and the apprenticeship program provided a vehicle for exhibiting the associate's administrative traits on the job. The associate, Harry Civik, was well liked by the faculty and staff, but the principal, although acknowledging his popularity, complained that the associate could not seem to carry out his assignments. The principal reported that he had to pull the associate off assignments repeatedly because they stalled.

The reason why projects bogged down was difficult to pinpoint. Civik always gave plausible reasons that placed the blame on persons and equipment outside his control. When school photographs were scheduled to be taken, the principal asked the associate to take charge of this activity. On the first day, the principal visited the photo area and discovered that the photographer was working very slowly. Students lined up in the hallways and interfered with traffic while waiting to be photographed. He advised Civik to instruct the photographer to bring two cameras the following day to speed up the operation. The next day the principal again visited the photo area and encountered the same confusion and crowding. The associate reported that the photographer did bring a second camera, but that "it blew" after they had taken only one picture. Obviously annoyed, the principal instructed Civik to phone the photo company to try to "get this thing moving." By the day's end, a second camera still had not appeared.

On another occasion, the principal instructed Civik to ask a special education teacher to represent the school at an important conference. Later in the day as the principal reviewed his mail, he came across a note that the teacher had attached to the invitation. It read, "I guess I'd better not go. I don't want to go nuts, but I am already." The principal knew that all the special education teachers were, in fact, "going nuts" trying to fill out IBM cards that described each student's individualized instructional program. In the principal's opinion, Civik should have explained to the teacher that her time would be better spent at the meeting than doing the clerical tasks which could be turned over to an aide. Furthermore, the associate should not have accepted this teacher's note but should have returned to the teacher to persuade her to attend the meeting. Civik was acting as a neutral go-between relaying the teacher's response, rather than as the principal's deputy whose requests should carry the weight of the principal's.

Growing more exasperated, the principal reluctantly concluded that Civik needed everything spelled out. The next morning, an occasion developed in which this hypothesis could be tested. He informed Civik that a delicate, valuable science exhibit would be in the school for a few days and asked him to set up a visiting procedure for science classes. The associate's responsibility was to "keep control of the situation," which included setting up a schedule for classes to visit the display area. The principal warned him not to give the teachers carte blanche in planning student traffic in the area. He took him aside and gave him specific instructions on what he might encounter: "You look this display area over carefully, seeing how the traffic might be best controlled."; "It should be a select group of students who will benefit from seeing this kind of display."; "The teacher must accompany the kids to the display area. Be sure the teacher is present and in control of his or her group."; "If there's any monkey business, you should ship out that teacher and the kids immediately."

With these bits of explicit advice in hand, Civik monitored the science exhibit on a daily basis. In general, according to the principal, things went reasonably well, although the associate's penchant for chatting with students and staff distracted his attention from his policing function. The principal appeared satisfied that his step-by-step, take-him-by-the-hand method of tutelage was finally paying off.

On another occasion, the principal asked him to supervise a wrestling match scheduled for an evening session. Hundreds of spectators packed the school gym. The principal had to attend a meeting downtown and did not arrive until 7:15. The meet was progressing well, but some of the students in the stands were becoming enthusiastic and starting to crowd down onto the gym floor. Civik did not seem to notice, as he stood at one end of the gymnasium with his arms folded, chatting with some friends. He was totally oblivious to the potential for trouble, even ignoring students sitting near him who were playing radios disturbingly loud.

When the meet concluded many spectators walked onto the gym floor and over the mats on their way to the door. Civik did not notice this either, and finally the principal told him to "do something," to "take a stand somewhere," to "take control." Under his breath, the exasperated principal commented, "You know, I'm just worn out trying to give him directions."

At the mid-point of Civik's second year, the principal summed up his performance in the following way: "He always walks around and chats in the halls. If a parent comes in, he'll sit and talk with them for an hour. He disappears for whole days at a time. When things have got to get done, he is never on hand. I've no time to chase after him."

On one "records day" the administrative team of the school turned to the task of helping teachers enter students' grades properly. This is a cumbersome process in which each teacher must locate each student's grade book and enter a course grade by hand. Civik never came to the library, where the grade books were centralized. At day's end the principal saw the associate and asked where he had been. Civik responded that he had been looking at the textbook claim sheets. The principal was shocked that he had spent the entire day shuffling papers when the teachers needed help. "Didn't it occur to you to come and help us?" he asked. The associate just hung his head at this reprimand and said nothing. Later the principal remarked, "I feel like I'm scolding a ten-year-old."

Elsewhere in this book, we have commented on the teaching function of the principal, a role that is conspicuous by its absence in the daily interactions of the principal with associates. In the case above, the principal formally assumed this role at the request of his superiors and trained his charge, the associate. One's own way of doing things comes to represent the "curriculum" of such a program; the principal in this example viewed his way as *the* way to do the job. He saw himself as an activist, directive, *I-am-the-boss* kind of school manager. He interpreted his role as one in which his authority was to be deployed constantly and in person throughout the school building. He believed in shaping events along lines he believed necessary to good learning, orderly discipline, and what the Navy calls "a taut watch."

His student, on the other hand, had a different orientation, a laissez faire attitude through which he hoped to coax his colleagues and subordinates into self-motivated and self-governed behavior. He believed that a principal's authority flowed out naturally and did not need to be explicitly exercised through directive commands. He assumed that highly educated professionals were capable of monitoring their own behavior and did not need a martinet supervising their every move.

In this instance, it is instructive to ask whether the teacher or the student was closer to defining the principal's role. Perhaps each was on target, manifesting his own interpretation of how a principal should behave.

Commentary The first example presents a perspective that developed from a series of administrative assignments. The arena in which Hartnett worked had expanded from her own classroom and department, to an entire school, and finally to the whole system. This extended setting formed the context in which the principal made choices among alternatives, established priorities, distributed resources, and maintained relationships with faculty and staff.

In the second example, we see some intangible qualities that principals exhibit in their dealings with other people. Civik's style is that of the principal who is charmingly passive, letting things float along without intervention and interpersonal direction. Another style is more aggressive, using the prestige of the position, the powers of persuasion, and personal presence to make things happen a certain way. This requires a knowledge of organizational dynamics and an understanding of the nature of power in institutional life.

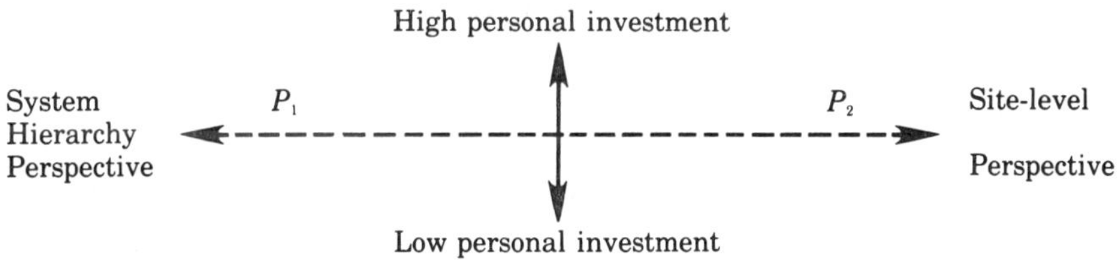

Figure 7.2 Organizational Perspective Continuum

The two cases also highlight different degrees of personal investment in the job. In one dimension, principals orient their work either to the total system and the organizational apparatus above them, or to the local school building and its inhabitants. In the other dimension, principals either plunge wholeheartedly into their work or become distant and detached in relating to their superiors, colleagues and students. This perspective is illustrated in Figure 7.2. Marilyn

Hartnett in the first example represents high personal investment in the system-wide perspective (P1). Considering herself part of the central administrative team, and throwing her energies fully into her hierarchical relationships, she belongs in the upper left-hand quadrant of the figure. The principal in the second example (P2) responds to the local situation but, like P1, is fully, personally committed to this role. He belongs in the upper right-hand quadrant. Harry Civik in the second example assumes a detached, uninvolved stance and appears to interpret principaling as a non-directive, "friendly observer" activity oriented exclusively to the local situation. This style belongs in the lower right-hand quadrant.

In summary, the examples reveal two paradigms of how principals are socialized into the role of principal. This patterning of behavior is effected by indirect pressures exerted by the bureaucracy itself and by a sponsor or mentor engaged in the overt act of modeling. In the former case, the socialization process is carried out through the inculcation of a belief system in which the primary commitment is to the larger system and its "party line": "my organization, right or wrong." In the latter case, the principal is taught the tenets of a micro-belief system: "here is how a good principal should act."

As we all know, the belief system sometimes does not "take," and the incipient principal marches to the beat of a different drummer. In these situations, new modes of principaling are created.

Shaping the Job to Suit: Maximizing Job Satisfaction by Design

Some of the episodes that make up a principal's day are interesting, personally satisfying and professionally fulfilling. Through these activities, principals feel they are actually leading an institution and making a difference in how things are done. At other times, however, they become bored, unstimulated, tense, or restless. No wonder, then, that principals select those tasks they find most pleasant to feature in their work days. In choosing which tasks to emphasize, they define what they want the job to be.

Redefining the supervisory role In our study, principals spent less than 10 percent of their time observing teachers. Most take very seriously their responsibility to evaluate teachers and improve instruction, and many are guilty and frustrated about not being able to do this. However, many feel that long hours in classrooms have little payoff and distract from many pressing demands. Rather than sit and observe, many principals spot-check teaching activity daily while patrolling the corridors. An example drawn from our observational log on high school Principal Dan Rutledge shows that teacher observation is often well integrated into the daily routine of overall school control and organizational maintenance.

7:55 A.M.	Rutledge finishes a cup of coffee and starts to leave the office for a walk through the hallways.
7:56	In the outer office, Rutledge glances through a sheet showing the attendance records of the school's teachers for the year.
7:58	Two teachers approach, one after the other, both asking brief questions about the scheduling of school events.
8:01	A male student approaches Rutledge, asks to speak with him, and mentions that he's having trouble getting along with one of his teachers. Rutledge admonishes the student to improve his attendance, buckle down, and make the most of the situation.
8:05	Rutledge enters the first floor hall, greets students, stops one student to ask for a pass, and stoops to pick up some paper scattered along a portion of the corridor.
8:08	Rutledge spots five students moving together down the hall and asks them where they're going. They explain they're on an errand to help set up the gymnasium for a special "festival" program later that day.
8:10	Rutledge enters the gym and looks over the preparations for the festival.
8:13	Rutledge moves again through the halls, looking into classrooms in session through the window in each door. He stops (8:17) in one class for 3 minutes to observe a teacher giving a geography lesson.
8:20	Rutledge leaves and walks to a departmental office to confer with a teacher chairing a committee preparing for a North Central Association visit.
8:26	Rutledge moves again into the gymnasium balcony and overlooks preparations for the festi-

val. A student approaches and informs him that a shop teacher is absent today.

8:27 Rutledge enters a music room, observes for two minutes, nods to the teacher and leaves.

8:29 Rutledge walks to the school office, gives some instructions to his secretary, and then begins some desk work in his inner office.

8:41 Rutledge returns to the hallway and is stopped by a teacher who tells him about a problem student.

8:45 A cafeteria worker stops Rutledge and asks a question. While talking, Rutledge sees a student wearing his hat and asks him to take it off.

8:47 A student approaches Rutledge to ask about his reward for winning a poster contest.

8:50 Rutledge re-enters his own office, makes a phone call to the school engineer, talks briefly with a student who pokes her head in his door, receives a teacher who informs him she'll soon be taking a maternity leave, and places a brief call to the district administrative office.

9:06 Rutledge walks again out to the hallway, up to the third floor, and enters a biology classroom to observe.

9:11 Rutledge returns downstairs to the school office and confers with an assistant principal regarding a teacher institute.

This log highlights a common activity of today's principals—a discretionary movement through the building designed to touch the appropriate bases, and establish only a brief presence at each base before moving on to the next encounter. The principal presumes that the duration of the encounter, usually less than five minutes, can be very brief; it is just long enough to establish the impression that the task is being performed. Thus, the principal, at least on a pro forma basis, can later document that he has indeed observed the teachers.

In most school systems today, a major constraint in fulfilling the supervisory role is the elaborate, legalistic and inflexible procedures controlling teacher dismissal. The cursory observation described above may be sufficient for the experienced teacher, but a more sophisticated form of observation is needed to dismiss the incompetent ones. A series of lengthy and sustained observations is required, and it must yield a "paper trail" of written critiques and evaluations of unsatisfactory performance. This regimen must usually be followed by a second opinion operation performed by a higher administrator, usually an assistant superintendent. Customarily, these visits and written reports must be carried out according to strict procedures and protocols. In many situations, principals recognize that getting rid of an incompetent teacher can become almost a full-time job, and that before proceeding on the dismissal track they must ask themselves, "In running this school, where is my time better spent—in building a case for dismissal against an obvious misfit, thus protecting the students from incompetence, *or* in devoting that amount of time to the other responsibilities of the position, including encouraging the other teachers to improve?" In most situations, the answer does not come easily. But principals in today's schools, beleaguered on all sides and pressured by other tasks, are increasingly unwilling to invest the time and energy necessary to get rid of the professionally unfit.

Anne Johnson, Principal of Mayfair School, reported that she had given a first notice to one of her teachers, but decided to drop the termination process for the year, giving the teacher more time to improve. Johnson explained that she "really would rather work on changing people who show potential but are not producing, rather than hanging people." George Alfero, another principal, complained that he already had one teacher who was formally terminated last year but had been in her classroom throughout this year, hanging on through a technicality. Alfero said this happened lots of times; people were dismissed but continued teaching. As they kept their jobs, other people realized that all the supervision, monitoring and carefully written ratings were meaningless. Alfero admitted, "I get very weary trying to keep the pressure up, especially when there don't seem to be any teeth in what I'm doing." The difficulty of standing firm on supervisory standards is illustrated in Case Four, page 290.

Principals sometimes swallow hard and decide to ignore the damage inflicted on students by a hopelessly unskilled faculty member. Although this is a criticism of educational administration, principals are not alone in directing their energies elsewhere. Throughout society, there is a noticeable ebbing of performance in almost every field. Managers seem unwilling to move against those who lower the effectiveness of our institutions, both public and private.

Getting things done Some principals redirect supervision energies into other areas that appear to have a better chance for some payoff. They concentrate on activities that have a positive end product of some sort, and give evidence of accomplishment.

Some principals devote considerable time to curriculum improvement, selecting textbook and instructional materials or rearranging the schedule and flow of learning activities, such as "walking reading" or "walking math" programs. Others take a special interest in pupil testing and evaluation, or spend their own time tutoring underachieving pupils. Still others turn their energies to program development that offers the hope of bringing new, outside resources to the school—perhaps a new program for the gifted, or a cooperative vocational education venture. Many principals take a special interest in the school bulletin boards, urging the display of student work throughout the school, and plastering the school with learning-related slogans.

Teachers' attention to bulletin boards and student exhibits often affects the principal's opinion of them. Nearly all principals wish their observation and evaluation of instruction to have an objective, measurable side; they make sure that teachers are on duty at the correct time and place, and that they prepare and file weekly lesson plans, keep accurate attendance records, and submit reports on time. Some principals consider this sufficient teacher evaluation.

Building staff cooperation Another alternative to direct supervision is building staff morale and cooperation. Despairing of ever being provided evaluation powers with "teeth," principals expand their within-the-school authority by taking an active interest in staff welfare and resource needs.

Although styles and degrees of openness vary, both elementary and secondary principals commonly balance their supervisory activity by attending to the individual and professional concerns of staff members. Nearly every principal waits at the front desk as teachers are signing in or out. Pleasantries are exchanged, messages are communicated, questions about schedules or procedures are asked and answered, concerns about friends or family are expressed, some bantering and joking occurs, and a few rumors are passed on. Nearly every hall tour includes exchanges with staff members, in which the principal either receives or answers a request for assistance.

In addition to helping with personal problems such as payroll or sick leave, principals also assist staff members professionally. A book order is all mixed up and the principal quickly arranges to borrow texts from a nearby school to insure each teacher enough books. An elementary school receives an unexpected increase in its teaching staff, and the principal decides to use the new positions to give some of his most heavily burdened teachers a non-teaching preparation period. The school suddenly runs out of ditto masters, and the principal runs out to an office supply store to purchase an emergency supply. A youngster in Miss Jones' class is large for his age, and Principal Smith spends part of one morning trying to locate an appropriate desk and chair for him.

The staff assistance provided by the principal, both personal and professional, can be just as effectively used as punishment as reward. The principal can conveniently decline to help those staff members who do not cooperate fully in meeting the principal's goals.

Focusing on yield Despite the reactive quality of the job, in which much of the day is spent responding to the initiatives of others, and despite the wide arena of managerial responsibility, principals nevertheless focus on personal and professional objectives. They find the time to emphasize things they are good at and that provide a measure of satisfaction in a role that seldom produces recognition for a job well done.

Arthur Robinson spent many hours over the course of two years striving to obtain a new hot lunch facility for Exeter School. The bureaucratic battle to get the facility authorized and installed was a source of much satisfaction to Robinson, who enjoyed recounting his effort. Similarly, Susan Collins was able, with much work and clever politicking, to get some vacant land adjacent to her Willow School designated natural prairie, to be preserved for environmental education. Other principals focused on community relations, new program development, principals' professional association involvement, or the school's instructional equipment. Principal Marmor pointed with great pride to the extensive computerized and programmed learning equipment he had secured over the years for Oak Lane School.

Expanding the role to meet responsibilities Principals also concentrate time on gaps in the organizational or procedural structure of the school system. Some of the most important elements of the institutional environment are, in some school districts, not under the direct control of the building principal: the janitorial staff, itinerant specialists such as social workers, psychologists, psychometrists, subject matter master teachers, and persons working in the schools who are paid by other city agencies (security officers, police personnel, and maintenance people). The principal must orchestrate the services of these outsiders to avoid disrupting the ongoing school program. Sometimes principals must serve in these capacities themselves to get the job done: wash a window, administer a test, fix a lock, clean off some graffiti in the washroom. One principal repaired the curtains in the auditorium on her own sewing machine rather than hassle with the appropriate repair personnel. Another spent many hours smoothing conflicts between school faculty and construction workers while the school was being remodeled in the middle of the school year.

Principals frequently must negotiate services with individuals or organizations that are needed in the school but are not readily available. One principal established a special relationship with one of the city's major teaching hospitals, and obtained psychological services for his students that, in his judgment, exceeded the quality and availability of regular school system resources. Another principal negotiated at length with the city park district to repair and improve some playground equipment serving the school but located on park district property. A third attempted through channels to bring an unattended, busy intersection to the attention of the police precinct. He eventually had to negotiate with local politicians to have a crossing guard stationed there.

Principals fill in gaps by taking on exceptional students, either problem or very able students, those who tend to fall through the cracks of the school's routine procedures. Both elementary and high school principals give a substantial portion of their day to student interactions. Many principals eat lunch in the student cafeteria and make themselves visible and available at passing periods. Although styles vary, a number of principals spend many hours in assisting students with individual questions. The problems are often school-related, such as class scheduling, teachers' grading policies, or credits needed for graduation. But they are just as likely to be personal matters of home environment, peer relations, psychological tension, or school-related stress. Returned runaways, drug or alcohol users, students with poor attendance habits, pupils with estranged parents—all become the personal business of the principal, particularly if they can be considered "nice kids" who simply need a bit of help. Exceptionally able students also receive the principal's personal attention through special awards and recognition ceremonies, an informal coffee hour with the principal, added educational opportunities, such as a weekly poetry reading group with the principal, or extra individual guidance from the principal about college plans. Thus, the principal seeks to make sure that both ends of the normal distribution curve, the very slow and the very gifted, do not slip away from the school.

Summary

Principals shape their jobs to suit their own occupational tastes, despite the norms and pressures common to all school situations. Principals, as do most teachers, enjoy seeing improvements in people—especially those improvements for which they can take some of the credit. They also take pride in program or physical changes in their schools; their pride is understandably increased when they can point out these changes to the superintendent. Even if principals cannot fully program their own success or insure the bottom-line yield of their administrative activity, they can at least program some of their own job satisfaction—which is perhaps the next best thing.

THINGS TO DO AND THINK ABOUT

1. Schedule interviews with several principals in a school system near you to learn whether they view the principalship from a System Hierarchy or Site-Level perspective. List ten questions you will ask to elicit their leanings on this point. At the conclusion of the interviews, consider the strengths and weaknesses of each perspective.
2. A recurrent theme in this book is that principals differ in the way they spend their time, energy, and resources. When you assume your first principalship, what three activities will command most of your attention? Why?
3. Select six principals who have been in the job for two years or longer. Ask each of them, "Has the principalship changed you as a person? If so, how?" Check their answers with their wives or husbands.
4. A strong ego has sometimes been mentioned as a prerequisite for handling administrative responsibility. What do you think of this generalization?
5. On page 196, we assert that the principals in this study spent less than 10 percent of their time observing teachers. On page 58, we offered some explanations for this. Is it possible for a principal to supervise and improve teaching performance through activities other than direct classroom observation? If so, what are some of these activities?

NOTES

1. William H. Roe and Thelbert L. Drake, *The Principalship,* 2nd Edition (New York: McMillan Publishing Co., Inc., 1980).
2. James M. Lipham and James A. Hoeh, Jr., *The Principalship: Foundations and Functions* (New York: Harper and Row, 1974).
3. Larry W. Hughes and Gerald C. Ubben, *The Elementary Principal's Handbook* (Boston: Allyn and Bacon, Inc., 1978).
4. William L. Pharis and Sally Banks Zakariya, *The Elementary School Principalship in 1978: A Research Study* (Arlington, Va.: National Association of Elementary School Principals, 1979).

5. Richard A. King, "The Principal and the Law," *Administrator's Notebook,* Vol. 28, No. 2 (1979–80), pp. 1–4.

6. P. Hill, J. Wuchitech, and R. Williams, "The Effects of Federal Education Programs on School Principals," A Rand Note Prepared for the U.S. Department of Health, Education, and Welfare (Santa Monica: The Rand Corporation, February, 1980).

7. K. S. Rogers, "Principals Discuss Their Roles: An Observational Study," Paper presented at the annual meeting of the American Educational Research Association (AERA), Boston, April, 1980.

8. Richard A. King, "The Principal and the Law," *Administrator's Notebook,* Vol. 28, No. 2 (1979–80), pp. 1–4.

9. See P. Hill, J. Wuchitech, and R. Williams, op. cit.; also Ursula C. Pinero, "Wanted: Strong Instructional Leader," *Principal,* Vol. 61, No. 4, (March, 1982), pp. 16–19.

10. C. T. Kerchner, D. Mitchell, W. Erck, and G. Pryor, "Labor Relations and the Muddling of School Governance," A Preliminary Research Report, Labor Relations Research Project, Claremont Graduate School, February, 1980, pp. 16–17. See also Susan Moore Johnson, "Collective Bargaining at the School Site: A Varied Picture," Paper prepared for a Conference on Creative Conditions for Effective Teaching, Center for Educational Policy and Management, University of Oregon, October 1981.

11. William L. Pharis and Sally Banks Zakariya, op. cit., p. 23.

12. Ibid. pp. 20–24.

13. Ibid. p. 5.

14. Susan Abramowitz and Ellen Tanenbaum, *High School '77: A Survey of Public Secondary School Principals* (Washington, D.C.: National Institute of Education, December 1978), pp. 93–100.

15. Karen N. Gaertner, "The Structure of Careers in Public School Administration," *Administrator's Notebook,* Vol. 27, No. 6 (1978–79), p. 2.

16. Ibid. p. 3. Gaertner's analysis is only indirectly applicable to this discussion. Upwardly mobile principals in the district from which these data were drawn frequently moved from elementary positions to secondary placements. The most important measure of a person's increased status was school size as measured by enrollment, regardless of grade level. Persons on the rise moved to larger and larger schools; principals losing favor moved to smaller ones.

17. Harry F. Wolcott, *The Man in the Principal's Office: An Ethnography* (New York: Holt, Rinehart and Winston, Inc., 1973), pp. 193–198. Wolcott cites Griffiths et al, attributing the use of the term "GAS-ing" to Griffiths' study of administrative appointments in the New York City school system. See Daniel E. Griffiths, John S. Benben, Samuel Goldman, Laurence Iannaccone, and Wayne J. McFarland, "Teacher Mobility in New York City: A Study of the Recruitment, Selection, Appointment

and Promotion of Teachers in the New York City Public Schools," A report, New York University School of Education, Center for School Services, 1963.

18. Ibid. p. 296; also A. Lorri Manasse, "Effective Principals: Effective at What?" *Principal,* Vol. 61, No. 4 (March, 1982), pp. 10–15; and Gordon J. Klopf, Ethel Scheldon, and Kevin Brennan, "The Essentials of Effectiveness: A Job Description for Principals," *Principal,* Vol. 61, No. 4 (March 1982), pp. 35–38.

19. Wolcott, op. cit., pp. 296–316.

20. Arthur Blumberg and William Greenfield, *The Effective Principal: Perspectives on School Leadership* (Boston: Allyn and Bacon, Inc., 1980), pp. 233–234.

21. Wolcott, op. cit., p. 306.

22. Blumberg and Greenfield, op. cit., p. 21.

23. Ibid. p. 248.

PART 3

Implications

8

Implications For Day-to-Day Practice

The picture of the principalship which we have painted is a busy canvas. One reason is that the principal is in constant interplay with four demanding constituencies: (a) students and teachers within the school building, (b) parents and layman in the community, (c) superiors in the organizational hierarchy at headquarters, and (d) his or her own ego structure, with its insistence on self-esteem, professional advancement and personal fulfillment. Another reason is that the principalship is a moving, dynamic occupation in almost a literal sense; the rhythm of the job, from arrival at the parking lot to the close of the business day, is typified by pace and movement, by frequent and abrupt shifts from one concern to another, and by the excitement pervading any institution dealing with young people. Finally, the principal's job is different from other managerial positions because it is essentially an oral occupation, a job of talking. The principal governs a school mostly by talking with other people, usually one at a time, throughout the day.

From this portrait, it is easy to get the impression that a principal always hovers on the edge of disorder. In some respects, this is true. The job is surrounded by uncertainty and by the need to respond instantly to others while simultaneously conforming to expectations of what the effective principal should be doing proactively. Teachers expect the principal to maintain disciplinary control and respect their autonomy as professionals. Parents expect good teaching and a caring relationship with their children. Superiors expect managerial efficiency and trouble-free control. Principals themselves want the feeling of a job well done and the satisfactions of having made a difference in the lives of young people.

But while we have a better picture of the principal at work, what does this mean for the practicing principal or the administrator about to take on these duties? What message does it send to the universities conducting principal training programs, and to the superintendents and boards of education who select individuals for this work and place them in particular schools? Are there some guidelines for practice, training, and selection that flow from these findings, and is there professional advice to illuminate the tasks ahead? We think there are, and devote Part 3 to this advice. In this chapter we examine the implications of the findings for working principals, and offer some operational suggestions on the daily management of schools and on the principal's position as middle manager in the organizational hierarchy.

IMPLICATIONS FOR SCHOOL-SITE MANAGEMENT

The conventional wisdom pictures the manager of any organization as a person centrally located, both physically and operationally, in the work flow. The manager has an office with clear indications of command such as a telephone switchboard, employee mailboxes, and a visitor receiving center. The manager is in and out of the office frequently and often supervises or even helps out with the organization's productive activity, particularly at times of peak customer load. But the manager's primary responsibility is to be on hand where (a) coordination of activity is most needed, (b) planning and record keeping are done, and (c) trouble is most likely to occur. In most organizations, the tasks of coordinating, record keeping, and trouble monitoring can be most effectively performed at a central point where customer requests are translated into work orders, where financial accounts are kept, and where clients or suppliers typically encounter the organization.

Similarly, in managing schools, there is a central location where the principal processes the flow of paper work, receives and distributes messages, handles parents and pupils, answers the telephone, schedules school activities, and orders supplies. In our investigations, principals spent about 50 percent of their time in their offices, including the immediate environs of an outer office; in these areas they perform the kinds of activities that managers in nearly all settings find necessary to a smooth operation.

But principals, unlike other managers, spend about 50 percent of their time outside the main office area, *away from* the executive suite and in face-to-face contact with their employees (teachers) and their clients (students). The management literature, for the most part, has not examined this phenomenon of administration on the run, and has dealt with neither its technology nor its implications for organizational governance. One suggestion often made is to stop running. Some scholars warn of the "activity trap" that surrounds the principalship, arguing that principals are too easily caught up in frenetic movement about the building, and consequently lose control over their own time as they scurry from one crisis to another.[1] We expect principals to keep on running, but they might benefit from some observations on how this running can do the most good.

Specifically, the findings raise three questions: What are the implications of the tendency of principals to perform half of their managerial tasks at the work stations of other persons? What are the implications of the predominantly oral, face-to-face character of principaling? And, what are the implications of the sizable percentage of their time that principals spend with the clients, their students?

Managing at Others' Work Stations

A busy principal covers a great deal of ground. In making these rounds, from office to corridor to classroom to gymnasium to boiler room to playground and back, the principal is managing the school. But it is management in a form unusual for most organizations because it is, in large part, administration at the work stations of other persons. This means that the principal carries the office around with him or her through at least 50 percent of the work day. A typical school is physically spread out, with many widely dispersed activities that are walled off from one another with closed doors, intervening hallways, and soundproofing. Most school staff members are much less mobile than the principal; someone must *always* stay with the kids. Thus, it is the principal who gets around, who visits teachers in *their* offices, who investigates areas of potential trouble, who smooths the flow of messages from one area of the building to another, who is on call and easily summoned by those needing assistance.

Three important implications for managers can be drawn from this behavior. First, this seemingly frenetic pace can be of vital symbolic value in school administration. We have earlier stressed the importance of "showing the flag" in the principal's movement about the building; this has been aptly referred to by organization theorist Karl Weick as "symbol management."[2] The principal's behavior provides a "glue" binding together the loose structure of the school. The glue provided is much more than the conventionally accepted bureaucratic rules and supervisory inspections of employee compliance. It is, more deeply, the communication of expections and visions that lead to a common understanding of organizational purposes. Weick writes

> The administrator who manages symbols does not just sit in his or her office mouthing clever slogans. Eloquence must be disseminated. And since channels are unpredictable, administrators must get out of the office and spend lots of time one on one—both to remind people of central office visions and to assist them in applying these visions to their own activities. The administrator teaches people to interpret what they are doing in a common language.[3]

A second and related significance of this behavior is that, in movements about the school from the work place of one person to that of another, the building principal is filling the role of managerial *broker*. While the conventional wisdom assumes that principals issue directives, provide organizational structure, and oversee school-site compliance with board of educational policies, the reality of the principalship tells us that administrative order is negotiated.[4] (See page 87 for an instance of brokering among CETA aides.)

Earlier we discussed principals' penchant for "peripatetic committee meetings." At the beginning of the day in a conversation with Miss Jones, an issue arises that the principal checks out with Mr. Green. Some time later, he shares the problem with Smith and Kirby. Kirby suggests a solution that the principal, many hours later, brings to another conversation with Jones, and the problem is on its way to a solution. In all of this, the principal functions less as the commanding general of a consolidated and disciplined army than as a messenger coordinating communications between several divisions. The building principal acquires authority over the school environment in large part by brokering relationships between people who are dependent upon, but not very closely coupled with, one another.

A third implication is that the portion of the working day spent at the work stations of other people leads to a feature of the job that is both trouble and opportunity—the extended responsibility that, for the most part, principals deliberately impose on themselves. As the principal makes the rounds in the school, he or she takes on a reactive mode of management. Indeed, we have earlier indicated the "search behavior" of the principal, suggesting that principals purposely place themselves in spots (on the playground at recess time, at the front desk as teachers sign in, in the halls as classes change) where something is likely to happen or where someone will come to them with a problem or a request.

This search behavior, with its reactive side effect, enlarges enormously the set of demands upon the principal. Whenever or wherever there is a problem, if the principal is nearby the responsibility becomes his or hers. Principals accept this as natural, and will without thinking often do tasks that could better be left to other people: supervising the loading of buses for a trip to the zoo, helping an aide find last year's fold-away Christmas tree in a storeroom, or repairing a duplicating machine.

While this "activity trap" apparently consumes much of the principal's time and emotional resources, the broad scope of the responsibility of the principalship presents an unparalleled managerial opportunity.[5] Administrators in other organizational contexts are much more deskbound. In schools, however, the principal experiences the environment first-hand. Many things convey important messages to a perceptive administrator: a sense of the mood of pupils as they enter the building; a quick glance through a classroom door at teaching in progress; a careful eye on a pair of perennial troublemakers at lunchtime; a measuring of changes in the noise level in the school corridors; a spur-of-the-moment drop-in at an after school dance. These episodes represent an information source that would not be available if the principal were not a constant presence in the organization. In a loosely coupled organizational environment, successful administration may be just as much a product of on-the-spot anticipatory reaction as of a principal's pro-active initiatives originating in the main office.

Managing Face-to-Face

Classroom teachers are accustomed to working with groups of people. In fact, students are often categorized by teachers in terms of their relationship to a group: keeping up with rest of the class, being placed with the fastest readers, working well with others, staying in line, performing up to grade-level, and being "mainstreamed." All are phrases in the lexicon of the teaching profession that imply a group orientation.

In contrast, principals manage all the groups in the school from a one-on-one perspective. Necessarily interacting with individuals, not groups, principals must develop skills that have not been necessary in classroom teaching. The most common medium of administration in elementary and secondary schools is oral communication carried on in close proximity to other individuals, usually one person at a time. The principal spends two-thirds or more of the day in verbal, face-to-face communication with other persons.

These exchanges seldom occur with advance notice. The typical principal maintains few scheduled appointments. Most interactions, even with parents, are drop-ins at the main office, chance conversations in the halls, or occasions when the principal decides to look someone up somewhere in the school. The subject matter is frequently just as unexpected. A parent may storm into the office with an accusation against a staff member, or a teacher may catch the principal on the run and request an immediate decision on rescheduling school activities for the day.

One central element in the reality of school-site administration is the importance of understanding what Erving Goffman has labeled "face-work."[6] Both the verbal and non-verbal (gestures, positionings, etc.) messages that people convey in conversation, and the many face-saving rites that are part of social interaction, are generally ignored in management texts that assume a tightly structured organization.

Perceptive principals realize very early in their administrative careers that not only students, but staff members and parents as well, must be given room to "save face" when they feel threatened. Perceptive principals also realize that a remark meant to be humorous may be taken seriously, that a neutral glance or expression may be viewed as disinterest and that a casual offhand statement may speed "like lightning" around a school building as rumored truth. Finally, perceptive principals are aware of the psychological importance of certain rituals or conventions in social interaction in their schools. For instance, teachers, like other people who serve clients, typically let off steam by sharing humorous incidents and "war stories" involving pupils and parents.[7] In making the rounds in the school, the principal becomes a vital outlet for his staff if he can sympathetically listen to grumbling, tales of woe, and put-downs of bothersome pupils and parents.

The importance of face cuts both ways. The principal presents an image to the faculty and students that communicates what he or she considers important to the organization. One female principal showed up at a social gathering wearing a stylish, expensive dress, the latest hair style and make-up, and driving an expensive sports car. In school, she usually dressed in an old-fashioned, schoolmarm style, with medium-priced dresses worn a bit too long in the hem, severely tied back hair, square cut low heel shoes, and no make-up. She drove to work in a well-traveled Volkswagen beetle. When we expressed surprise at all of this, she admitted, "Oh yes, there are two me's."

A second and related element in face-to-face managing is the opportunity it provides for the manipulation of rewards. As Dan Lortie has discovered, the predominant element in the reward system for classroom teaching is a cluster of intrinsic, or subjective, benefits that vary from individual to individual. Reaching a difficult student, watching a young face light up, generating an exciting class discussion—these are some of the teacher's rewards. Extrinsic rewards such as money, prestige, and power, although important and certainly worth an occasional strike or two, are so thoroughly standardized within the profession that little incentive is added to extra individual effort.[8]

One important consequence in this patterning of rewards, notes Lortie, is that the rewards teachers receive come primarily from within the confined space of their own classrooms, away from the controls exercised by administrators and peers. A teacher's key rewards, he concludes, "are largely independent of administrative action." Thus, the teacher's relationship to administrative superiors can move "away from subordination towards exchange."[9]

In the face-to-face management of the school, the principal often facilitates, through an exchange relationship, teachers' opportunities for reward. Although largely independent of hierarchical authority, teachers nevertheless enter into what amount to quid pro quo bargains with their principals. Principals agree to handle difficult discipline cases, buffer teachers from intrusive parents, schedule duty-free periods for lesson planning, hold down paper work demands, and see that plenty of supplies are available. In exchange, teachers concentrate on their teaching and on the day-to-day management of boys and girls under their charge. Uncooperative teachers may discover they have been given the slowest pupils, assigned the noisiest classroom next door to the cafeteria, allocated the school's most dog-eared textbooks, and placed on restroom patrol as an on-duty, non-teaching assignment. They are the losers in the exchange process.

The exchange process is idiosyncratic, varying from one person to another. Also, the form of exchange is typically a verbal give-and-take that depends as heavily on nuances of tone and expression as on content. Perceptive principals learn quickly to interpret signals. A slight hesitation when agreeing implies that Miss Jones has reached her limit in accepting new pupils. The highly regarded Mr. Green's reluctance to chair a new committee indicates that the topic is unpopular with many in the faculty. The usually friendly Mrs.

Gardner's avoidance of the school's main office shows that she is upset by some administrative decision.

Managing Through Interactions with Students

In few organizations do we find the administrative head of a unit engaged in continuous, direct interaction with the clientele of the organization. There are usually intermediaries such as salespersons, tellers, and clerks who deal directly with clients, leaving the administrator the task of overseeing the flow of work and guiding the improvement of work processes. Only intermittently, and usually only in especially problematic situations such as that involving an irate customer, do we find administrative heads handling clients themselves.

In schools, teachers are intermediaries. Yet building principals spend roughly one-fifth of their own working day in direct contact with students. The styles and nature of this contact vary. Some principals are their school's most active disciplinarians; others are seekers and helpers who establish a personal assisting relationship with the brightest or neediest pupils. Still others manage unstable schools where human relations are volatile; in these circumstances, the principal interacts with students to take the pulse of the organization and to head off trouble. Finally, other principals are cheerleader types who, amazingly, remember the first names of hundreds of youngsters; they roam the halls dispensing much encouragement and motivational good will, and an occasional word of censure.

One explanation for the relatively large amount of time spent with students is that the immaturity of the clientele makes such close supervision necessary.[10] Students are compelled to attend school while they are engaged in the difficult process of maturation and adjustment—growing up. As agents of society acting in loco parentis, educators bear a heavy responsibility for the protection and socialization of their young charges. A second explanation is that principals simply enjoy kids; we often heard, "The children make it all worthwhile," or "The kids come first." Principals are usually successful former teachers; they often express a nostalgia for the classroom and still rationalize their professional duties in teaching/learning terminology.

Each of these two explanations implies something critical. The control of a potentially troublesome or unpredictable clientele requires student interaction as part of an anticipatory managerial strategy. Principals learn to be good reactors; in fact, as we observed earlier, they conduct search routines during the course of a day, looking for trouble in places where experience says something often happens.

As anticipators and reactors, principals not only learn to be where the trouble is, but also learn how to interpret trouble when it occurs and decide what remedies will work best. Although not engaged in planning in the traditional sense of setting goals, selecting alternatives, etc., principals plan in the nontraditional sense of establishing limits to the range of outcomes that can occur. One high school principal, as a precautionary measure, added extra security personnel and limited entrance and exit privileges for a school dance. She had learned through a student confidante of tensions between students at her high school and a neighboring school and was determined to reduce the chance of trouble.

On the other hand, the anticipatory managerial skill required by unpredictability among students may leave the principalship with too much reaction and not enough action. The hectic pace of daily activity, the undifferentiated jumble of events, the ever-present possibility of uproar may, in combination, have a narcotic effect on the school administrator. When they are absent, the principal feels a strange uneasiness. In our investigations, we noted that some principals seem to become disoriented when, without warning, peace and serenity set in. There was nothing to react to; "What do I do now?" they thought. With obvious relief the principal, temporarily disengaged from the environment, would receive the next phone call or visitor and jump back into the hurly-burly of activity.

Principal behavior motivated by an enjoyment of youngsters has another implication. This rapport with young people may be an entree to the supervision or evaluation of teachers. Principals do not spend much time directly observing classroom instruction, but they do know what their teachers are doing, in large measure, from the youngsters. An elementary principal who spent a full hour guiding students through the cafeteria line at lunch explained, "This is where I pick up most of my information." A high school principal who frequented the same busy intersection in the school corridor each day received occasional notes or comments about teachers as the students passed. An elementary principal who tutored youngsters in reading kept abreast of activities in the classroom. Her teachers thought a high school principal was wasting time helping individual students with course selections and schedule conflicts. But she was quietly picking up tidbits of information about teachers' homework assignments, instructional activities, and testing and grading policies. In all of these contacts, the principal is making use of thc natural tendency of children to be candid about their school experiences, and to supply more information than the attentive principal is actually asking for.

The teaching profession's norm of teacher autonomy often collides with the managerial tradition of supervision and evaluation of employees. When this confrontation is deadlocked, the principal is forced to find out what is going on through direct contact with the clients. In effect, principals have to gather information about the organization from the customers themselves, an unusual situation generally not found in other organizations.

There are obvious hazards in making the client the primary conduit of information. In bypassing the teacher as intermediary, the principal can be caught between teacher and pupil. Teachers can become frustrated when they think the principal has been fraternizing too much with the students, or when they feel the principal is not protecting them from parents' complaints.[11] Principals may come to depend on students for information, but relying too much on this can easily lead to managerial headaches.

IMPLICATIONS FOR MIDDLE MANAGEMENT

The conventional wisdom puts the building principal at a lower rung of a long ladder of bureaucratic control. Although admittedly critical, first-line supervisors, principals are nevertheless several steps removed from top management, where decisions are really made. They are expected to carry out the policies that have been made well above their level of responsibility. Like the shop supervisor in industry, the building principal fulfills the vitally important function of linking the organization's management and production.

Traditionally the production-line manager's job has been characterized as (a) tightly bounded and compartmentalized, (b) provided with limited, delegated authority commensurate with a clearly delineated realm of responsibility, (c) carefully guided by instructions, rules and regulations from bureaucratic superiors, and (d) easily evaluated by observing products or outcomes of employee performance.[12] As Leonard Sayles writes, the traditional view of the site-level manager is:

> Each person has a *job* to do with a clear beginning and end, and for which he is responsible (and by which he can be measured). The individual makes discrete decisions within the confines of his delegated authority.[13]

Recent research on what administrators really do has revealed that production-line managers, such as school principals, are positioned and function within their organizational hierarchies in a manner quite at odds with the tradition described above. First, principals make broad decisions within a loosely structured system of authority; they engage in what may be called the discretionary definition of their own administrative roles. Second, their position in the middle of the organization does not fit the model of a hierarchical ladder. The educational middle manager is better described as situated in the middle of an intricate system of relationships. The principal responds simultaneously to multiple constituencies rather than to the simple dyad of the boss above and the employees and clients below. Each of these aspects of job reality in the educational organization has managerial implications which we will examine separately.

The Use of Discretion

The layman's image of the public school bureaucracy is of an organization typically bogged down in a mass of restrictive, tightly woven rules, regulations, and standard operating procedures.[14] Principals themselves tend to cultivate this impression, perhaps out of a protective desire to shift responsibility to the system for their conduct of middle management. However, although some rules are, in fact, explicit and tight, much of the procedural policy used in site-level administration exhibits considerable looseness and flexibility. Principals' complaints about central headquarters are more likely to center on the vagueness of language and lack of clear-cut administrative direction than on the rigidity of tight rules which permit too little managerial freedom.

For example, during a budget cutback period, principals were instructed to begin laying off teacher aides. Nothing in the order, however, specified *how.* Were the layoffs to be based strictly on seniority, or was there room to be selective, perhaps keeping the more competent workers? Little additional help came from district offices. Some principals used a seniority criterion and others used the merit approach; many complained about the lack of guidance from above.

In this and other instances, many observers are struck more by the lack of specificity in the organization's rules and procedural guidelines than by their rigidity, comprehensiveness and pervasiveness. The most competent principals are fully aware of their freedom of action. They not only protect it but endeavor to exploit and enhance it through site-level initiatives and pre-emptive interpretations of instructions from headquarters.

There is, we conclude, a considerable degree of *managerial discretion* built into the public school system's administrative structure. It is important to remember that the discretionary spheres of school management are the areas most revealing of administrative competence. Three implications can be drawn from this finding.

Open-ended The scope of the job of building principal is significantly open-ended; the job is largely what each principal makes of it. Some principals enjoy working with teachers and tinkering with strategies for instructional improvement. They often experience frustration and defeat in these initiatives, but they find fulfillment in making the effort, hoping that there will be some pedagogical change for the better. Other principals avoid projects with no end product, and direct their energies toward activities which seem to promise some observable payoff. They raise funds, procure materials or equipment, or develop extra-curricular activities such as assemblies, festivals, or sports events. Still other principals seem to enjoy the "law enforcement" or pastoral aspects of their job. They devote energy to student counseling, school discipline, and straightening out miscreants and directing them into positive channels of adult life. Finally, some principals enjoy the quasi-political aspects of their position. They like to "work the streets", spending time with community people, PTA mothers, and local politicians, and try to parlay this public affairs activity into high visibility for their schools and themselves.

The principal's own values and preferences color the job. Principals share with one another a kind of upbeat gregariousness; they are usually neither reflective nor intellectual. They generally prefer person-to-person relationships, most of which are direct, verbal, and face-to-face. Nevertheless, they demonstrate their gregariousness in different ways. Some enjoy spending their time with teachers, others prefer interacting with youngsters, and still others face outward to the community, local politicians, and their superiors. Every principal has things he or she enjoys most. Although all principals spend time doing all parts of the job, the typical principal concentrates on those activities that are the most fulfilling.

Which sector is most important? Leonard Sayles writes that one of the most serious mistakes stemming from traditional, tightly-bound notions of organizational behavior is the use of *end-result measures* to assess managerial effectiveness. It is misleading, he says, to rest one's case on profit and loss figures or pupils' test scores, or on such things as the percentage of high school graduates going on to college. Such a tally of accomplishments according to some overarching notions of organizational goals can easily be accompanied by a "concomitant failure to observe and evaluate how the game was played."[15] Learning how to make teachers and pupils feel good about themselves, building supportive relations with parents, and establishing a physically attractive atmosphere for learning are samples of "process" that may be more significant than final product. This approach assumes that the manager is the only causal agent in the mix. However other factors are at work, some of them beyond the principal's power to control. At best principals can play an intermediate role; they influence the "machinery" of production, participate in the process, and influence organizational outcomes. The central objective of the bureaucracy, as Gordon Tullock suggests, should be to encourage people below the apex of the administrative pyramid to intervene, use discretion, and "give it a try."[16] Peter Drucker some time ago suggested that a simple rule for determining how much discretion the firing-line manager should exercise is to stand the old Prussian notion of a citizen's rights—"Everything that is not expressly allowed is forbidden"—on its head. His suggestion: Spell out only that which the manager is *not* entitled to decide, that which he or she must leave to top-level administration. All else may be considered within the site manager's domain of experimentation, authority, and responsibility.[17]

A balancing act The discretionary behavior concept yields a second implication. The term 'middle' in middle management is best defined neither by notions of hierarchical position nor by the tugging and pulling of competing interests. Rather, middleness is the balancing act the site manager performs in negotiating between organizational expectations of stability on the one hand, and the quasi-political requirements for change and reform on the other. As Leonard Sayles observes, the production-line manager is under pressure to exert leadership, motivate subordinates, be creative, and innovate. But the manager is also under simultaneous pressure to detect disturbances in the work flow, minimize deviations from established patterns, and "hold the organization together."[18] Principals play a similar role, balancing organizational maintenance and process/product enhancement.

For example the principal is expected to be responsive to but protect the organization from parents and community. Teachers expect the principal to shield them from parental harassment. However, both teachers and principals want parents to be involved in the instructional program. As we have reported earlier, in balancing parental involvement and institutional autonomy, principals use discretion to mold parental expectations, guide parental contact, and reward influential or helpful parents who seek special assistance. By paying attention to neighborhood information (and by adroit handling of the "crazy mother"), principals anticipate the problems and try to ward off trouble before it gets out of control. Some "creative insubordination" may be also necessary to neutralize bureaucratic insensitivity with neighborly common sense or to delay a central office directive until local resistance dies down.

Similarly, principals are expected to promote their schools as successes, but also protect the hierarchy from any conflict or embarrassing publicity. Each of a school district's buildings is a subunit of the larger organizational system. Power and status are not equally distributed, and principals compete with one another. But there are limits on this competition. Promotional tactics must not threaten other principals or irk superiors who must explain everything to the public.

Another hazard lurks. Sometimes system officers or headquarters staff push their mistakes down to principals to correct quietly, so the boss escapes the blame. Clever principals can carry this off, especially if they know how the system really operates. Nevertheless, much of a principal's time may be required to cover up the bungling or inertia of the central office. They might have to negotiate for some needed kitchen equipment several months overdue or schedule a long-delayed rehabilitation of the school building held up by misplaced paperwork. These inherited problems usually take precedence over the principal's own projects.

Teachers cooperate to improve instruction at least in part because the principal can protect teacher welfare (paid leave days, summer contracts, position security) by manipulating bureaucratic rules. However, a principal's attempts to improve the school can go too far. If the attempts lead to unfavorable publicity or turf battles at headquarters, the principal could lose influence, be censured or even be transferred to a less desirable school.

Rewards A third observation is that principals may make decisions based more on the reward system of the educational organization than on its rules and regulations. Although it is generally believed that production-line managers are guided by explicit instructions from superiors, many principals, conscious of opportunities for reward and advancement, learn how to exploit the rules to enhance their own or their school's fortunes. The unwritten but widely recognized expectations of the organization, plus its traditions for advancement ("This is how you really get ahead."), often outweigh official policy statements.

Advancement usually is a transfer to a larger or more prestigious school; it may also be a shift to a magnet or specialty secondary school. Or, advancement could be an appointment to an administrative position at headquarters. Even those principals less concerned with career advancement are still interested in holding on to what they have, avoiding transfer to a "dead end" administrative job, or, worst of all, being sent back to the classroom.

Neither the criteria nor the procedures employed in evaluating principals are clearly specified. Nevertheless, building principals take care to present as glowing a picture of their school as possible. Most principals understand that the system expects each school to be under control and free of sticky problems that require the superior's attention. Thus, principals take steps to suppress teacher grievances, parental complaints, or teacher dismissal proceedings that would require their immediate supervisors to act. Similarly, such extra-bureaucratic maneuvers as short-circuiting regular supply channels (see page 156), or even the occasional act of creative insubordination, are in response to a well-recognized "do it yourself" norm of school-site management. Finally, the ultimate discretionary act is when the principal takes the heat for the organization in some politically troublesome situation. All principals hope that this self-sacrifice will be rewarded on some future day.

Handling Multiple Constituencies

It is simplistic to conceive of the school as a place where teachers teach and pupils learn, supported by at least a principal, a janitor, and a librarian. In a modern school psychologists, social workers, community relations experts, speech and hearing specialists, reading consultants, experts on gifted children, and Title I coordinators are all present. Also, there has been a major increase in the use of non-professional personnel. Many kinds of aides are now employed: Attendance aides, teacher and library aides, bilingual aides, departmental assistants, and security aides. The increased transportation of pupils has added cafeteria workers and bus drivers to the mix; government programs have spurred the employment of additional secretarial personnel; even the janitor frequently has specialized assistants. Finally, parents are doing much more than running the PTA and chaperoning field trips. They often actively volunteer in the instructional program.

Outside of the school's immediate environment, the courts, state and federal governments, private businesses, community interest groups, and other agencies of local government such as police, welfare workers, and health officers, have become involved. The media, street gangs, drug pushers, union representatives, lawyers, and parole officers add to the mixture.

The school principal responds to a multiple rather than simple constituency. One central implication, treated thoroughly by David K. Wiles, Jon Wiles, and Joseph Bondi in *Practical Politics for School Administrators,* is that the school setting can be viewed as a political arena where managerial decisions must be negotiated amid many competing interests rather than promulgated from bureaucracy on high.[19]

The school context is fluid; actors on the political stage are constantly changing, contradictions abound, and solutions to problems often do not last. One group of parents may oppose another. Factions may develop among the school staff, and some of these will ally with outside groups. Even the controls exercised by the organizational hierarchy may change as chief officers come and go. The rules of the managerial game will be altered by the decisions of federal bureaucrats, the whims of the state legislature or the judiciary, and the initiatives of local politicians. The pressures that force a change in policy from above may be met by an equally powerful counterforce from staff members and parents below. To bow to one is to alienate the other; to compromise by bending a rule may alienate both.

The principal is pulled by competing interests, and must blend these interests into a working unit. It is dangerous to assume that the organizational world possesses bureaucratic harmony, with the political problems of policy making solved. Arthur Blumberg and William Greenfield suggest that effective principals have a high tolerance for ambiguity; they learn to function effectively where power is limited and the direction of the educational system unclear.[20]

A second observation on the handling of multiple constituencies is that beyond the problems of practical politics, the central dilemma of the school principal is answering the question of allegiance.[21] To whom does the principal owe his greatest loyalty? Which of the many categories of constituents is the principal's primary reference group? Each group has a legitimate claim upon the principal. The local community represents the aspirations of parents for their children, as well as the struggle of a neighborhood to gain good schools, qualified teachers, and a livable environment. Teachers and other staff members have a tradition of professional autonomy and standards. The principal usually shares the teacher's view of the importance of instruction and the value of independence.

The board of education and the larger society require other loyalties. Loyalty to the board is at least in part self-loyalty, for the principal's future depends on the board's evaluation of his or her performance. Furthermore, the board is the legal authority and makes policy for the community. The society demands allegiance to certain values and enforces constitutional safeguards. Society's values —freedom of speech, a tolerance of ethnic and religious differences, equal treatment, a right to learn—take precedence over local narrow-mindedness.

Blumberg and Greenfield, in analyzing the phenomenon of allegiance, have found that principals working within turbulent relationships experience a feeling of relative isolation.[22] Responsibility takes its toll.

1. Broken glass on the playground may be ignored by a classroom teacher, but it threatens a lawsuit for the teacher-turned-principal.

2. A few cases of upset stomach following lunch do not concern busy instructors. But the principal worries, "Food poisoning? Is lunchroom sanitation adequate?"
3. Broken windows overnight suggest more to a principal than after-dark vandalism. "Is the neighborhood failing now to support and protect its school? Have I done enough to reach out to the community, to make them proud enough of the school to care for it?"
4. While loading up for the bus trip home from the zoo, two youngsters cannot be found. The teachers in charge throw up their hands in frustration. It is the principal's job to find them, to inform the parents, to take charge.

Principals experience a quantum leap in responsiblity when they assume managerial control. Suddenly, they inhabit a much larger, more complex administrative world. The organization wants obedience, but its demands occasionally conflict with the interests of teachers or parents. Doing "what's best for the kids" may sometimes require considerable courage in the face of hierarchical or political counter-pressures. A teacher in the wrong and at odds with parents may need the principal's support. But how much? At what point does collegial loyalty yield to admitting and correcting injustice? What does one do when implementing one federal program conflicts with another, when a provision in the teachers' contract causes inadequate service to children, when a direct order from headquarters disturbs a fragile agreement with local parents? Peter Drucker has suggested that the site manager's job is not so overwhelmingly large in terms of what to do, but is burdensome in having so many things to do "without knowing which are most important."[23]

"I can't work for everyone—equally," muses the principal. "I'm forced much of the time to make a choice. But whose side do I come down on? Where do my loyalties lie?" It is a haunting and sometimes irresolvable problem, one that is often answered by overidentifying with the special welfare of the school-site. Principals sometimes refer to their charges as if they owned them: "*My* teachers, *my* kids, *my* parents, *my* school." The isolation and fluidity combine to create a primary loyalty to *their* school, *their* kids. A problem that has its roots in an excess of discretionary choice leads to a restriction of choice; principals are tempted to center their attention on one small piece at the bottom of the organization pyramid. Facing a myriad of pressures, the principal comes to value most the loyalties of those closest to him—the teachers and students in the school.

THINGS TO DO AND THINK ABOUT

1. Principals walk a lot; they have to in order to carry out the tasks of management. In the design of a school building, an architect might wish to take this into account. What advice could you give a school architect on the physical layout of a school?
2. A central concern of the principalship is the question of allegiance. As a school administrator, how would you address this question? To whom do you feel you owe the greatest loyalty?
3. Observe people in conversation as they fulfill occupational roles—a clerk with a customer, a flight attendant with passengers, a nurse with patients, a teacher with pupils. Describe the "face-work" of these occupational performers. What faces must they put on; what behaviors are required of them? What face-saving messages are involved in the conversations?
4. Principals manage, for the most part, face-to-face with one person at a time. What are the special skills necessary for these kinds of interchanges? How does a prospective administrator learn these skills?
5. Principals sometimes supervise and evaluate teachers indirectly through their contacts with students. What are the strengths and weaknesses of this unorthodox approach to employee evaluation? How could principals be trained to use this approach effectively?
6. You have been asked by a local superintendent of schools to develop an instrument to assess principal "effectiveness." What in your judgment should go into such an instrument?

NOTES

1. Larry W. Hughes and Gerald C. Ubben, *The Elementary Principal's Handbook: A Guide to Effective Action* (Boston: Allyn and Bacon, Inc., 1978), pp. 344–345.
2. Karl E. Weick, "Administering Education in Loosely Coupled Schools," *Phi Delta Kappan,* vol. 63, no. 10, (June 1982), pp. 673–676.
3. Ibid. p. 676.
4. The notion of administration as "negotiated order" has been explored most notably by Anselm Strauss and his colleagues. See Anselm Strauss et al., "The Hospital and its Negotiated Order," in E. Friedman, ed., *The Hospital in Modern Society* (New York: The Free Press, 1963), pp. 147–169.
5. One of our professorial colleagues, an experienced school administrator, suggests that a substantially enlarged scope of responsibility is one of the most important defining characteristics of the principalship. But it is also that which provides one of the greatest "shocks" to new administrators—who have previously experienced only the very limited scope re-

quired of the classroom teacher. Per discussion with Professor R. Bruce McPherson, University of Illinois at Chicago, June 1982.

6. Erving Goffman, *Interaction Ritual: Essays On Face-to-Face Behavior* (Garden City, N.J.: Anchor Books, 1967).
7. See Michael Lipsky, *Street-Level Bureaucracy: Dilemmas of the Individual in Public Services* (New York: Russell Sage Foundation, 1980); also, Willard Waller, *The Sociology of Teaching* (New York: Wiley, 1932).
8. Dan C. Lortie, "The Balance of Control and Autonomy in Elementary School Teaching," in Amitai Etzioni (ed.), *The Semi-Professions and Their Organization: Teachers, Nurses, Social Workers* (New York: Free Press, 1969), pp. 1–53.
9. Ibid.
10. See Charles E. Bidwell, "The School as a Formal Organization," in James G. March (ed.), *Handbook of Organizations* (Chicago: Rand McNally and Co., 1965), pp. 973–975.
11. See Howard S. Becker, "The Teacher in the Authority System of the Public School," in Amitai Etzioni, ed., *Complex Organizations: A Sociological Reader* (New York: Holt, Rinehart and Winston, 1961), pp. 243–251.
12. Leonard R. Sayles, *Managerial Behavior: Administration in Complex Organizations* (New York: McGraw-Hill Book Company, 1964), pp. 24–25.
13. Ibid. p. 25.
14. See David Rogers, *110 Livingston Street* (New York: Vintage Books, 1968).
15. Sayles, op. cit., p. 26.
16. Gordon Tullock, *The Politics of Bureaucracy* (Washington, D.C.: Public Affairs Press, 1965), p. 141.
17. Peter F. Drucker, *The Practice of Management* (New York: Harper & Brothers Publishers, 1954), pp. 141–142.
18. Sayles, op. cit., pp. 46–50.
19. David K. Wiles, Jon Wiles and Joseph Bondi, *Practical Politics for School Administrators* (Boston: Allyn and Bacon, Inc., 1981).
20. Arthur Blumberg and William Greenfield, *The Effective Principal: Perspectives on School Leadership* (Boston: Allyn and Bacon, Inc., 1980), pp. 246–247.
21. Our professorial colleague, R. Bruce McPherson, suggests that deciding to whom the greatest degree of allegiance is owed is *the* most difficult task for the practicing school administrator. We owe a word of thanks to McPherson for his insights into the problems of allegiance growing out of the scope of responsibility involved in principaling.
22. Blumberg and Greenfield, op. cit., p. 233.
23. Drucker, op. cit., p. 322.

9

Implications for Training and Selection

The principal's job, as noted in the preceding chapter, requires ad hoc thinking and situation-specific decision making. Site-level administration requires fast reflexes, one-to-one communication skills, a good memory for details, a facility for solving problems quickly, *and* strong legs and solid shoe leather.

We now raise the question of how to best teach these skills and, perhaps more important, how to detect and measure them in individuals who are considered for available principalships. Can these traits be developed in university programs for administrators, and can they be identified and evaluated by superintendents and boards of education looking for the right person to fill a vacancy? We believe the answer is yes.

TRAINING PRINCIPALS

Before any university establishes a training program for school principals, it should consider admission requirements. The program planners should ask, *What kind of people do we want for this program?* This question means two things. *What kind of individual can benefit the most from what we can offer?* And, perhaps more critical, *What kind of person can succeed in university studies, complete the program fully certified, proceed into the administrative labor market, and become a credit to our institution?*

The answers depend partly on what the program is to be. Most departments of school administration have some expectations about the job of training principals. Moreover, we find from the research for this volume that the principal's job itself makes demands on both the trainee *and* the program designers. The first step in planning a program should be describing the kinds of students a faculty wants to invest its time in.

We assume that applicants will be, for the most part, working professionals who have already spent some years in the classroom. Most of them will have only their bachelor's degrees, although a few may have completed a master's degree program and may wish to earn an administrative certificate or a second master's degree in school administration. In this pool, who are the likeliest candidates?

Previous educational record Training programs for educational managers should require a strong academic record. Customarily, this is measured by grade point average at the undergraduate and graduate levels. There may be some variation in standards from school to school, but most universities will seek only the A and B students. Some colleges still provide a class rank. In any event, the screening committee should evaluate the candidate's institution, recognizing that A students from X University may not be as strong as B students from Y College.

Test scores The most common nationally normed graduate level tests are the *Graduate Record Examination,* which measures scholastic achievement, and the *Miller Analogies Test,* which measures intellectual ability. Here also, institutions may differ on their cutoff points, but applicants should score at the 50th percentile or higher.

Goal statement Graduate students should have a career direction, an overall professional objective. Some institutions ask the applicant to prepare a statement of 300–500 words explaining his or her long-term plans and how the training program would contribute to that goal. By studying these statements, experienced admissions officers can often detect clues about the individual's motivation and, more important, whether his or her goals are realistic and achievable.

Writing sample Educational leaders need to write well. Some institutions ask the applicant to write an impromptu essay of 300–500 words on some general topic in education. The applicant may not use any reference materials; such an exercise can reveal a great deal about the individual's language ability.

Interview Most educators agree that it is difficult to predict a candidate's future performance from an interview. If an interview is used, it is important to structure the encounter carefully and ask all candidates the same questions. Open-ended questions reveal the most about someone's ability to articulate ideas orally and extemporaneously. For example, "Here is situation X; how would you handle it?", or "Here is Policy Y; what is your critical estimate of this policy?" In designing such questions, the interviewing team should decide on some sort of scoring system, so their post-interview judgments will be as objective as possible.

Letters of recommendation With today's freedom of information, screening officers have mixed feelings about the value of letters from outside parties. Since such referees are usually selected by the applicant, it is safe to assume that they were chosen because the applicant expected a favorable letter. Moreover, writers of such letters are notorious for their artful dissembling and obfuscation, and it is sometimes difficult to separate the sincere, straightforward referee from the inveterate blower of smoke. If possible, a follow-up phone call might be worth while. On the telephone, as Marshall McLuhan pointed out in *The Medium Is the Message,* people are willing to say things that they would feel uneasy about putting in print. It is still possible, though, to get an inaccurate impression over the phone.

Solicited referees Perhaps the most reliable information about an applicant can be obtained from a colleague or superior where the applicant works. Such individuals have to be found in the information provided on the application and should be telephoned "cold" and asked for their critical estimate of the applicant.

In all of the above, we assume that no single measure by itself will be decisive. Taken together, however, they could be decisive. A prudent selection committee could critically discuss each individual's cluster of "scores" to determine admissability.

The administrator of the program and the admissions personnel should keep data on all such decisions. In subsequent years, they could assess how well the admissions criteria predicted winners and losers. Did the admitted students succeed? Did they deliver on the promise indicated by their cluster of scores? The admissions process should be overhauled if it is not working well.

Turning to the design of the program itself, we must issue a few warnings. First, the educational profession is only now beginning to get around to the vital task of identifying the special attributes of the educational manager. The range of abilities involved in the job is very wide, and the number of skills manifold. In our discussion of how universities should prepare school principals, therefore, do not expect a set of curricular prescriptions in the form of course titles, program requirements, and grade point specifications. But we do offer a few procedural observations which any program planning committee ought to consider.

It is also useful to remember that *job-relatedness* is now the watchword in our certificate-oriented society. Licensing bodies expect that preparation for the job will resemble the activities of the job itself. Preparing to become a firefighter may include study of the chemistry of combustion, but it must also include more prosaic elements like climbing unsteady ladders, wrestling errant nozzles, rescuing trapped people, and resuscitating unconscious victims. Likewise, any university program for school principals must involve real-life exercises in what principals actually do.

The job-relatedness imperative leads naturally to a final, more comprehensive, and perhaps decisive obligation of program planners—the need to bring school and university closer together. In any significant rethinking of principalship training, the practitioner's concern for hands-on effectiveness must join with the scholar's concern for generalization and theory. Other professions, most notably medicine, have effected this union with internships, externships, and apprentice residencies. It is imperative that some of the same elements appear in university training for educational management.

Direct Observation

The strongest impression we gained from our direct study of school administrators is this: A great deal can be learned by watching managers in action. This conclusion should not come as any surprise, since we have apparently known it all along. Students studying to be teachers, for example, devote a large share of their undergraduate studies to directly observing teachers and children in classrooms. Indeed, in recent years the requirements for on-site observation have been sharply increased in most states, and the certification of teachers has come to depend on how much time has been spent inside schools, observing and participating. Why has it taken so long for the administrative community to catch on?

Observing the manager in action should be the occasion for witnessing professional behavior. The interchanges between the principal and others in the school environment are dynamic episodes of human interaction. The observer is the privileged witness to this action and has the opportunity to examine both its verbal and nonverbal content. The observer can use the experience not only to understand what is happening, but also to participate vicariously in the life of the chief actor, the principal.

Trainers of principals must remember that observation is a learning device which must be closely monitored and evaluated. Most important is preparing the student observer prior to an excursion into the field for on-site observation. Perhaps a set of training films of administrators in special situations, like those for student teachers, could be part of the preparation for direct observation. The university professor should also instruct students what to watch for, and help them compare their expectations of what they will see with what they actually see. When they review the observation, we recommend that students and professors critique what they have observed, evaluate the behavior, assess the outcomes, and determine what they would have done differently. In a group, such a critique of each student's observation would provide options and alternative courses of action to be evaluated.

On-site observation requires the principal's cooperation; such a principal should not be intimidated by a stranger in his or her presence for several days. Although some managerial tasks are sensitive and would be disturbed by the presence of an outsider, most of the school manager's work day is open for inspection. More administrators are sharing their work with outsiders. Principals are more willing to take part in observations if universities invite these "host-administrators" to the campus to participate in the seminars and group critiques of their or others' managerial behavior. If practicing school administrators can become part of the training team, their willingness to be followed about will increase.

Internship

The internship is used extensively in medicine, law, and nursing, and, to a lesser extent, in social work, architecture, and career government service. In teacher education, it has been institutionalized as student teaching, during which the trainee gradually assumes full responsibility for a classroom of youngsters.

Internship is very valuable in training principals because it is difficult to teach the job in the conventional campus-based course sequence. Book learning, although vital for understanding concepts of administration, is unable to train the student for the practice of managerial activity. Accordingly, direct participation in administrative duties, closely supervised by an experienced professional, is a natural complement to the graduate seminars conducted on campus. Moreover, internship experiences are a natural follow-up to observation, especially those observations which are followed by systematic critique and discussion.

The major hazard of internships is the difficulty identifying and isolating specific, concrete administrative problems on which the intern is to work. He or she is, of course, only a temporary participant in the management network. Moreover, in most cases the trainee will be an outsider and probably a stranger to most of the staff. In medicine, the intern's assignment is an actual hospital patient, or group of them, under the care of a training physician; in teacher education, the intern's assignment is a class of pupils under the supervision of a teacher. In both instances, the trainee progressively assumes more responsibility for delivering the institution's service to the client, until he or she assumes almost full responsibility by the end of the internship period.

In managerial settings, however, the work assignment is not so easily separated from the universe of things which principals do. Moreover, the managerial service sometimes involves professional staff people (not hospital patients or school children) as the recipients. This means that the internship experience may be complicated by the superior-subordinate relationship. Faculty members are generally reluctant to take orders, or even friendly direction, from someone without authority. (Medical interns seldom have this problem.) Accordingly, administrative internships must be designed so the trainee may function in place of the principal in certain relatively limited and problem-specific areas. The host or critic principal must insure that the faculty and staff understand clearly that, in that particular area or on that specific problem, the intern functions as a deputy principal and speaks for the principal.

An opposite danger, the temptation to trivialize the assignment to limit disturbance to the managerial environment, must be avoided. Here the intern receives something unimportant to do, to give the appearance of participation, but receives no authority or responsibility. This tactic may indeed neutralize the subordinates' resistance to working with the outsider, but it destroys the purpose of the internship—to induct a newcomer into real managerial responsibility. Interns must be assigned real tasks and be allowed to make real decisions. They must be given the opportunity to make something happen, to make mistakes or to achieve results, and be held accountable.

As for examples of such special tasks, here are some possibilities:

- ☐ Directing the faculty in preparing for a formal visit by a regional accrediting association
- ☐ Directing the preparation of a school handbook for use by both faculty and students
- ☐ Serving as coordinator of programs drawing volunteers from outside the school in areas of special instruction: university students in foreign languages serving as tutors in Russian, Chinese, Japanese, or Arabic; investment counselors providing special sessions in economics; nutritionists from local hospitals conducting classes in home economics and biology; policemen, firemen, architects, psychiatrists, entertainers explaining the work world
- ☐ Conducting planning sessions of faculty and staff to draw up specifications for building rehabilitation

One-on-one Communication

Anyone who watches principals in action for any length of time will be struck by the fact that they manage schools primarily by encounters with one person at a time. In this book, we have commented on the degree to which the principal moves about the school to run it. This is no doubt because in schools, unlike hospitals, business firms, government bureaus, and other institutions, subordinates cannot easily be pulled away from their work stations for a meeting in the principal's conference room. Thus, management in a school must be conducted from person to person. Each exchange is a unique event in administrative life, and a message that might be delivered to a group of people at once must be transmitted over and over again to each person.

Communicating this way is inefficient and hazardous. The principal must be careful to give precisely the same message to each individual so there will not be complaints of dissembling or favoritism. On the other hand, this avenue of exchange enables the principal to deal individually with each recipient of the message; the message may be the same, but the medium of delivery can be adjusted for each listener. This ad hoc delivery can be especially helpful whenever the principal may be delivering some bad news.

In any event, university faculty designing a program might include some attention to management through one-on-one, face-to-face encounters. This raises the question of whether this skill can be developed and taught. Social psychologists do not know. As noted in the previous chapter, Erving Goffman has written extensively on this form of human interaction and has described several features of both verbal and non-verbal communication in face-to-face encounters which influence the administrator's effectiveness. Program planners should explore this literature for clues on how the trainee can become adept in this critically important area of human interaction.[1]

Conflict Management

Running a school yields its share of little and big problems. By far the most troublesome, time-consuming and unpleasant (and most critical) are those in which individuals are in conflict. These are the problems that no one else wishes to handle; they wind up almost immediately on the principal's desk.

As you learned in Part 2, a principal's discretionary decision making impinges on four main constituencies: the school building personnel, parents and lay outsiders, hierarchical superiors, and the principal's own psyche. The principal is the quintessential middle manager, not merely in a hierarchical sense, but in a political sense as well. Constituencies are everywhere, whispering (or shouting) into the principal's ear their values, aspirations, and expectations. The principalship is made-to-order for conflict, and this is especially true because the primary client, the child, is everyone's sentimental focus. The pupil is small, psychologically defenseless, and heavily dependent on the institution's continuing good will toward him or her. This means that the principal's constituencies can gain leverage for their own self interest by emotionally appealing to "the needs of children." The principal must be able to sort out the educational arguments from the merely political ones which may be advanced in confrontations.

In most cases, conflict originates in disagreements between individuals. A student or parent complains about a teacher, a teacher objects to the continuing presence of a student, two students get into a fight, two teachers lock horns over classroom allocations, a counselor disagrees with a teacher on the handling of a youngster, or two assistant principals tangle on a jurisdictional matter. The occasions for dispute are numerous and familiar to anyone who has spent any time in a school.

But what specifically can the principal-in-training do to prepare for these episodes? Unlike teacher evaluation, curriculum planning, or course scheduling, conflict management is a task that earlier experience does not usually prepare one for. Managing children in a classroom is perhaps the closest approximation to supervising adults in an organization. Some claim that adults are sometimes more like children than children, and that they require the same kind of hand-holding, ego-stroking, and tender loving care as young people. If this is the case, then social psychology may again provide some answers on how to resolve confrontations in the workplace.

The literature on conflict management is extensive and program planners should consult it. Here is a short bibliography:

Robert C. Owens, "Conflict in Organizations," Chapter Nine in *Organizational Behavior in Education,* Second Edition (Englewood Cliffs, N.J.: Prentice-Hall, Inc. 1981), pp. 276–304.

Kenneth E. Corey, "Structures in the Planning of Community Change: A Personal Construct," Chapter 7.1 in W. Bennis et al., eds. *The Planning of Change,* Third Edition, (New York: Holt, Rinehart and Winston, 1976), pp. 265–275.

Herbert Cohen, *You can negotiate anything* (Secaucus, N.J.: Lyle Stuart, 1980).

Roger Fisher & William Ury, *Getting to yes: Negotiating agreement without giving in* (Boston: Houghton Mifflin, 1981).

Anselm Strauss, *Negotiations: Varieties, contexts, processes, and social order* (San Francisco: Jossey Bass, 1978).

William Zartman, ed., *The 50 percent solution* (Garden City, New York: Doubleday, 1976).

Technology of Principaling

By this we mean the conceptual nuts and bolts of professional knowledge. Every principal, somewhere in the training program, must learn the state's school codes. These are the statutory bylaws that govern schools, and they stipulate the conditions under which schooling is to be provided, and the protocols governing relationships between professional educators and students.

Principals must also become familiar with school law, especially that which bears directly on student rights in discipline and suspension cases. In addition, the principal must be familiar with laws that provide the basis for the union contract, if there is one, and the ancillary legal literature on teachers' rights. Finally, it is imperative, especially nowadays in our litigation-minded times, that the principal be operationally familiar with the body of law, such as Public Law 94-142 on Handicapped Children, which influences the actual functioning of a school.

The competent principal must take an increasingly more active attitude toward educational research, not only that reported in the journals by university professors, but also research which is conducted in schools by system specialists at the direction of their boards of education. Curriculum design, instructional strategies, and innovations in evaluation techniques are being generated throughout the profession, and today's administrator should study them.

There is also a growing body of knowledge about administration itself, and the special applications of psychology, sociology, and political science to institutional management. The principal must be adept at interpersonal communication, and also be able to represent the educational establishment to the outside world. The principal is the energizer of professional effort inside the school, the motivator of achievement among students, as well as the shaper of lay opinion toward education in the wider society. This means that the social and behavioral sciences are intellectual spheres in which the modern principal must be able to move competently.

Finally, computers are entering the schools. Computer literacy must be developed and schools are the best places to do it. School administration, especially at the site level, must explore ways to insure that children entering our schools will encounter computer learning as universally and commonly as they do basic skills like history, biology, and geometry. Computer learning, contrary to popular belief, is only indirectly connected to mathematics; it is something genuinely new. It represents a method not only of generating and communicating information, but essentially a new method of understanding the world. We do not overstate when we say that languages like FORTRAN, ASSEMBLER, BASIC, and COBOL represent different orderings of the brain, and new alignments of perception and cognition. They are strategies that open up totally new fields of exploration.

The Career Ladder Concept

Finally, we recommend a form of training that must augment pre-service preparation—continuing education while pursuing a career. As with other professions, it is too often assumed in school administration that administrators can afford to stop learning. The importance of professional development and life-long learning must be affirmed by administrators.

On assuming the first principalship, individuals may be temporarily overwhelmed by the demands of the job. But after they have mastered the basic procedures, they experience a new burst of energy and ambition. Administrators should turn this energy into new learning; the true professional is one who wants to go on improving.

As practicing professionals know, school administration has its ideology. There is the faith in the idea that the administrator *can* make a difference in the way a school works. Recent evidence has shown that this is not just an article of faith but an empirically established fact.[2] Moreover, administrators have different roles: instructional leader, secular pastor, chief of police, corporate executive, Secretary General of a mini-United Nations. To develop that style of administration that best suits him or her, the conscientious principal must continue to go to school. We mean this not in the literal sense, but in the sense of sharpening managerial skills, developing new performance options, and sensing novel ways to measure effectiveness. It is a form of going to school to oneself.

Such continuing education could be developed in informal seminars with other administrators, in advanced theoretical investigations at universities, or in research projects in management directed by scholars. The practitioner's contribution to these investigations is extremely valuable, as we have learned in our own studies of principals. In one school system, this form of advanced learning in school management is called "Administrative University," a district-sponsored, externally funded local think tank for practicing administrators.

Several institutes of advanced study are now operating around the country. The George Peabody College for Teachers at Vanderbilt University has established what is known as The Principals' Institute, "designed to improve school effectiveness by preparing principals to be more successful educational leaders." The Institute is offered each year in a three-week summer program concentrating on leadership skills and the knowledge base required of educational leaders of the future.

The University of Maine and the state department of education, in collaboration with two principals' associations, have created the Maine Principals' Academy which "focuses on training practicing principals in the state to be both effective instructional leaders and able managers." The major activity of the Academy is a two-week summer institute during which participants study and discuss problems of mutual interest.[3]

Harvard University has established the Principals Center with offices and conference rooms adjacent to the Cambridge campus. Principals come together to discuss their strategies for handling administrative problems and write up their experiences in publishable manuscripts for other school administrators to study. The Harvard Principals Center publishes a newsletter which reviews the activities of the Center and carries professional articles from participating principals.

The Connecticut School Management Institute at the University of Bridgeport "aims to strengthen the leadership and organizational development skills of principals and other middle managers, so that they will be more effective in achieving educational goals at the building level."[4] Perhaps the most sophisticated of these agencies, the Bridgeport facility offers a full year program concentrating on diagnosis of administrative style, training in specialized skills, and coaching the principals in introducing special programs in their schools.

The Charles F. Kettering Foundation of Dayton, Ohio has established the I/D/E/A Principals' Inservice Program to assist principals with personal professional development, school improvement, and the development of collegial support groups.

In the early 1980s The Chase Manhattan Bank of New York City awarded the New York Public School System a grant of over $400,000 to establish a principal renewal program, designed to benefit the more than 1,000 school principals in that city.

Finally, the National Institute of Education in Washington, D.C. maintains a directory of in-service training programs for principals. These agencies are operated by state departments of education, local school districts, universities, professional associations, and foundations.

The site level administrator has become, whether intended or not, the key figure in providing educational services in the United States. Most of the managerial decision making resides in this office. This means that the managerial wisdom of this individual is critical to the integrity of the entire enterprise. We expect that continued training in the handling of this office will increasingly concern the profession.

The principal's growing expertise will eventually benefit others; the principal was at one time a teacher, and continues to be. The best way to learn anything, they say, is to teach it. What better way to prove this axiom than to instruct others in the administrative art?

SELECTING PRINCIPALS

People become administrators for a variety of reasons, usually because of the desire for more responsibility and a higher income. As they conclude their training programs on the way to a principal's certificate, they request to be considered for principalship openings. Every school system has a pool of individuals who annually emerge from the teaching ranks and announce their availability for administrative assignment. How should a superintendent and board of education go about identifying the best prospects for this position?

Present Performance

A conventional place to look is the applicant's competence in his or her present job. If this happens to be a quasi-administrative position such as department head, program director, or curriculum coordinator, the assimilation of a principal's duties may be relatively easy and straightforward. If the candidate is presently a classroom teacher, the transition may be more difficult.

But in either case, the evaluator should focus not on overall performance as required in that position, but only those aspects of it which are transferable to, and predictive of, performance as a principal. A good teacher will not necessarily be the best administrator; the skills for the two jobs are not all the same.

We can make one qualification to this generalization—the special skills of coaches. Over the years, many coaches have become principals. Many faculties have developed a mild scorn for these individuals, usually male, who make the transition from coach to principal. Allegedly less intellectual and biased in favor of the "jock" sub-culture, these individuals, so it is argued, are inappropriate cultural role models for academically oriented faculties and student bodies. They symbolize the wrong values. Their identification with physical prowess, sport spectacles, and public hoopla seems somehow out of keeping with the aims of a scholastic enterprise.

All of these observations are valid, and it is not just unreconstructed fuddy-duddyism to want our educational leaders to be among the best and the brightest. Moreover, the ex-coach as principal stereotype has come to represent to many in the profession a denial of opportunity for those who pursue other routes into administration, particularly women.

Nevertheless, we may be able to learn something from this phenomenon. The responsibilities of persons holding the two positions are remarkably similar. Both:

- ☐ organize disparate elements—people, equipment, money—into a self-sustaining enterprise.

- ☐ coordinate individuals in an intricate division of labor, each person performing a specialized task.
- ☐ motivate highly skilled individuals, some of them prima donnas.
- ☐ take care of wounded egos and serve as counselor and parent figure to troubled subordinates.
- ☐ maintain frequent, easy-going contact with the public.
- ☐ keep a cool head under provocative and stressful circumstances.
- ☐ answer to the school and the community.
- ☐ identify with the whole school.

This does not mean that coaches necessarily make good principals, but that the requirements of the two jobs are similar. These are the job features that should be studied to measure an individual's performance. What about the person's present job most resembles the principal's daily work? How well does the person perform in these areas? This is the way to find future principals.

The Principal's Exam

Identifying promising prospects depends on personal judgment, and evaluating people on the job is an inexact science. Moreover, protective clubbiness among top administrators can sometimes cause biased judgments. Recognizing this, some school systems have recently turned to the candidate examination as an objective screening device. The education industry is saturated with examinations on all levels and for all skills. Why not evaluate administrators the same way, through some form of standardized test?

Early attempts at this, beginning in the 1950s, resorted to the kind of examination educators know best—the paper and pencil test. Prospective candidates were brought together for up to six hours and given a battery of short-answer, true-false, open-ended essay tests. Unlike the National Teachers Examination, such tests have not been standardized nationally, but in their local application they have been systematically refined to focus on specific professional skills administrators are expected to have and on specialized skills and abilities of managerial importance. Understandably, the exams have focused on a working knowledge of all disciplines taught in the school curriculum, and professional knowledge usually taught in university administrator training programs. It has been conventional wisdom that someone who is generally familiar with the school's curriculum and has a specialized knowledge of school administration is ready to become a principal.

The political advantage of such examinations is that they are objective, free of color and gender bias, and yield quantitative results enabling comparisons of candidates. They treat all comers equally and, at the same time, provide merit rankings of practical use to superintendents and school boards. In some systems, eligibility lists are drawn up using examination scores as the only or dominant criterion. When a vacancy occurs, the superintendent weighs the credentials of the top three names, consults with aides, evaluates other criteria, and recommends to the board one of the three.

It has become clear in recent years, however, that the conventional paper and pencil test, no matter how artfully designed, is only a part of screening candidates. We have seen in this book that only a portion of the principal's work requires a working knowledge of the curriculum, and that a principal makes only infrequent use of the knowledge acquired in university courses in school administration. So, as a starter, any principal's exam would have to include new components: skill in face to face communication, agility in ad hoc, situation-specific decision making and adaptability to the peripatetic nature of the contemporary principalship—in short, all of the job skills described in Chapter 8.

What kind of examination would measure such things and be able to detect the presence or absence of such skills in a candidate? As indicated earlier, such tests are only now under development, but it is possible that some of the following suggestions may be useful to test developers:

The in-box exercise Some innovations in job-related test design place the test taker in a real-life situation. The examinee is asked to pretend to be the principal of a junior high school, spending a Sunday morning at the office to clear the desk of paperwork before flying off to another city for an important conference. It will be necessary to be absent for three days, with return scheduled for the following Thursday morning. For background, the "principal" is provided a three-page brief on the school—its history, current faculty, the mix of students, some of its major problems—and a paragraph or two on immediate staff superiors in the superintendent's office.

Without using the telephone or seeing anyone, the examinee is asked to handle the mail that accumulated during the preceding week. In the in-box is a short pile of memos, reports, handwritten notes, formal letters, a set of keys with a note attached, a grasshopper taped to a three-by-five card, forms to sign—the usual amalgam of a principal's mail. In the stack are the following:

- ☐ (A handwritten note) "Dear Mrs. P, Clarence is acting up again in my room, and all of our (yours and my) efforts to calm him down have failed. Tomorrow, Monday rather, if he starts up again, I am going to send him to you to deal with. Let me know if I can be of any assistance. Signed, Gladys T."
- ☐ (A letter on the system letterhead) "Florence: When the grade reports are all in for the month of February, would you kindly direct your department heads to prepare a report for my office showing the grade records for your school, by subject, by teacher, for the month of February for each of the preceding five years. Signed, F. Arbuckle, Superintendent"
- ☐ (On the back of the three-by-five card) "Florence, I found this critter in the faculty men's washroom as I left the building Friday. Thought you should know about it. Signed, Charlie" (an assistant principal)
- ☐ (A typewritten memo from a teacher) "Mrs. P, I have been trying my best to work out an accommodation on rooms with Mr. J. He says he needs 201 third period and will not take no for an answer . . . says this is the only time in his schedule when he can begin to rehearse the mixed glee club for the spring festival. I need this room all day long—it's MY ROOM—and I can't give it up even for one period. I know it's the only room at that end of the second floor with a piano, but Mr. J will just have to work something else out. Please get him off my back! Repeat OFF! Signed, Peggy M."
- ☐ (A handwritten note wrapped around the set of keys) "Dear Mrs. P, I found these under a radiator in the hallway leading to the parking lot. I don't know who they belong to. When I left at 5:30 (Friday), I noticed Miss Haskin's Oldsmobile still in the lot. Maybe they're hers. Thought you should be the one to get them back to the right party. Signed, Hubert T." (the janitor)
- ☐ (A stack of purchase vouchers, with a note attached) "Mrs. P, here are the vouchers for the new lunchroom tables, also some for chairs. They need your signature.

> But please note that Jake at central office says that this order will be filled from used tables in the warehouse. *We don't want used furniture,* so I wouldn't sign these if I were you until we clear that up with Jake. Have a good trip. We need these forms in by Tuesday to make this month's allotment. What should I tell Jake? Signed, Sylvia" (clerk in the outer office)

The entire stack contains approximately twenty-five such items. After the two-hour period, the examinee is asked to return the materials with her disposition of each item attached, and any other notes to herself or general instructions that would be helpful on her return Thursday. A panel of test graders drawn from the superintendent's staff then reviews the material and, employing criteria worked out by them and the superintendent in advance, gives the examinee a grade.

Personal conference simulation Since much of a principal's actual managing is conducted in personal conversation, and since one of the middle manager's key tasks is to evaluate subordinates' performance, the examinee is once again asked to pretend to be the principal of a high school preparing for a personal conference with an assistant principal in thirty minutes. A two-page brief on the school and another two-page statement detailing the AP's behavior over the preceding six months are provided. The latter document says the AP has grown lax in insisting on accurate, detailed, on-time lesson plans from the teachers. The principal called the meeting to see if the situation can be remedied.

In another room a former principal, now a member of the superintendent's staff, is preparing to play the role of the AP by studying the same two documents. At the end of the thirty-minute study period, the role playing AP enters the "principal's office" and is greeted by "the principal." The conference between the two of them is scheduled for fifteen minutes, with the "principal" responsible for ending it on schedule. By prearrangement, the interchange is tape-recorded.

Seated off to one side in the "principal's office" are two observers, hired for this purpose from a neighboring school district. Their job is to evaluate the examinee's handling of the AP conference, paying special attention to human relations factors, persuasiveness of argument, professional poise, and the degree of compliance he is able to obtain from the AP. At the close of the conference, the examinee is excused and the role-playing AP joins the two observers to evaluate the examinee.

The presentation simulation To measure an individual's ability to deal with laymen outside the school, it is sometimes helpful to place the examinee in a hypothetical situation of public contact. In this circumstance, the examinee is a junior high school principal; the assignment is to make a ten-minute presentation to the school's P.T.A. Real P.T.A. members are the audience.

The examinee studies material on the history of the school for a half-hour. It describes the problems of the former principal and how he handled them, the particular concerns of parents about the school, and includes a few paragraphs on the political forces at work in the community, including recent communications between the parents' group and the office of the superintendent. During the study period, two P.T.A. members and a member of the superintendent's staff study the same materials. At the close of the study period, these three convene in the "meeting room," greet the examinee role-playing as the principal, and sit down to hear the presentation, again tape-recorded by prearrangement.

The presentation is limited to ten minutes and delivered ex tempore, with the examinee using only the notes taken during the study of the materials. At the close of the ten-minute presentation, the three people role-playing as the "audience," raise questions as if in a public meeting, and the "principal" is asked to handle these questions. At the end of a ten-minute question period, the simulation is concluded and the examinee excused. The three members of the "audience" then discuss the presentation, paying particular attention to such criteria as the "principal's" grasp of the problems, ability to articulate possible remedies, stage presence, poise and speaking ability, and personal fitness as a role model for adolescents. Together they arrive at a grade.

Some informal measures Whether or not these testing devices are employed, there are other approaches a superintendent and staff might use in assessing the *behavioral,* in addition to the intellectual, qualifications of a candidate. These informal approaches are less precise and more difficult to measure than test criteria; they attempt to sketch a profile of an individual by examining his or her personal attitudes toward self and work, particularly those attitudes that refer to professional service, as against merely holding an income-producing, eight-to-three job:

1. Self-organization. Is the person well organized and disciplined in carrying out professional duties? Are resources systematically gathered together and coordinated, are they used properly, and are they maintained and kept in good condition?

2. Closure orientation. Are jobs done? Are they done on time? Are schedules kept and deadlines met? Is there a task orientation and does the individual maintain focus on the task at hand? Is there a steady, patient interest in seeing something completed?

3. Energy deployment. Is there a willingness to exert extra effort, to work longer hours, and to expend more emotional energy in seeing that the enterprise as a whole succeeds? Without being a workaholic, is the individual prepared, when others slacken, to call on reserves of energy and pull more than his or her own weight?

4. Managerial imagination. In any organizing effort (a committee assignment, coaching a drama club, or planning a school dance) when the accepted procedure doesn't work, is the individual capable of coming up with alternative solutions? Is the person willing to take risks and try new procedures?

5. Capacity for growth. Is the individual professionally inquisitive about his or her own work? Is he or she curious about how to make it better? Does the individual respond to instruction and learn from criticism and experience? Is the individual *growing* in present pursuits?

6. Low-profile good nature. Are the individual's emotions under control, and is the ego sturdy enough to accept gracefully the brickbats of subordinates and the critiques of superiors and turn them into occasions for self-appraisal? Is the individual willing for others to receive the credit? In the end, is there a personal warmth that enlivens every encounter?

These suggestions are certainly not quantifiable in the usual statistical sense. Yet they represent character traits that are important in school administrators.

The assessment center These selection procedures, however imaginative, are only estimates of administrative performance. In the late 1970s and early 1980s, these measurement efforts were gathered together, empirically refined, and institutionalized in the assessment center concept—an agency created to measure managerial potential through specially designed exercises.[5]

From a research design standpoint, the questions are straightforward enough:

1. What are the tasks performed by the school principal?
2. What are the skills required for performing these tasks?
3. Do individuals scoring high on these skills perform better in the principalship than individuals scoring low?

Taking the questions in sequence, assessment center architects have approached Question 1 by performing a careful job analysis of the principalship through systematically prepared inquiries to practicing principals, superintendents, teachers, pupils and parents. Once this catalog of activities is refined and edited to remove vagueness, overlap, and redundancy, the job analysts also inquire about the relative importance of these activities, and the amount of time principals spend on them. (This book would be appropriate for this exercise.)

Question 2 is more elusive; unlike tasks, skills are not directly observable in a strict empirical sense, but have to be deduced from overt behavior. According to Paul W. Hersey, Director of the Assessment Center Project of the National Association of Secondary School Principals, continuing research points to twelve skills involved in the principal's job:

1. Problem analysis
2. Judgment
3. Organizational ability
4. Decisiveness
5. Leadership
6. Sensitivity
7. Range of interests
8. Personal motivation
9. Stress tolerance
10. Educational values
11. Oral communication
12. Written communication

What is the working definition of each of these skills, and what would count as evidence that a candidate possessed the skill? Hersey's group asserts that the answers to these questions can be discerned from a candidate's performance in four explicit exercises:

1. Leaderless group activities, in which a group without a designated leader is asked to solve a problem
2. Fact-finding and stress exercises designed to exhibit behavior under pressure (e.g., a simulated speech to the P.T.A.)
3. Paper and pencil "in-basket" tasks (similar to those outlined on pages 243–245)
4. A structured personal interview

Hersey reports

> . . . while completing the assessment exercises, each participant is observed by a specially selected group of assessors who are trained under rigorous standards established by the N.A.S.S.P. In a typical assessment project, 12 participants are observed by a team of six assessors who record behavior relating to the [above] skill dimensions. Each participant's observed behavior and skills are discussed by the team of assessors who reach a consensus regarding performance in all 12 dimensions.
>
> Finally, a comprehensive assessment report is prepared describing strengths, improvement needs, and developmental suggestions for each candidate. This performance summary is then given to the participant during an intense feedback session.[6]

What about Question 3? Do persons with the identified skills actually perform more effectively in administrative roles? Due to the recency of the program's development, the evidence is still coming in. Advocates of the assessment center concept claim that early findings indicate a connection between the twelve skills and effective job performance. In the early 1980s an independent validation study was conducted by a Michigan State University team on the N.A.S.S.P. project. The results of this investigation were positive enough to encourage the Association officers to extend the project and even set accreditation standards for a national chain of such centers—a sign that the movement has come of age.

As assessors have become more sophisticated in listing specific strengths and weaknesses for each candidate, assessment strategists and university trainers have turned to a fourth question: Are the twelve skills learnable and teachable?

If a candidate measures up well in written communication, sensitivity, and personal motivation, but is below average in problem analysis, decisiveness, and stress tolerance, what happens next? Are there instructional sequences or experience assignments that could correct the deficiencies?

This question would have to be answered for each of the twelve skills areas, and assessment theorists and university study teams are currently at work on this project. The Association is developing a satellite system of assessment centers throughout the country, sponsored by a consortium of school districts, universities, and research laboratories. It is an understatement to say that the assessment center approach to administrator selection and training would be frightfully expensive for school districts and university training programs.

Does this approach actually yield more competent school administrators? This question remains to be answered.

PLACING PRINCIPALS

We come finally to the question of school placement. What can superintendents and boards of education learn about the assigning of qualified individuals to particular schools?

We have emphasized in this book that the principalship is a highly political job. But this can be understood two ways. On the one hand, the recent rise of community awareness on matters of educational policy means that a new principal must be politically acceptable to the school attendance area and especially to the parents of the school's youngsters. The superintendent must avoid alienating community people in appointing a new principal and must provide the new appointee with a receptive work environment.

But the principalship is political in a more sophisticated sense; the principal encounters powerful constituencies *other than* the parents and laymen surrounding the school, and must have the political know-how to work with these other groups. There are few tests of this ability except prior experience in mobilizing other people in a group enterprise. Accordingly, political adroitness may be one of those skills best learned on the job. Since the politics of any principalship is unique, perhaps the skill must be learned on a particular job. Job-specific political ability may not be transferrable to other sites.

Closely related to political skill are the personality factors that influence the administrator's work. These traits, some of which have been touched on in previous sections, are perhaps unteachable; they are subtle personality elements that have been shaped from childhood. Just as the politics of a given principalship is idiosyncratic, so are the personality requirements for each school. A lax, doin'-our-own-thing faculty may require a firm, take-charge type whereas a well disciplined, smooth-running "factory" may benefit from a more flexible, person-oriented individual.

This observation leads to a final question of site-person matching. In small school districts, such meticulous principal placement is perhaps not possible; in these situations, the next available principalship typically goes to the most qualified individual who has been waiting the longest. In larger systems, however, the site of the principalship vacancy may need some special study. The special needs of the school, the entrenchment of old-timers, the preparedness for change and new leadership—the superintendent should study these and other variables to "make book" on a specific opening. When these data are in, and their significance has been weighed by the appointing officers, only then should the screening process begin. By this time, the appointing officers should have also digested the data on the candidates: their credentials, job histories, abilities in test situations, and the personal factors revealed in their interviews and conferences with system officers, including members of the board of education.

When the particular requirements of the site are fully assessed and compared to the special qualifications of the candidates, the empirical method has reached its limits; the next step is judgmental. One candidate is chosen over the others, and a new administrative career begins.

THINGS TO DO AND THINK ABOUT

1. In your educational experience, both as a student and educator, what do you believe are the primary behavioral requirements for the position of school principal? Make a list of these requirements, and for each, write a short paragraph on how such behavior might be taught in a principal training program.
2. In this chapter, examples were given of the In-box Exercise, the Personal Conference Simulation, and the Presentation Simulation. You are a test reviewer and are asked to rate these three testing techniques for *job-relatedness*. What is your analysis?
3. Schedule an interview with a school district superintendent to solicit his or her views on the ideal training program for prospective principals. Write up the results of this interview and share it with your classmates.
4. Schedule personal interviews with five or six school principals to determine what their own training programs were like and which elements of these programs best prepared them for the job as it is actually performed. Write up a summary of this small survey, and compare it with your classmates' evaluations of your own program.

5. In this chapter, we described some informal measures of administrative potential. How do you personally rate on these measures? Mark yourself from one to ten on each of these characteristics. Are there other measures that should be added to the list?
6. Schedule an interview with the president of your local school board to discuss the board's policies for principal selection and placement. Specifically, how do they evaluate the superintendent's ability to fit the right person to the right principalship? What elements of the site and of the candidate command the greatest share of their attention?
7. Talk with some teachers, students, parents, librarians, janitors, and one or two upper-level school district administrators (e.g., an assistant superintendent). What are the expectations of each of these groups regarding how a "good" principal should behave? Do these expectations differ significantly?

NOTES

1. The new discipline of *semiotics* (the study of signs) may be of some help in this endeavor. One scholar defines it as "the discipline of studying everything that can be used to lie." More generously, it is the study of nonverbal signals we send to one another through the way we dress, the cars we drive, the houses we live in, the magazines we read, and the toys (stereos, sailboats, skiing equipment) we play with. What we believe we mean to other people is revealed, in some small measure, in our life style. See Maya Pines, "What's the Real Message of *Casablanca*," *New York Times*, September 28, 1982, p. 20.
2. For a review of this evidence and the studies that have produced it, see W. L. Boyd and R. L. Crowson, "The Changing Conception and Practice of Public School Administration," in *Review of Research in Education*, Vol 9, D. Berliner, ed. (Washington, D.C.: A.E.R.A. 1981), pp. 321–326, 355–356. Copyright 1981, American Educational Research Association, Washington, D.C.
3. Gordon A. Donaldson, Jr., "Rx for School Leadership," *Phi Delta Kappan*, February 1982, Volume 63, Number 6, pp. 400–401.
4. Joan Shoemaker and Hugh W. Fraser, "What Principals Can Do," *Phi Delta Kappan*, November 1981, Volume 63, Number 3, pp. 178–182.
5. The technique is reported to have originated with the Germans, but during World War II, American intelligence officers used it in intensive sessions at a secret site near McLean, Va. to screen candidates for sensitive spy operations. Later, private industry adapted the concept to selecting managers.
6. "The NASSP Assessment Center Project—Validation, New Developments," a brochure published in 1982 by the National Association of Sec-

ondary School Principals, pp. 1–2. For more information on assessment centers, write to Paul W. Hersey, Director, NASSP Assessment Center Project, 1904 Association Drive, Reston, Virginia 22091.

PART 4

Instructional Case Studies

As a conclusion we offer a series of cases depicting principals in action. In these episodes, administrative behavior is presented in an unedited form, allowing you to study managerial decision making in the real-life atmosphere of a school.

The cases in Part 4 have been drawn from the daily logs we kept in the course of gathering data for this book. These real schools and people have been given fictional names, and the situations portrayed are actual events, with the dialogue sometimes reproduced verbatim.

Following each case is a set of questions designed to help you analyze the administrative behavior exhibited in the case—specifically, the situation encountered by the principal and the response to it. In anticipation of these case-specific questions, you may want to keep in mind the following general questions:

1. What is going on in this episode? Who are the chief actors and what do they want?
2. What forces influence the flow of events? Are there motives at work? How much of the agenda is hidden, how much open and overt?
3. What outcomes are produced by the principal's behavior? Are these the intended outcomes?
4. What would you have done in this situation? Why?

With the above as prologue, Chapter 10 offers two *contextual* cases, so labeled because they provide an extended narrative on the managerial environment within which the principal works. They depict principaling behavior throughout the work day.

Chapter 11 offers six *episodic* cases, so named because each portrays a management episode in dealing with a particular situation. In these cases, the principal confronts a specific problem which requires making a decision.

10

Contextual Cases

CASE ONE

Attendance: Keeping 'Em in School

Mondale High School serves an all-black student body in the inner city. A large percentage of the students live in a public housing project whose high-rise buildings march in a straight line southward from the school's southern boundary. Many good students from Mondale's attendance area have chosen to attend other high schools, either through open admission transfers or to take advantage of magnet programs. The principal at Mondale, Trudy Green, is in her first year. A veteran of inner city elementary schools, she is still learning the ropes of secondary school administration.

It was Green's habit to spend a few minutes at the start of each day sitting at her desk reviewing her schedule. This morning, in the third week of November, she reached for two folders. One was marked "Security," the other "Student Attendance." Opening the security folder she saw a copy of her recent memo to the deputy superintendent. It began with the sentence, "We did *not* have a riot at Mondale High School today." She was referring to a situation in which too many students had arrived at the lunchroom at the same time. Too few seats, too long lines, and too close quarters had led to pushing, shoving and food throwing.

As a result of this incident, Green had developed a proposal for a new lunchroom security system which she wanted to try out on her faculty. Since students' ID cards indicate their scheduled lunch period, students would be required to show their IDs when entering the cafeteria. By controlling entry, the lunchroom would be restricted to those scheduled to be there, and there would be enough seats for everyone. Students at Mondale also skipped classes and study hall during the four lunch periods. If they did not congregate in the lunchroom or leave campus for one of the nearby fast food restaurants, where would they go? The second part of the Green plan was designed to take care of this problem. A general study hall would be open and available during each period of the day in Room 147. Although students might not go there voluntarily, at least there would be a place to send students wandering about the school, particularly during lunch time.

As Green reviewed her notes, she was mentally preparing for a meeting of her faculty union committee; this was the first group to hear the plan formally. The committee had been discussing various problems with school security since the year began. Now the winter holidays were approaching and seasonal excitement often spurred disturbances in classrooms and hallways. The committee was ready for some serious discussions of this problem, and Green speculated that the lunchroom situation was the place to begin.

When the committee meeting began later that morning, she put the plan before the committee members. They discussed it in detail for about twenty minutes, finally concluding that it should get a trial and that perhaps the best time to start the new system was after the holidays.

With that out of the way, Green spoke more generally about security, sharing with the committee members her concern over the effectiveness of study halls as holding pens for students not attending their specified classes. In particular, she was anxious about problems in supervising these study halls. Students did not show up according to their schedules, but then neither did the teachers! Repeatedly, she checked into study halls to find the teacher arriving late or not at all. Furthermore, even teachers assigned to hall supervision did not demand that students produce ID cards. Once again, Green heard herself saying, "Every teacher in this school should be involved with hall supervision. When people look the other way while students freely roam the halls, there are going to be repercussions within the classrooms. The mood of the students has changed." Green reminisced, "The rebellion we faced a few years ago has diminished. They seem to be more willing to comply with the rules, so now it's up to the teachers to insist that students meet the rules and regulations within the school."

The meeting was now moving down a familiar track. The teachers responded to her argument with a well-worn refrain. "These students think that they can come into a class whenever they get around to it. They fool around in the halls and then wander into class ten, fifteen, even twenty minutes late. It does not make sense to interrupt the entire class to ask each straggler where he has been and whether he has a pass. Most teachers think that we should shut the door when the bell rings and get on with teaching those who have made the effort to come to class on time."

"But where are those students to go?" Green asked. "I need to be able to count on conscientious supervision of hallways and study areas. I cannot encourage students to roam free on campus."

This was countered by the expected round of questions. "What about those security guards? What do they do all day? Aren't they supposed to supervise the hallways? Do the teachers have to be responsible for everything?"

The discussion wearied Green. In most areas, she enjoyed easy relations with her faculty, but this issue seemed to be a dead end. Rather than proceed through each predictable point in the script, she raised the next item on the agenda—an item involving basketball games. The following discussion was desultory and aimless, so Green brought the meeting to a close.

As Green said goodbye to her colleagues returning to their classrooms, she noted she had a few minutes before her next appointment. She looked at the student attendance folder. Like the security issue, the attendance problem provoked feelings of frustration and helplessness. She tried to describe her discomfort, sharing her thoughts with a visitor. "We want the students to come to school. We need the state funds that are allocated on the basis of school attendance. But then when they are in school, we cannot seem to get them to class. We need them to stay in school, even if they do not go to class. Punish them for cutting by suspending them, and attendance drops. Truly enforced, it would drop a great deal. But if we can't send them home, and they won't go to class, then what are we to do with them?"

Green opened the folder. She had been collecting various items concerning student attendance since the deputy superintendent informed her that she was expected to improve student attendance this year. She reviewed the file's contents as she waited for her appointment to arrive.

There was a chart of "Average Daily Attendance by High Schools, 1977."[1] Based on a national survey of high school principals, the chart reported the year's average student attendance:

Percent of Average Daily Attendance	Percent of Schools
Under 59	0.0
60 to 69.9	1.0
70 to 79.9	5.0
80 to 89.9	21.0
90 to 94.9	55.0
95 and above	17.0

From the same publication, she had also reproduced a chart entitled "Drop Out Rate of High Schools 1977, 1965."[2]

Percent of Drop Outs	1977	1965
None	5.0	8.0
Under 9.9	62.0	54.0
10–24.9	28.0	27.0
25–35.9	3.0	7.0
More than 36	2.0	3.0

Green reviewed the attendance figures at Mondale High School for the current school year (1977–78).

	% Attendance
September	87.4
October	85.4
November	83.6

In comparison with the national figures, Mondale's attendance was in the lowest third. The drop out rate at Mondale was one of her major concerns. Only one-third of each freshman class reached the senior year. A prospective dropout was signaled by poor attendance. At Mondale, the attendance of many students was so poor that 10 percent of the school's 2700 students were currently classified as chronically truant.

Attendance was taken each day during a special homeroom period. Absent students were listed by name the following day on an attendance list. About 400 students appeared on this list each day. To maintain these records, the school had an Attendance Office staffed by thirteen office workers with eleven student aides.

Green was further troubled because she knew these official Mondale figures only scratched the surface. Since the start of the school year she had conducted classroom observations of several teachers each week. On each visit she had inspected the teacher's class book which logged student attendance as well as marks on school work. She discovered that class attendance was lower than school attendance might suggest. The teachers with high and low attendance records in their homerooms had been targeted for observation and interviews related to the attendance issue.

In the meantime she had established two general approaches to the issue of student attendance. She would initiate programs that rewarded students who came to school; in this way, students might stay for four years and come more often. She would also initiate programs that tried to contact and bring back to school those who were chronically truant.

Finally, she looked at the information she had compiled on students with perfect attendance. For the first 10 weeks of school, there were 73 ninth-graders, 69 tenth-graders, 50 eleventh-graders, and 43 twelfth-graders. Her plan was to reward students at the end of the tenth week, again at the twentieth week, and again in June. All seniors with perfect attendance would receive a free prom bid worth about thirty dollars. At each other grade level there would be a drawing for a prize. She planned to conduct a drawing today, based on the attendance records of the first ten weeks. Ten dollars in cash or credit in the school store would be awarded to a student in each grade level drawn from the pool of students with 100% attendance. Another drawing would be held after the twentieth week. If a student's name was drawn after the second ten weeks who also had perfect attendance during the first ten weeks, the award would be doubled.

Green's secretary interrupted to tell her that her appointment had arrived. The secretary showed in a sophomore girl, a reporter for the school paper. Green explained the plan to reward school attendance. She asked the girl to write an article about the plan and leave blank the names of the ten week winners. "We will draw the winners' names this afternoon, and I will pass them along to you when your article is ready." She confirmed with the student that the article would appear in the next issue of the school paper.

When the student left, Green checked her attendance file for the list of teacher interviews she had targeted. She looked immediately at the name of Thomas Grey, whose homeroom attendance average was a startling 58 percent. Putting the file away, she decided to observe his class during the next period and get his views on the attendance problems.

Upon leaving her office, Green turned a corner and encountered a girl in the otherwise empty corridor. "No class?" Green asked. The girl explained that she was scheduled for study hall that period. "Which room?" Green asked. The girl replied that she did not know, she had never been to the study hall. Green waited as the girl consulted her schedule and then sent her on her way to the study hall.

Green then headed for the mathematics department office. The teacher, Thomas Grey, was just finishing his preparation period. Her plan was to meet him in the office and walk along with him to his Pre-Algebra class scheduled for the next period. When Green arrived at the departmental office, she saw Grey talking on the telephone. She went back into the hallway to wait for him. The passing bell rang. Suddenly the halls were filled with activity. Ms. Mathis, president of the Parent, Teacher, Student Association greeted her and they talked for a few minutes. Mrs. Mathis said that she was involved in resolving a conflict between two parents active in the Association. Mrs. Mathis had arranged a meeting, but neither parent showed up. "I'm afraid they are still bickering," she said sadly.

Green saw that Grey was off the phone. She gestured to

him to join her in the hall, calling to him to bring his class book. Green waited for him in the hall as he looked for his book. A newcomer to the faculty, Grey had been assigned in October as a Full Time Substitute Teacher in 10th grade science and math. His classes were made up of slower students. Green had a hunch the poor attendance in his homeroom was related in some way to his students' ability level. She suspected also that these students were also "over-age," a system term used to refer to students whose courses are at the underclass level, while their age group is at the upperclass level. Often these students register for school in September, but do not show up after the first week or so. Still, they must be registered, programmed and placed in classes. If too many students in this category show up, it is necessary to open a new homeroom unit, and employ another teacher to handle it. If this had occurred with this group, it would explain why Grey's position was created and activated in mid-October; it would also help to explain the poor attendance Grey was experiencing.

Grey joined Green in the hall and they walked together toward his classroom. He handed her his class book, but said nothing. They entered the classroom a few minutes late. No students had yet arrived. Grey began to complain that he could not put any of his equipment in the classroom cabinets because he had no keys. He also wanted a key to the classroom door. Green explained that keys to many cabinets were lost when the school was rehabilitated the previous year. She suggested he could put a padlock with a chain through the cabinet handles, or he might go out and buy a lock and chain, and give the bill to the business manager to get reimbursed. At this suggestion, Grey appeared to back away from the subject and lost interest. Rather than continue, Green carried the class book to a seat in the back and began to look through it as she waited for students to arrive.

Green knew of an outreach program for over-age truants soon to be initiated in the nearby housing project. She suspected that most of Grey's students were over-age, and saw an opportunity to identify some of them for this program. She searched through the book for addresses of over-age students with poor attendance living in the project.

She noticed that some students had not been in class since September or October. She made a written note that these students "should be dropped," rather than carried on the record. To Green's surprise, most of the flagrant truants turned out to be girls, and although she identified several truants whose address was in the project, she found only four who were over-age.

By this time eleven students had arrived. Grey had written a homework assignment on the board. He initiated class by asking questions regarding yesterday's homework assignment. He called on students by name, asking them about the problems. Green glanced at the grades and noted that more than half the students had received a D or F for the first grading period.

Grey wrote some problems on the board. As the students turned their attention to these, he moved among them checking their work and answering questions individually. It was soon clear that the problems on the board were beyond the students' ability. Grey commented, "Most of you need practice in reducing fractions." He promised to give them "some work sheets on that." He asked several more questions of individual students, and then began a mini-lesson for the class on long division. He gave some long division problems, but most students did not know how to proceed. The class ended with Grey still trying to explain long division. He commented to the students as they gathered their things and edged toward the door, "I see you all need more practice on this kind of thing."

Green joined Grey by the door and returned the attendance book. As they walked into the hall, one student remained in the classroom, slumped at his desk sleeping. Green asked Grey about tardiness in his classes. He responded by saying that in the class just observed there was not much tardiness, but in some other classes tardiness was rampant. He added that there was a high degree of absenteeism in all his classes. Students seemed to be intelligent and seemed to grasp concepts explained on a one-to-one basis, but with so much absenteeism it was impossible to establish the continuity a course demands. He was aware of teaching material below course level, but he found that they really needed experience with basic math. Grey estimated that his sophomore students in pre-algebra were really functioning at or below the seventh grade level of mathematics.

Regarding tardiness, he said that when he first came to Mondale in October, he would challenge students who came late to class. Most students balked at this, and simply turned and walked out of class. He tired of being left standing there and decided he wasn't going to challenge them anymore. "If they want to come in late, they can come in late. If they want to wander in and wander out, they can do that. I can't concern myself with that," he explained. By this time, Green and Grey had reached a fork in the corridor. Grey turned left and said good-bye. Green turned right, proceeding to the lunchroom.

Green ate lunch with two assistant principals and a counselor. She explained to them that she needed to know more about faculty gripes concerning school policy. They decided to ask each department to make a list of complaints and forward them to her. She would respond to the most widespread complaints at the next faculty in-service day.

After lunch, Green returned to her office for her next appointment, Ms. Brown, a teacher whose homeroom attendance was excellent. As Brown entered and took a seat, Green began by mentioning the program for over-age, chronic truants who lived in the housing project. "Do you have any students you would suggest for this program?" she asked. Before Brown could respond, Green explained the program more fully and then began to share some of her own observations about the absentee issue. "You know, I have found no pattern of chronically absent students. I had thought that most truants would be over-age, but this doesn't seem to be the case."

Brown then offered the names of several students she believed would qualify for the program. Consulting the teacher's class book, Green picked out the name of a sixteen-year-old girl. "Do you have any contact with this student?" she asked. Brown explained that the student had a small baby and the baby was ill. Often the student took the baby to her grandmother, who lived in another part of the city. In Brown's opinion, this student was not very happy about coming to school. Her life revolved around the world outside school.

Green said there was no leverage in getting students to come to school once they were over sixteen years of age. She asked Brown exactly what she did to get students to come to class. A glance at Brown's class book had informed Green that few students were chronically absent from her classes.

Brown explained that when a student was absent, she phoned the parents immediately. She did this for any student who did not come to her homeroom or any class. She said that in general students who did not come to homeroom were not likely to be in school. "Students do their best to get to their homeroom if they are somewhere in the school, even when they cut their other classes."

Green praised Brown for her students' excellent attendance record. Then she asked, "How do you handle tardies in your classes?" Brown responded that she was very firm on the issue of tardies. "I always start my classes on time," she explained. "If students come to my class late, I embarrass them by asking them directly in front of the class why they were late. They do not like the fuss or the moment of embarrassment, so they make sure they get to class on time to avoid the unpleasantness. This was my policy from the start of the year. I stress it over and over and am continually firm about promptness in getting to class. You have to start this in September."

Green asked Brown how she explained her policy to students, to which Brown responded by saying that she tells her students, "I am here on time and so it is up to you also to be here on time." She also stressed, "Students only have forty minutes to accomplish their tasks, and if students are not present for the full forty minutes, they are losing valuable time that should be applied to course work. If I can meet my responsibility to be in class on time, then they can meet their responsibility to be in class on time." Also, she had a policy that "three tardies are converted into an absence." She emphasized that she followed this rule. Green said there were so many tardies in the school that "it seems something has to be done."

Green complimented the teacher on her classroom manner. "You know, whenever I go by your classroom, I see you are actively involved in working with students. It seems to me that where teachers are active, students get involved." Brown replied, "I think that I am able to convey my concern for my students to them. I let them know that I have been through the same thing they are going through. I came from a similar environment to theirs. I know how hard it is to meet the requirements of school when you have competing interests. I tell them that I know how hard it is, but that even though it is hard they must meet their responsibilities within the school."

Green told her she thought it was right to show concern for one's students. "Students will respond if they feel that the teacher is concerned about them." Brown replied that in the time she had been at Mondale she had never once been threatened by a student. She found with most problems, the best way to handle it is to contact the parents. "I call up the parents and ask them to come to the school. I tell them what the problem is and in almost every case the student straightens up," she explained.

Green then asked her about her grading system and how students achieve in her classes. Brown responded that most of the students who come to her class "don't know how to read when they walk in the door." For this reason, she teaches them through materials other than the textbook. "This is important if you want to reach them," she told Green. "Because they don't read, I do a lot of work with charts, I write a lot on the board, and I work orally with the course material.

"One of my biggest problems," she offered, "is during the last period of the day. My sophomores watch the older students, many of whom are in work study or on shorter days, leave school at the end of the seventh or eighth period. They resent the fact that they've got to stay for extra periods as underclassmen. This makes it hard to teach classes because the students are restless. They cut a lot at the end of the day. It is hard to motivate students during ninth period when they look out the door and see the upperclassmen going home.

"There are specific students who just resist these late classes," she continued. "They just don't want to come. I have a student whose mother has been to see me several times. Then there was one student who came into class, I told him the rules I run my class by, and I haven't seen him since. He heard the rules, but instead of meeting the challenge he just decided not to bother."

Green told Brown that she was very happy to have her at

Mondale. Earlier in the year it looked as if she would be replaced. A teacher with more seniority whose position had been eliminated in a school elsewhere was given the option of moving to Mondale. She refused the assignment, so Brown was able to stay on.

During the next several weeks, faculty met in departmental meetings and drew up lists of complaints which they turned in to Green. Items which pertained to the attendance issue included the following:

1. Teachers from several departments wanted to send tardy students away from class to an office where they would be disciplined.
2. Teachers complained that students who were not scheduled for a class loitered in the hallways during school hours. This problem was greatest at the end of the day when upperclassmen were leaving school.

Green considered the first complaint to be the more serious. In her opinion the problem of the students in the hall was exaggerated. After several spot checks throughout the day, she was unable to find many students congregating in hallways.

The tardy issue, however, raised serious concerns of enforcing the board of education policy. Her understanding of the board policy was that it was not permissible to bar students from class unless they had been formally suspended from school. Sending tardy students away from class effectively barred them from class. Furthermore, she realized that teachers were lowering academic grades on the basis of school attendance. This, too, violated board policy. The rules stated that absent students were allowed to make up work; in fact, it was the teacher's responsibility to help them do so.

At the next faculty meeting in March, Green informed the teachers she had reviewed minutes of both department head meetings and the union committee and learned that the issue of tardiness has "always been with us." Her plan was to organize a committee to deal with both this problem and also with school security.

She explained her position, "A lot of people say that students who are tardy should be given either a study hall or detention. But who is going to supervise these activities? I have been knocking my head against the wall on this issue for a long time. If there are any on the staff who want to join the committee and knock their heads against the wall on the same issue, I would be glad to have you around. I don't know the answer. If you lock the door, the students stay in the hall and there is nobody to supervise them there. But not all teachers have this problem. There are some teachers who are small in stature and with little teaching experience who nevertheless seem to be conducting their classes without either absences or much tardiness. How many of you have walked in late yourself? Maybe we need to take a good look at ourselves."

She continued her speech. "You cannot bar students from class because of tardiness. If you do, this is in effect a suspension and all suspensions must now be cleared through the office of the deputy superintendent. When you bar students from class without going through the suspension process you ignore student rights." Finally, she concluded, "Frankly, I feel that we have come to a dead end on this tardiness issue. Unless somebody has some original thinking about it, I cannot imagine what else can be done."

In early April the faculty-student Committee on Tardiness and Security met in the social room of the school. Each teacher had been asked to bring a student to the meeting who was often tardy, so that the students' point of view could be heard. Green was the first person to arrive. The assistant principal in charge of security arrived a moment later with a female teacher. Two male teachers arrived shortly thereafter. A female teacher joined them and said that she had to arrange for someone to cover her class. The assistant principal went to "see who's around" so that they could "look in on this woman's class." Another male teacher arrived, joking, "I really hate to be tardy to the tardy meeting." Green commented that "I hope some of our students show up." After a few more minutes of casual talk about a recent school dance, the meeting was called to order by Green.

Initially, the teachers shared some comments on why students did not show up at the meeting. Each teacher said that his or her "invited guest" had agreed to attend. Then they began to speak about the problem itself and what they thought should be done about it.

One said that he did not feel he could do anything about the chronic tardies in his classes. "Our goal should be to get the bulk of the students here on time. We should not worry about the chronic tardies." He also suggested that a bell be rung at 7:50 A.M. "Now students think they should enter the building at the 8:00 A.M. bell and get on to their rooms as soon as they can make it," he explained. "If they rang a bell at 7:50, that would be like a warning bell. Then the 8:00 bell would be understood as the time when students are supposed to be *in* class, not on their way to class."

The assistant principal said she thought students should be admitted to class up to ten minutes after the 8:00 bell. She said, "You meet the same people coming to school late every day." Another teacher said that there should be people in the Attendance Office who keep records and follow up on the tardies. "They should do something if students are tardy. Right now nothing happens if they are tardy and the students know it. So they just get to class as soon as they find it convenient."

Green observed that when she visits classes, she does not see that much tardiness. "Maybe I am in the wrong place at the wrong time, but in most instances there are very few tardies. When students arrive tardy, in most cases the teachers seem to ignore this." She asked, "Where is the problem with tardiness? Absenteeism I can see as a problem, because only half of the students are in the classes I visit. Tardiness doesn't seem to be a problem."

One teacher volunteered that first period was the worst time for tardies. She again raised the idea of a 7:50 bell. Another added, "Tardiness itself is not the problem, it is the disruption of the class that occurs when the teacher has to go back and explain everything. When students come in late, they've missed the instruction about how to go about the day's work."

Another commented that what the school really needed was a Tardy Office. Tardy students would have to go there to get a pass. When they brought the pass to class, they would be admitted. Green asked him, "What does that accomplish?" He replied, "If students know that they have to get a pass, then they might get out of the halls and get into their classroom, rather than facing a trip to the Tardy Office." The assistant principal wondered, "What do you do with the tardy passes when you get them? What do the teachers do with them when the tardies start bringing them into the classroom?"

Another teacher replied, "You keep track of them. If any student has too many tardy passes, then you contact the parents and say that this is a consistent chronic problem of tardiness." Green asked, "I wonder whether teachers would bother reporting tardies to a tardy office? They don't report cuts now, so why would they report tardies?"

A female teacher said, "They should already have a pass when they arrive tardy, so what would be accomplished by requiring a special tardy pass? The pass system we have now is not being utilized. What we should do is send late students outside the building until the next class period starts."

Green explained, "The board of education does not allow teachers to bar students or fail them for reasons of attendance. It is the teacher's responsibility to provide make-up work for students who miss class work and instruction. Tardiness is part of the whole attendance problem. You cannot bar students from class simply because they are tardy." Then she added, "We can sit and talk about all of these extra amounts of paperwork and so on, but does this really address the problem? The real problem is how to reach the freshmen. Why is it that only about 60 percent of the freshmen come to school?"

The teachers responded in unison that teachers want to

lock the door when the bell rings because it is effective. "When you only allow the students who come on time to stay, students learn they cannot come late to class."

The assistant principal asked, "Doesn't a student have to have an objective to come to class in the first place? Shouldn't we be concerned about the students who don't even try to come?" A teacher said, "What we are really talking about is re-educating students to new attitudes. I have students who tell me there is no advantage for them to come to school and do school work. They tell me that they don't need to know how to read because they are going to have a baby and go on ADC or welfare. That is going to be their ticket. Their ticket is not going to be through school and learning skills in school."

Green told them, "I'm disturbed that kids go to the elementary schools, but many do not make the transition to the high school. I want to know why that is. Why is it that students who have been regular in attendance in the eighth grade don't come to the ninth grade?"

The group turned to this wider problem. One explanation offered was the structure of both schools. In this system, many eighth graders are placed in an elementary school. Students only have one classroom teacher. In high school, where instruction is departmentalized, students move from teacher to teacher every forty minutes. One member of the group voiced the view that one problem with freshmen is that "they want the teacher to be mother." Another says that the student is much more anonymous in the high school: "In the eighth grade they have been known for years by the teachers, other students, and the administration." Green said that something must be done to help more students make the transition to the high school.

Another told the group it was her experience that many of the students do not understand the concept of separate classes with attendance for each. "They don't understand that they have to be in attendance at each class. They think that if you are in the building that is enough."

The assistant principal suggested, "Maybe we need to set up something for longer homeroom periods so that teachers can use this time to build relationships with students."

Suddenly they realized that they had no more time for the meeting. They quickly decided on a 7:50 A.M. bell, and that the school door would be locked at 8:10.

* * * * *

In the preceding January, Green had sent a list of overage truants to the Director of the Student Outreach Program in the housing project. By March, Green learned that fourteen Mondale students with good attendance had joined the program as CETA employees. Their job was to contact truant students from the list Green had supplied.

In early April, Green received a report from the program's director, explaining what had been done with the names and what had been learned. First, a letter was sent to each of the ten students. Five did not respond. Of those who did not respond, three were reached by phone. The other two, it was later learned, never received the letter because the address had not included an apartment number. Follow-up on the five "no response" students revealed the following information.

- ☐ One student had moved; there was no forwarding address.
- ☐ Two households were reached by phone. The students were not there. Word was left for the students to phone the project office.
- ☐ A fourth student was pregnant and uninterested in attending school.
- ☐ A fifth family had moved to another building in the housing complex.

Students who responded to the initial letter were contacted personally. In one case, the mother said that her daughter was still in school. The mother was unaware that she was truant.

In another case, a male student told the project representative that he wanted to come back to Mondale "as soon as possible." It was recommended that he be reinstated forthwith. In the third case, the mother said that the girl "goes to school every day." She claimed that there was no problem with her daughter's attendance.

A fourth student was found to be watching television and babysitting her niece. She told the representative that teachers at Mondale are "pests." The representative recommended to the director that they continue to contact this girl and talk to her mother, if possible, about counseling for the girl.

As an innovative development, a teaching outpost was opened. Classes in English, Social Studies, and Mathematics were offered during the day in an apartment on the second floor of the project. Teachers from Mondale went there to teach these classes. The idea was to offer a casual atmosphere in an attempt to reduce truancy and increase attendance for some students.

In mid-May the administrators at Mondale prepared the Administrative Bulletin for the following school year. Several items spoke to attendance issues. Under the heading "Classroom Management" was the following:

> "No student should be denied admission to class even if he is tardy or without a pass."
>
> "Teachers are responsible for the students assigned to them during class, division, study, and other extracurricular activities."
>
> Under the heading "Use of Passes":
>
> "Students must have an official pass to be sent from a room into the hall during class time."

A memo entitled "Attendance Office Information and Procedures" had also been drafted. The duties of the Attendance Office were listed:

> "To confer with students and parents, personally, by phone and letter."
>
> "To issue early dismissals."
>
> "To conduct attendance checks for parents, teachers and social workers."
>
> "To call home for ill students."
>
> "To issue a daily attendance bulletin."
>
> "To keep records on student attendance."

Also listed were duties the office "does not perform":

> "To serve as a detention room."
>
> "To handle cases of misbehavior."
>
> "To accommodate unprepared students."
>
> "To bar students from classrooms."

The draft also contained the following statement:

> "The only legal means by which a student can be kept out of school is through suspension following all guidelines of the board of education. A bar is an illegal act, serving no useful purpose. To bar a student from the class he has not been attending is impossible because we have no detention center. To bar a student from all his classes, pending a parent conference, only causes his absence from classes he has been attending."

A few weeks before school closed for the year, Green and her assistant principal in charge of security completed plans for a truant counseling program. Students with a history of truancy would be given a code 500 when their schedules were programmed. These students would be placed in a special homeroom. A letter would be sent to these students asking them to come for counseling during the second week of school.

Green also compared the attendance records of freshmen to their eighth grade records. She found that students who came from a departmentalized junior high school had a superior attendance record, indicating that the structural similarities might account for the better attendance record. These students were already accustomed to switching from teacher to teacher. She decided to initiate a program bringing freshmen and their parents to an orientation day before the school year began. She hoped the high school's structure could be explained to freshmen during this session.

STUDY QUESTIONS

1. How does the principal define the nature of the problem in this case? How do teachers define it? What would *you* delineate as the central issue to be resolved?
2. Review the actions taken and decisions made by Principal Green. Evaluate the effectiveness of her activity to date. What would you have done differently? What should be done next?
3. What forces outside of the high school seem to be serious barriers to an improvement in attendance? Can anything be done about these? Review some of the steps taken by Principal Green (e.g., an "outreach" program), and suggest additional options or ideas.
4. How do you explain the decision to ring a bell at 7:50 A.M., and lock the school door at 8:10? What's likely to happen as a consequence? What would you have done about the problem of student tardiness?

NOTES

1. David R. Bryne, Susan A. Hines, and Loyd E. McCleary, *The Senior High School Principalship, Vol. 1 The National Survey*. Publication of the National Association of Secondary School Principals. 1904 Association Drive, Reston, Virginia. 22091, 1978, p. 40.
2. Ibid. p. 41.

CASE TWO

Transfer and Tension in a City School

Hawthorne High is situated close to the city's suburbs and has a suburban ambiance and atmosphere. The student body, however, is diverse, reflecting the changing population of the neighborhood. About a fifth of the students are black, another fifth Hispanic, another fifth from third-world countries such as Libya, Syria, India, and mostly Korea. The remaining students, about a fourth of the total, are white.

In recent years, the population had been shrinking, and the Board of Education had designated it a receiving school in a system-wide plan to balance enrollments in the schools. The Stabilization Plan, as it was called, specified that if the enrollment in any high school exceeded a certain designated capacity figure, then students in excess of that number would be given the option of transferring to receiving schools of their choice, with free bus transportation provided by the district. Hawthorne was expected to attract many of these students. Moreover, the socioeconomic status of the student body, although changing in ethnic and racial composition, remained middle class. Students showed a high degree of acculturation to middle class values, used standard English as the common language of the school, and worked hard in their academic, college-prep programs. The occasional presence of inner city patterns, such as gang slogans on an outside wall, was dismissed as the work of "outsiders."

After several months, it appeared that the Stabilization Plan was working. A sizable group of students, many of them of high academic caliber, were transferring to Hawthorne. By the second year into the plan, more than 15 percent of the student body were taking the bus to Hawthorne from their homes, often many miles away.

When the plan was first initiated, some black parents

filed suit against the Board of Education claiming that it discriminated against black students. Since the all-black schools were the most overcrowded, it turned out that it was always black students—never Hispanic, Asian or white—who were expected to be the guinea pigs of the scheme and accept the inconvenience of being bused many miles each day to stabilize the schools. After many months of study, the judge ruled that the plan was acceptable as long as the Board of Education provided transportation to schools that were of equal quality to the originally assigned schools. Nevertheless, transportation did represent a problem for some of the incoming students. They were expected to catch a bus at their neighborhood school at 6:30 A.M., ride to another high school, and then transfer to a second bus for the final ride to Hawthorne. The tedium of the twice-a-day trips made student riders restless, as expected. Accordingly, the superintendent's office employed aides to ride the buses to maintain order.

One morning, Charles Coleman, principal of Hawthorne, was informed by one of the aides that she was having trouble controlling the students; they were playing their radios loudly and using "a lot of profanity." Coleman sympathized and told her that he would set up a meeting with all students in the transfer program, together with all the bus aides, to talk over the problem.

Coleman left his office to tour the corridors and courtyards of the school. On the way he encountered a tall, handsome male dressed in a three-piece suit and walking with a quiet, self-assured manner. He might have been mistaken for a teacher or administrator. Coleman, however, knew he was a student who was late for class.

"Mr. North," Coleman addressed him, "you know, you need to be in class to get the material."

"I'm on my way now," North replied.

Coleman sent the youth on his way and then stopped by "counselors row," a string of offices used by the guidance staff. To one of them he said, "You know, that fellow North aspires to get a Ph.D., but he doesn't seem to see the steps toward that goal which he must take. He seems to think that being careful about your appearance is the ticket. See if you can have a talk with him. Get him to see that a well-dressed appearance is only part of it—he's got to *learn* something in school, too."

Coleman returned to his own office at the far end of the hallway. Almost immediately, a woman who worked in the cafeteria burst in. She was very agitated. With a shaking voice, she said one of the boys from the school hit her car from behind in the parking area. Her car was not damaged. But the fellow did it, she claimed, on purpose and then threatened her and yelled at her. She had apparently been driving more slowly than he thought she should. He was trapped behind her, so he tapped her car's rear bumper slightly. Then, as she got out of her car, he drove by, yelling, "Watch your feet, or I may drive over them." She said that she had failed to get the boy's license number, and she did not notice the color of his car. "I hope the kids aren't going to vandalize my car now," she said. Coleman calmed her down, saying that he would try to track down the culprit.

After the woman left, Coleman gathered his thoughts and papers and settled in for some desk work. A few minutes later, Mrs. Wagner, a teacher aide, came in to announce, "Crawford and I are not going to get along," referring to a female student in the Stabilization Program. "She just ignores me." Wagner said that earlier in the morning she had asked Crawford to leave an area and that Crawford had responded by "showing and wiggling her ass," and asking, "You want some of this? This is what you like, isn't it?"

Coleman did not register surprise, but only said, "Okay, we'll send her home."

Wagner continued, "When she said that to me, I said to her that she sounded like a whore." Coleman responded, "Well, Crawford is somewhat unpredictable. We had a similar incident with her last spring. When I called her in she was very contrite, but I guess that she hasn't changed her ways."

Wagner left the office, and Coleman asked his clerk to call Crawford to the office. A few minutes later Crawford appeared; almost immediately she informed Coleman, "A teacher aide hit me this morning."

Coleman asked, "Well, what did you do?"

Crawford explained, "The aide told me I could not be in the hall. But there were about fifty other students there, and she wasn't bothering them. She told me I was acting like an ass and that I was acting like a whore."

"Let me tell you what the aide told me," Coleman broke in. "She said you were using vulgar actions."

"I called her one name and that was a 'bitch'."

"Well, the aide told me you gestured indecently, and said 'you want some of this?' Without using words you were more vulgar than if you had used words."

Crawford asked whether she should bring her brother as a witness. "Look," Coleman told her, "Mrs. Wagner has been here at the school for a long time. She has always been a kind lady and has never had any problems with students. You, on the other hand, have had run-ins with teachers before."

Crawford continued to argue. "Why was it that she told me to move? There were other students doing the same thing I was."

Coleman said, "Look, I'm sorry. You can't do this. You were in the wrong and you were asked to behave properly. That's all that's important, not whether there were other students doing it wrong too."

Crawford became more upset. "Why am I the one getting into trouble?" she demanded. "That teacher aide shouldn't have called me a whore." Then she added, "I did *not* do what she said I did."

"Well," Coleman told her, "I'm going to bring her in here. I believe what she has told me. She has been dependable and reliable for the past ten years. That's why I believe her."

He got up and invited Wagner back into his office. Crawford blurted out to the aide, "I see you didn't tell him that you called me an ass."

Coleman motioned to his Assistant Principal, Mr. Palmer, to join them. Palmer was in charge of student discipline. When Palmer entered the office, Coleman shut the door.

Coleman explained that he would "go through the whole thing now." Looking at Crawford he added, "And I'll probably go through it again when your parents come in."

Wagner began by saying it all took place at about 7:35 A.M. "Crawford was in the hall and was told to move three times. Crawford ignored this, although she was standing right by my station in the hall."

Denying this, Crawford claimed she responded to Wagner's requests by moving toward the elevator, explaining that she was waiting for Mrs. Jones.

Wagner responded that she may have made a slight move out of the hall, but she "wasn't hurrying herself at all to get out of the hall."

"Why weren't you telling Curtis to move?" Crawford asked Wagner. "He was in the hall too."

Wagner replied that Curtis had not been in the hall as long as Crawford had.

"Is that when you made the gesture?" Coleman asked Crawford.

"You called me an asshole and a whore!" Crawford shouted at the aide.

Wagner said, "I did say that you were acting *like* a whore when you did what you did."

Coleman interrupted them, "I know Mrs. Wagner does not challenge or confront students."

"I only told the girl to move," Wagner said, pointing her finger at Crawford.

"No, you pushed me. You pushed me first," Crawford claimed.

"No," Wagner replied, "you pushed me. *Then* I pushed you."

Coleman turned toward Crawford. "You know, you have a history of cussing out people in this school. You've done it to this lady before my eyes and you've done it to me."

"Well, what kind of a school is this that when a teacher hits a student, nothing happens?" Crawford demanded to know.

"You had better bring your parents in here to talk," Coleman told her. "We'll talk with your parents. I can't permit a student to treat a teacher like this."

Then Palmer addressed Crawford. "You know, you're blaming everybody but yourself. You're blaming the other students who weren't doing the right thing. You're blaming the aide, and you're blaming everybody, but you are not facing the fact that you were doing something that you should not have been doing, which was standing out there in that hall."

Crawford began to cry. "Okay," she said, "call my mother. I don't care." With angry tears she asked Coleman, "Are you sending me home?"

"Yes," said Coleman, "you're going home today."

"Are you going to give me bus fare?" she asked. Before he could answer, she said, "I'll call my mother right now."

Coleman told her, "Sure, go ahead and phone your mother." Turning to Palmer, he asked him to escort Crawford out of the building.

* * * * *

A student and her mother were waiting outside Coleman's office. He invited them to enter and sit at the conference table. The mother seemed ready for a fight. She said, "I'm not afraid of any kid in this school. I grew up in a city neighborhood. I moved out of that area, but I can still fight." Then she compared herself to her daughter. "My daughter has a reputation for being afraid to fight, but I'm not afraid to fight." Her excitement was explained as she told Coleman about a girl at school who had been instigating a fight with her daughter. Nancy, her daughter, had been attacked by the other girl. "I want that girl suspended from school," the mother demanded.

Coleman learned that the other girl's name was Jeanne. Coleman left the office to have Jeanne called out of class. Returning he turned to Nancy and asked her to tell him what happened. "Jeanne approached you on the street, right?"

"Yeah," Nancy replied. "She started talking. She said that I had called her a slut, and then she pushed me against a car."

Coleman learned that Nancy and Jeanne were both in chorus. "Are you friends or are you enemies? What's your situation?" he asked.

Nancy said they used to be friends, "but not any more." They were enemies in the seventh grade, then became friends in the eighth grade, and now were enemies again.

Coleman spoke with Nancy's mother while they waited for Jeanne to arrive. The mother insisted, "I don't want a kid laying a hand on her." Coleman explained that he could not suspend the girls. He could not take punitive action without meeting first with the parents or without first giving a warning to the girls. Because the fight took place on the street before school, the girls could not be suspended. The fight had to occur at school. He felt that some fault was probably shared by both students. "It is very rare when one student physically assaults another unprovoked," he said. "All I can do now is warn the girls. Perhaps the threat weighing over them will affect their behavior and keep them from fighting in the school."

Jeanne arrived and began to give her side of the story. She claimed that Nancy said she had a gang of three people ready to beat her up.

Nancy interrupted saying, "Well, that was to scare you."

"The problem with Nancy," Jeanne said, "is that she has a mouth that won't stop. Oh, I have so many witnesses from girls' chorus. There was somebody in there who was taking a look at school pictures, and somebody pointed out my picture and said I was pretty. Then Nancy said that I was a slut. Everybody heard her say that."

Coleman asked Jeanne, "Did you hit Nancy this morning?"

"Yeah," Jeanne said. "I went to her and I said I heard she had three guys on me."

Nancy answered Jeanne, "I was told you would beat me up."

Nancy's mother told Jeanne, "Look, if you don't like my daughter, you stay the hell away from her." As they talked together, it became clear that Nancy and Jeanne had been swearing at each other on the street in front of the school.

Coleman began to be annoyed at this kind of talk. He turned to Nancy and Jeanne and said, "What you both need is to be spanked, both of you, and put to bed without any supper." They began to giggle. He gave them a friendly smile and said, "You should be friends or you should find a way to get along in chorus, even if you don't like each other the rest of the time. I'm going to send you to class," he told them. In a kidding way he added, "If you come back I'm going to spank you both with a stick." At this Nancy's mother told Coleman, "Well, you have my permission. In fact, I'll even get you the stick." As the girls left, Nancy's mother admitted to Coleman that her daughter had a "very big mouth."

An hour later, Coleman announced over the P.A. system that all students in the Stabilization Program were to meet in the auditorium during homeroom period. A few minutes later, as students entered the hall, Coleman asked them to sit close to the front since there were too few in the group to fill the auditorium. In all, about fifty students showed up. The counselor to whom Coleman had spoken earlier regarding North, the well-dressed student, came into the hall, as did all of the bus aides. Coleman distributed pink sheets of paper listing the rules for traveling on the charter buses.

Opening the meeting, Coleman reassured the students that a bulletin was being sent to all homeroom teachers "to be sure that no student will be marked absent for coming to this meeting." Then he added, "If you have a problem with this, let me know."

Through these introductory remarks, the students continued to chat with one another, not giving Coleman their attention. Finally, in the hubbub, he asked the students, "Please be quiet," but this request went unheeded. Expressing some irritation, Coleman raised his voice, "I'll do the talking. Now keep quiet." But the students kept on chattering as though he had said nothing. Finally, he exploded. "Look! Either you be quiet or you get out of here!"

As they gradually quieted down, he began to address the group. He told them that if the bus was late in the morning, and they were late to class for that reason, "I feel you should not be penalized for being late. If it's the bus which was late picking you up, here's what you must do: When the bus arrives at school, you must go to the attendance office with the bus aide. The attendance office will issue a pass so you can go first to your locker, and then be admitted to class. Now remember you won't have all day to get to your class, but you will have five minutes to get to your locker and then to class."

He continued discussing morning tardiness. "However, if you come to school on your own and are late, then I'm sorry, you're late and must accept the penalty." He then added, "If you are penalized because of late buses, see your counselor for assistance."

A girl lazily raised her hand. Coleman looked at her and nodded for her to speak. "I want a transfer," she said slowly, without expression. "I'll talk to you later," Coleman told her.

He continued to review bus policy. If the bus arrived early, students were to go to the cafeteria and get breakfast, which was served until 7:45. He said if students did not have a first period class, they were to go either to the library or the lunchroom. These were the only two places a student without a first period class should be. He stopped his presentation to address a young man who had been talking. "Ephraim, will you leave, please." Ephraim left.

Coleman continued, "How many of you do not have an eighth period class?" he asked. Nine students raised their hands. Coleman said, "If you don't have an eighth period class, the place to go is one of the study halls." This was greeted by a loud guffaw from the group.

Coleman continued, ignoring their response, "If you don't

have a ninth period class, you should go and wait in Room 116. Or, you can go and wait outside the building."

He told them that any students found wandering the halls during eighth or ninth period would be suspended. He said that students found "not where they're supposed to be would be asked to leave, not for the day but for the week." This last statement was greeted with laughter by the students. "Now if you leave the building, that's okay, but you can't come back in. You will not be allowed to leave the building and then go in and out." Coleman then asked whether there were any questions.

A young man asked, "What happens if you don't have a seventh period class?" Coleman wrote down his name and said, "We will work something out."

Coleman told the group, "Look, I want to tell you personally what is expected. If the bus is late, you are expected to see your teacher about making up the work. They have to let you make up the work, but it's up to you to see them and find out what you are expected to do." He promised to tell the teachers the same.

Regarding the end of the day, he said, "The bus leaves every day at 2:45 whether you're on it or not. The drivers have been told to leave at that time. Now that is nine minutes after the last bell rings. If any students want to join an athletic team and if they are not able to catch the bus because they're at practice, then we will reimburse you money so that you can take public transportation home." He explained that each coach would give him a list of student athletes who regularly attend practice.

Next, he raised the issue of behavior on the bus. "The bus aides have their job and their job is to see that the bus is both orderly and quiet. Anyone who is smoking or who fights or causes a disturbance will not be permitted on the bus. Then you can come to school at your own expense. The general rule is good manners. If you don't follow the rules I'll tell you and write a letter to your parents. You will be suspended for a week or for two weeks or for a month or for good, if I find out that you aren't behaving on that bus."

He then recognized Mrs. Jones, the bus aide who spoke with him earlier about student misbehavior on the bus. She added, "There should be no swearing." Coleman reminded the students they were not to bring radios on the bus. Turning to the aides he said, "If they bring a radio, first warn them, and if they keep bringing the radio, don't let them on the bus." At this last statement there was a loud verbal protest from the students. Coleman continued, "I can appreciate enjoying a radio coming back and forth. But if it's disturbing people, you should not get into the bus. The purpose of riding the bus is not to play a radio loud and disturb people. And radios do not belong in schools."

Another aide asked to speak and was recognized by Coleman. "The buses we are using are new buses. Students are marking on the back of the seats. The things they write are disgraceful. Also, I find spit and cigarette butts on the floor at the back of the bus." Again, there was a loud verbal protest from the students as she spoke.

Coleman then admonished them about their manners. "Toward her (looking at the aide), toward me, toward each other. It's disgusting. Everything is a big deal. It's all funny. You can act like this if you want, but I'm going to tell you something. The reason you're here is to learn and to go to school. That's what the purpose of this whole thing is supposed to be. That's what we're here to do, to go to school. You want to have a good program? Well, we want to give you a good program. But if you don't act reasonably, then you don't belong here, and you aren't going to be here. I know that it's a hardship for you because you have to come a long way to get to school. But we're not going to goof around on this. You're expected to follow the rules. If you don't we'll have your parents in here. This stuff that you're doing on these buses is completely out of line. You know better and you can do better."

Turning to the pink sheets that were distributed during the meeting, he explained that they contained regulations for students. He reviewed the attendance procedures for the late arriving students. Then he asked whether there were further questions.

A young woman raised her hand. She said that she missed the bus on Tuesday and the teachers marked her absent. Coleman told her, "If you're at the pick-up on time and the bus is late there is no penalty. But if you miss the bus altogether then it's your responsibility to get to school on time. If you're late the teacher is correct in marking you absent from classes that you missed. However, if you're mostly on time, the teachers will probably help you out on an occasional time you may be late. If you have a habit of being late and this is just one more time, they're probably not going to be very sympathetic." He said he also understood that students from Hawthorne shared the bus with students from Washington High School. "Sometimes it's the Washington students who cause the problems." He promised to speak with the principal at the other school to make sure the same kind of behavior is required from the students at both schools.

The young woman who spoke earlier of a transfer raised her hand. She said she was tired of getting up so early in the morning. She said she also wanted to get to school on just one bus, rather than having to switch at Washington High school.

Rather than commenting on her statement, Coleman recognized a young man who wanted to know about hall guards. Coleman said the hall guards were teacher aides or teachers who had hall supervision. Impatiently, one of the students cried out, "Look, we know that. That's not what we want to know." Coleman bristled at this. He said, "You just keep quiet and listen, and I'll tell you what you want to know. This school is going to be quiet and orderly so that teachers can do their job teaching to the best of their ability. Hall guards have the job to keep the halls quiet. You may think this is funny, but it's not. This may be funny to you, but it's not funny in terms of the order that has to be maintained in the school."

A young girl asked why students were not given tokens so they could take public transportation to school, instead of having to take the charter buses. Coleman replied that the court order which spelled out guidelines for the program specified that the Board of Education had to provide a bus. He said he could not give students tokens. He could only provide a bus in compliance with the guidelines.

A young woman asked why the high school did not accept credits earned at night school. Coleman said that this was an issue to bring up with her counselor. "Every case has to go through the counselors and they will make the determination." A young man said, "Yes, but we want to know which credits can be accepted and which credits cannot be accepted."

Coleman told him, "Go to your counselor and your counselor will look at the credits you've got." There was a lot of derisive laughter when he said this. Coleman's voice grew louder; he said the reason he invited the counselors to today's meeting was so that they could hear the kinds of questions students had. "If you have some credits, take them to your counselor. If they are not adequate, the counselor will give you a reason."

As he continued his explanation, the bell rang, and all the students jumped up and walked from the auditorium without waiting to be dismissed.

Coleman was approached by the young woman who wanted the transfer. He told her, "You picked this school. I can't transfer you out." She told him that when she was making her choice there weren't any schools near her house that had openings. She wanted to go to one of the other high schools near her house. She mentioned several other high schools with excellent academic reputations that she would have preferred. She complained she was not given those choices, she had to choose from schools "way on the other side of the city." She also explained she had a medical problem that made it difficult for her to get up in the morning and travel a long distance to school.

Coleman told her, "Well, I'll talk with your parents, if your parents want to call me."

She said, "My first period class is killing me for sure. At least, can I change my schedule if I can't get a transfer?"

Coleman replied, somewhat condescendingly, "Well, I know it's hard, sweetheart."

The girl tried one more time. "Mr. Coleman, I'm working and I'm getting my life together. I know if I've got to stay here, at least maybe I can get a schedule that will be easier for me."

Coleman did not reply and, moving a few steps toward the exit, was approached by the school's truant officer. They began to discuss a list of students who had not yet attended a single day of school although they were registered as students. With this interruption, the girl sensed that her conversation with Coleman was over. He did not notice as she turned to walk away.

* * * * *

The previous spring, Coleman had called together a similar group of students at a special homeroom assembly. As with the bus riders, the purpose was to remind students of certain school rules. A day or two before the meeting, Coleman had been presented a T-shirt listing the names of each senior about to graduate. As a softening-up tactic, Coleman decided to put on the T-shirt before speaking to the students in the school cafeteria where the senior homeroom assembly was regularly held. He arrived early at the cafeteria and helped the teacher set up the microphone system. As the students began drifting in, some of them noticed him and commented on the T-shirt.

When the microphone was in place, he attempted to open the meeting. In a joking manner, he called out, "Hey, guys! Shut up there!" They did not quiet down. He tried again, "Hey—that means I'll talk and you'll stop for a couple of minutes, okay?" He was trying to be a good guy, but they continued talking. Showing annoyance, he began to call out the names of specific students, telling them to be quiet. Finally they began to settle down.

As Coleman began his remarks, he complained about their taking so long to settle down. He commented that many other students were still wandering in late to homeroom. He was rattled as he spoke and shook the microphone, causing the end to flip from its holder and fly across the room. Setting the holder aside, he continued to address the group. The students, however, had started to talk among themselves again. "Now this is seven times," he shouted. "Take the hint, won't you. It doesn't take a lot of brains to be quiet for four minutes." Exasperated, he turned to the homeroom teacher and said, "Okay, I want the teachers to send home people who come in late to homeroom. Important announcements are going to be made, and they are going to miss these announcements if they just sit there and chatter to each other."

"Now, where is the senior class president?" Coleman asked. "I want him to come up here." A long silence ensued as everyone turned around looking for the president. But he did not appear. The students began to chant, "Send him home. Send him home." Finally, the president walked in, and the students broke out in loud laughter, as their chant rose to a new crescendo.

Coleman called for their attention. He ignored the laughter and chanting and turned to his main topic, "My reason for coming up was to thank the senior class for this T-shirt. I'm going to wear it when I play racquet ball. When I play tennis, I'm going to wear it to show that I'm associated with the Hawthorne High Senior Class." The senior class president then took the microphone, which had been retrieved and reassembled, and announced procedures for the purchase of prom tickets.

The bell rang and the seniors jumped up to leave. Coleman checked the microphone and found it undamaged. The school engineer joined Coleman for a moment. They spoke of how the homeroom teachers were letting things deteriorate because they were not enforcing the tardy rules or other discipline.

STUDY QUESTIONS

1. This case presents a number of episodes involving a high school principal's interactions with students. Evaluate the principal's behavior in each episode. What appears to be happening? How well does the principal seem to be handling himself?
2. The student transfer busing program does not seem to have settled down very well at Hawthorne High, even though the program is now in its second year. What would you do, as principal, to smooth out the adjustment process?
3. What principalship qualities and/or behaviors, in your estimation, are necessary in gaining the respect of and control over students? Should the high school principal interact fairly often with students or should this be left to subordinates?
4. High schools have many rules, regulations, and eventually punishments (e.g., suspension) designed to guide and control student behavior. Identify the rules in operation in this case and evaluate their effectiveness. How would you, as principal, establish and enforce a set of rules for students?

11

Episodic Cases

CASE THREE

Bugging the New Teacher: Beetlemania in the Parking Lot

Columbus Junior High School serves a solid, mostly white working class community. Ms. Haskins, a black teacher newly assigned to the school, thought that the year had gotten off to a good start and that she was getting along well with her students. Then, abruptly, she began finding her Volkswagen Bug moved to areas from which there was no driveable exit, when she left school for the day. Since the car had been locked, she was puzzled how this levitation had occurred. More than that, she was confused and discouraged, hurt and afraid. What was going on?

Mrs. Harris, the principal, began an investigation immediately and soon learned, along with Haskins, that a playground leader had reported witnessing eight students picking up her car and depositing it in a walled portion of the playground. Harris was able to identify the students, and she suspended them. Ms. Haskins agreed to file a police report, and the parents were notified and asked to come to the principal's office the following Monday morning.

On the Friday evening preceding the scheduled meeting, an open house had been scheduled at the school. As the students and their parents began to show up, one of the culprits approached Harris several times, saying that his father wanted to speak with her. Finally, the father approached her himself. The boy, in his father's presence, immediately began to deny that he had anything to do with lifting the car. Harris spoke to the father, explaining there had been a witness who saw the car being lifted by the boys. As she spoke, the boy grew increasingly anxious and began to cry, repeatedly denying his participation in the stunt. His father turned to Harris. "Look, Mrs. Harris," he said, "if Clarence was involved, I want you to know that I will support you in whatever action you decide on."

Harris confided to the father that the entire incident had her "very upset." She did not understand why these kids had done such a thing. "Why are they picking up Ms. Haskins' car?" she wondered. When he heard this, the boy piped up, "Because her car is little and light enough for us to carry." They could not lift a heavier car.

The father, recognizing this outburst as the boy's admission of guilt, agreed to come to the school on Monday to discuss it further. He said he had been involved in a similar prank as a boy, and often told the story to entertain his friends. Perhaps his own son had overheard and decided to repeat his father's antics. He said that if there were any damages, he would be glad to pay for them.

Harris responded by saying that she felt that any damage should be paid for by the boys themselves. The boy turned to his father and admitted that his hand was on the car when it was being lifted by the other boys. "But my hand was only there," he claimed, "I wasn't actually lifting it."

At this, Harris turned to greet other parents and to see that the open house proceeded on schedule. Later, as the boys and their parents said goodbye and left the building, Harris returned briefly to her office. Sitting at her desk, she pondered a number of things: the creative impishness of her students, the organizational skills of the ring leaders, the hurt feelings of Ms. Haskins, and the amusing craziness of the whole affair. But most of all, she pondered how to handle the Monday morning meeting.

STUDY QUESTIONS

1. Consider some alternative ways in which Principal Harris could approach the meeting on Monday morning. What are her options?
2. How does each individual or group of central figures in this episode expect the issue to be resolved? Ms. Haskins? The students? The students' parents? Principal Harris?
3. Are there special considerations in this episode (e.g., race, harassment of a new teacher) that make it too important to dismiss as a prank?
4. What would you do as principal in this situation?

CASE FOUR

Teacher Supervision: The Belligerent Subordinate

Early one morning, as the school office personnel settled into their daily tasks, Mr. Samuels, the principal, reminded his staff that he had summoned Ms. Vickerson, one of the school's problem teachers, to his office for a personal conference. Since she would be arriving shortly, and since they knew about the complaints against her, he wanted them available on short notice. He informed his secretary that during his talk with Vickerson, he was not to be disturbed by phone calls or personal visitors.

When Vickerson arrived, Samuels invited her into his office and asked her to be seated. After some pleasantries, Samuels got right to the point, informing her that several students had complained about her. In particular, he mentioned complaints about the way she graded the students' work.

At this, Vickerson became indignant. She demanded to know the names of the students who had complained. She spoke vehemently, calling them liars. "If charges are to be made against me," she said, "I want specific facts." She said she would not be intimidated by "lies by people who won't even give their names to me."

Samuels told her that his assessment of her teaching showed areas of great weakness. He felt that in the classroom there was "not enough instruction." He tried to reassure her by saying that the main reason he had called her to his office was to help her prepare for next year. "You'll have your program for next year before you leave," he told her, "and I expect to go over your September lesson plans first thing in the fall. I also expect to see that you follow your instruction plans very closely when you're teaching your classes."

Samuels continued, "I get reports that your students feel they're being given a lot of busy work." At this point, Ms. Burdin, an assistant principal in charge of counseling, entered the office and sat down with the two of them. The AP repeated the report of students complaining about Vickerson's classes. "They come running to their counselors saying that 80 percent of the grade will be on the final exam," explained the assistant. "As you know, Barbara, this is contrary to school policy."

Vickerson began to explain her grading system, going into detail on how she marked every assignment and allotted various weightings to the several exercises during the semester. Halfway through her remarks, she interrupted herself, complaining that her students often intimidated her, verbally harrassing her when she entered the building or when she walked through the hallways. She voiced the suspicion that her students were "out to get her," and that she found it necessary to deal with them firmly in class. As she spoke, Samuels and the AP detected an unseemly vindictiveness; Vickerson apparently tried to gain leverage in her relationships with her students by threatening to punish their undisciplined behavior with failing grades.

At the end of Vickerson's commentary, the AP refocused the conversation by saying that, from her perspective, too many students had formally complained for the administrative staff to ignore the problem any longer. She registered the concern not only of the principal, but of other administrators, saying that something had to be done.

At this Vickerson became more aggressive. "Students complain all the time about teachers, not just me," she said. "Students always complain about teachers. They come to me and say they don't understand what this one does or that one does, even after the teacher has said it plainly. They are not sincere students, they blame the teacher, but they really don't *want* to understand." Then, lowering her voice, she said to Samuels, "These other teachers they complain about, I'll mention their names to you, okay?"

Samuels cut her off. He said he did not want to discuss the other teachers. He was giving her notice that she should follow the school's grading policy and be better prepared to teach her classes the following year.

The meeting concluded and Vickerson left, walking with heavy, angry steps. The assistant turned to Samuels and said, "No matter what you say, she has an answer."

"She rationalizes everything completely," Samuels agreed. Then he added, "We can't let her fail those kids. We'll have to watch her grades as they come in."

STUDY QUESTIONS

1. What next steps would you take as a principal? Is the principal justified in this case in deciding to wait and "watch her grades as they come in"? What would you do as principal if the teacher does "fail those kids"?
2. How would you have handled the personal conference with Vickerson? Did the principal approach the problem in the right way?
3. How have the actions and behaviors of students influenced the flow of events in this case? As principal, how are student complaints best handled?
4. What sequence of actions, in what time frame, should be taken to determine if Vickerson is truly an incompetent teacher and should be dismissed?
5. Put yourself in Vickerson's shoes. What would you have done in the situation?

CASE FIVE

A Teacher Responds to a Pay Cut

Mr. Samos, principal of a medium-sized high school, had developed an extensive career education program and had hired several teachers to staff it. Because the program required teachers to supervise students in their job placements for several hours each week, these teachers were assigned reduced course loads. They also received extra pay for the after-school hours devoted to visiting student placements.

Halfway through the school year, the board of education was forced to make financial cuts in most school programs. Cuts in career education were decided on early; they were deep and severe. First to go were the additional stipends for supervisory time. Since Samos wanted his students to continue to be visited on the job, he decided to retain the same format, but reduce the number of students for whom each teacher was responsible. Of course, their pay had to be cut by the amount of the stipend cut.

Together with the associate principal in charge of teacher schedules, Samos worked out new reduced assignments for career education staff, who would now be expected to work at a lower salary level. The teachers in the program were called in individually, informed of the board's budget cuts, and given a revised schedule. Understandably, staff members were angry over their reduced pay.

One teacher was convinced that Samos was not telling the truth about the cuts. After their conference, she wrote a letter to Samos, claiming that a friend of hers, a principal at another high school, had given her different information regarding the cuts. The other principal had told her that, under the new policies, she could expect a better deal as a result of the cuts. She accused Samos of singling her out for unfair treatment because she had disagreed with

Samos in the past over how the career education students should be supervised.

Samos met with his assistant principal to discuss the teacher's letter. He felt the teacher had misunderstood what the other principal had said. Together they re-read their instructions from the board of education. The policy seemed clear. Samos asked his assistant what he thought. "Should we try to convince her she had been treated fairly?" he asked. They decided they could not satisfy this teacher with more personal conferences. Instead, they would invite the teacher to gather the evidence which supported her points of view. They agreed she would not succeed in finding such evidence. They concluded, "She should waste her time looking for it, instead of us spending our time documenting support for her schedule change."

STUDY QUESTIONS

1. Is the principal justified in this case in sitting back until the teacher makes the next move? What would you have done?
2. Why, and for what reasons, might a principal decide that additional discussion ("personal conferences") with a disgruntled teacher would not be appropriate?
3. What are the principal's objectives in this episode? The teacher's? Are the two sets of goals incompatible?
4. What is likely to happen to the career education students? What would you do in resolving the issue to insure continued quality in student services?

CASE SIX

The Ruler and the Ruled

It was just after 10:30 A.M. Marilyn Robinson, principal of Jefferson School, was in her office, where a meeting with the school social worker had just concluded. A mother came into the office with her child, Jordan Russell, in tow. Mrs. Russell told her that Jordan came home last night with dried blood in his nose. When she asked him about it, he told her that his teacher, Mrs. Briggs, hit him on the nose with a ruler.

Robinson asked Jordan to come to her. She sat in the chair beside her desk and he stood directly in front of her. Her tone was soft and gentle as she asked him to tell her what happened.

Jordan answered, "That boy was talking to me."

"What boy?" asked Robinson.

"Tony," he said.

"What was he talking about?" she wanted to know.

"Casper."

"A cartoon?"

"Yes."

"What were you supposed to be doing?"

"Doing work," he answered.

"And the teacher, she did what?" she asked.

"The teacher hit me across the nose with a ruler."

"Did it hurt?"

"Uh-huh."

"Did it bleed a lot?"

"A lot of blood came up."

"What did the teacher do?"

"Put a towel on it."

"Was your nose swollen?"

"No."

"She hit hard enough to make your nose bleed, and there wasn't any redness or swelling?" Robinson inquired.

At this point the child's mother interrupted. "It was red last night." Robinson turned back to Jordan and asked him, "Did you cry?"

"Yes."

"How much, a lot?"

"No!"

"Did you cry when she hit you?"

"No," he replied, reversing his position.

"All that blood, and none on your clothes?" she asked.

Jordan said nothing, but started to say, "uh, uh, uh."

"Did the other children see it?"

"Yes."

"What will they tell me, will they tell me the same thing?" Robinson inquired.

"No," he shook his head.

"You know what I'm going to ask them, don't you think they will tell the truth?"

"Yes," he said.

"Well, then, what will they say?"

"The teacher hit me across the nose."

"What were you doing when she hit you?"

"Nothing."

"You mean that you *weren't* talking and she hit *you,* and Tony *was* talking and she *didn't* hit Tony?"

"I don't know," he said.

"Did the teacher hit you before?"

He said, "Yes, right here," and pointed to his leg.

His mother interjected that the last time he complained the teacher had hit him she found a mark on his leg that stayed for a week. Russell explained that she did not come to school the first time because Jordan was hit on the *leg*. She added, "But I don't think she had any business to hit his face." Robinson turned to Jordan and asked, "Did she ever hit you on the face before?"

"No," he replied.

Robinson stood and said, "Let's go and see the teacher." She explained to Russell that Jordan's class was taking achievement tests now, so they would have to wait about ten minutes before they could talk with the teacher. Robinson asked the mother, "Can you wait that long?" She said she could.

Jordan and Mrs. Russell left the office to wait in the hall. Robinson returned and sat at her desk, rubbed her eyes, and thought, "Darn it! I've told her before, 'Put that ruler down. If you teach with a ruler in your hand, it's only a matter of time before something happens!' "

STUDY QUESTIONS

1. Choose some colleagues to join you in role playing a meeting between Mrs. Russell, the teacher, and Ms. Robinson. You are the principal. How would you conduct this meeting?
2. What are the apparent expectations of each of the actors in this episode? What solution would please the mother? The principal? The boy, Jordan? The teacher?
3. Assume the teacher is found to be guilty of hitting the child. What action would you take? What action is best if the teacher claims innocence?
4. This case raises the everlasting question of corporal punishment. What are your views on this larger question? Are there ever any circumstances in which it is appropriate, maybe even necessary, for a teacher to strike a child?

CASE SEVEN

Discipline and Desegregation: Voluntary and Involuntary Transfers

During the period covering the research for this book, a large school system was under pressure from federal authorities to desegregate school enrollments. In pursuit of this goal, the Board of Education established permissive transfer programs that enabled elementary students to elect voluntarily to attend schools outside their own neighborhoods. Schools considered to have a deficit of students were designated as receiver schools for these programs.

The case presented here is drawn from an elementary school admitting students on a permissive transfer basis. Many elementary principals came to believe that permissive enrollment and the consequent use of busing to facilitate the transfers generated discipline problems that would not have occurred without these added factors.

When it was first announced, elementary school principals seemed to welcome the idea of increasing the number of students on their rolls through permissive transfer. Such enhancement of enrollment figures could only work to their advantage, since resources were allocated on the basis of attendance statistics. There was a general feeling, however, that, regardless of race, students seeking to enter on permissive transfers were different from the regular student body and had to be watched closely. Many of them, an inspection of their applications revealed, had long histories of behavioral and academic problems. In one case, a student had been in a special education class for students with behavioral disorders in the neighborhood school. The parents had not mentioned this when the newly designated receiving school accepted the boy as a regular student. In another case, a high school student's record revealed fewer course credits than the student's application form had claimed.

In the behavioral area, many of the transferring students proved difficult to handle; many suspected that transfer was motivated by discipline rather than programmatic concerns. Moreover, parents of such students were sometimes militant advocates for their children, determined that they should have a fresh start and a chance to do well in a totally new environment.

Monroe School was one of the well-regarded elementary schools in the system that still served a largely white, middle-class community. In recent years, some Asian, Middle Eastern and Hispanic students had moved into the neighborhood and joined the student body. Under the permissive transfer plan, a few spaces were opened to students from beyond the community. Most of these spaces were filled with Hispanic applicants and children from racially mixed marriages.

When the number of Hispanic students in the school became larger, the principal, Ellen Parker, found a bright, energetic Hispanic CETA worker to help her build good relationships with the students and their parents. Switching from English to Spanish at opportune moments, this CETA worker, Mrs. Ruiz, translated and interpreted school programs and policy to parents. Parker included Ruiz in all disciplinary matters concerning Hispanic students. The following example involves a Hispanic permissive transfer student.

Parker was in her office when Luis burst in. Excitedly and loudly Luis told her that he and another boy were fighting and that during the fight, a teacher had had to restrain Luis. "I called my mother," he said. Calmly, Parker called for Ruiz and told Luis to go and talk with her.

Ten minutes later Luis's mother entered the outer office with her pre-school child. Parker heard her announce herself and went to the outer office to greet her. "Good afternoon, Mrs. Franco, would you please come into my office," she said. They took a seat in the principal's office. Parker told the mother that a teacher had interrupted a fight between her son and another boy. "I think that Luis is angry about that and is trying to get the teacher in trouble," Parker speculated.

"Luis told me that a teacher hit him," Franco retorted. She seemed ready for a fight and would not be pacified easily.

Luis had been at the Monroe school only for a few months, but they had been stormy months for Luis. Parker had suggested that Luis might benefit from placement in a special education class for students with behavioral problems. Franco had refused.

Parker spoke calmly and firmly. "Mrs. Franco, no one touches a child in this school. I just saw Luis and he seems to be all right."

Franco was not reassured. "Well, Luis told me something different," she replied.

"Well, I knew that he had told you something," Parker responded, "because he burst in here and said 'I called my Mom'." Parker continued to seek out a reasonable common ground with Franco. "The teacher involved is a good teacher. He is trying to work successfully with Luis. I am trying to help your son stay in a regular classroom. You should appreciate this."

Franco stubbornly refused to budge. "That teacher had no right to touch my son," she reaffirmed.

"But Mrs. Franco," Parker answered, "If the teacher restrained Luis it was only to keep him from getting into a bigger fight with the other kid."

"I want to see my son," Franco demanded. "And I want to talk with Mrs. Ruiz."

Parker went to the intercom and called for Ruiz. As they awaited her arrival, they discussed another Franco child who was enrolled in the school. Parker informed her secretary that Luis should be brought from his classroom to the office. Soon Luis, his mother, Ruiz, and Parker were seated in the principal's office.

Parker began to speak with Luis. "Maybe you were getting into it a little bit with the other boys on the way to the cafeteria," she suggested. "You know that I don't want anyone hurt. You can't be acting up in the halls and so on. You know what I mean when I say safety on the stairs." Parker and Luis continued to talk about what happened as the mother listened. Luis explained that he had been at the other boy's house for lunch. Upon hearing this, Franco became very angry.

"Luis, I gave you 50 cents for lunch. What are you doing taking the 50 cents and then not spending it and going to somebody else's house for lunch?"

Franco yelled at Luis about this for several minutes. She seemed to forget about the incident with the teacher. Her anger turned away from Parker and the teacher as she vented her rage at Luis.

Parker attempted to quiet Franco by bringing the discussion back to the original issue. "I instruct teachers in the school to physically restrain children if they are in danger of hurting themselves or someone else. In this school, all the teachers are the teachers of all the children. Just because a teacher is not a student's classroom teacher doesn't mean that they can be ignored when they tell you what to do." She speculated, "This teacher probably saw the students scuffling on the stairs and was afraid that someone would slip. He got involved in order to help."

Luis disputed this. "No, that isn't what happened. He threw me against the wall."

"Luis, aren't you exaggerating?" Parker asked. "Perhaps you're trying to get the teacher into trouble. You don't want to be in trouble with your mother and the school, so maybe you're protecting yourself in this way by trying to get someone else into trouble instead."

As Luis and Parker talked, Franco listened carefully. Then she threw up her hands in exasperation and said to Luis, "So what happened on the stairs?"

Luis immediately replied, "He almost threw me down the stairs."

Parker told Luis, "You know, I think that you and this teacher are going to sit down and talk about this."

Franco seemed to ignore Parker. She continued to speak to Luis. "Why are you so nervous? You're just sitting and fidgeting with that pencil there."

Following Parker's comment about the teacher, Ruiz began to speak. She explained that she had already talked to the teacher. He was upset because Luis called his mother instead of going through the chain of command. "If Luis had any complaints he should have come to the principal instead of calling his mother and having her charge down here."

Parker turned to Luis. "You know, when you think that you've done something wrong, you can't cover up by calling up your mother. We have an open door here. Your mother has worked two years to get you into this school. I won't let you use any techniques to keep yourself out of trouble if you have been misbehaving. Now I think that you should go back to class."

Franco suggested that Luis should run around the block before returning to class to "let off some steam." Parker said, "He can run if he wants, but he should run in the gym because it is so cold outside."

Luis, his mother and Ruiz left the office. "You know," Parker commented, "this could blow up and take all week. That mother could have had the police and everybody else here today. This is the kind of situation that has to be defused as rapidly as it comes up."

A few minutes later Ruiz returned to the principal's office. She told Parker that she had talked to Luis's classroom teacher and he reported that he had seen the entire incident with the other teacher. "He said that the other teacher did throw the boy against the wall, because the boy swore at the other teacher." Ruiz explained to the teacher involved that Luis' mother came to school and complained. The teacher replied that he would not be intimidated by Franco.

"You know, that teacher does not have a pattern of physically abusing children," Parker commented. "Still, I think that I should talk with him immediately."

Later in the day a white male teacher stood in the outer

office waiting to speak with Parker. Parker invited him into her office. She explained how angry Luis' mother had been because he had "knocked her child against the wall." She told him that the mother was very close to going to the police, "but luckily she came to the school first instead."

The teacher responded, "This group of boys is hard to manage. They are constantly pushing one another. We have to tell them to go back and walk down the stairs. This time one boy said 'no' and then started to swear at me. So I pulled strongly on the boy's arm. I did not bang the child on the wall."

Parker told him, "You cannot touch a child in the school even if they swear at you. I had to have a long conference with the mother because of this incident."

The teacher said, "Just now I saw Luis in the hall. He apologized to me for having sworn at me."

Parker told the teacher, "This boy doesn't come to the office when something happens to him. Instead, he calls his mother directly and makes charges to her there and then. After that, he comes to the office and tells me he just called his mother, that his mother is on her way. When mother arrives, she is very angry."

Parker turned toward the teacher and asked him directly, "Did you knock him against the wall?"

The teacher replied, "No, I took him by the arm."

Parker ended the conversation. When the teacher left, she commented that the student was really a special education placement. "He belongs there but his mother will not approve of that placement."

STUDY QUESTIONS

1. In light of the continuing experience with transfer students, what advice would you pass along to the superintendent of the school district concerning the workability of the transfer policy?
2. Ruiz plays a special role in the school—combination interpreter and mother hen to Hispanic students. What complications can arise in a principal's discipline policy by having a third party involved in all discipline cases of Spanish-speaking students?
3. Imagine a role-playing session involving Luis, Franco, Ruiz, the teacher who grabbed Luis, and yourself as the principal. How would you handle this session?

4. A week after the incident reported in the case, Luis is overheard using profanity in the lunchroom and directing it at another teacher. He is brought to you by this teacher, and the three of you decide on a course of action, without the help of Ruiz. How do you want this meeting to turn out?

CASE EIGHT

The Vigilantes

You are the principal of Hanford Elementary School in School District 101X in the State of Americana, a midwestern state. One Tuesday morning in early fall, you open your mail and find the following:

Mr. R. Jones, Principal
Hanford Elementary School
School District 101X
Crossroads, Americana

Dear Mr. Jones:

Please be advised that our daughter, Gloria Lunt, is only permitted to be tested on basic academic skills and knowledge. Parental permission is required for all psychological and attitudinal tests, evaluations, questionnaires or surveys, written or oral. If you plan to use any of the following, please:

a. Call us or write personally and include a sample of the test or program, questionnaire, handout to be administered.
b. Wait for our express written permission before including my child in the test, program, or survey.

In addition, we hereby request that you advise us of all classes which will utilize the techniques known as values clarification, moral dilemmas, role-playing, sensitivity training, group therapy, rank order, survival games, and the extent to which they will be employed.

Sincerely,

Gerald Lunt

P.S. Please place in our daughter's permanent file. Also please notify any school personnel that will come in contact with our child of this letter and our instructions for our daughter's education.

Thank you,
Gerald Lunt

cc: Superintendent
District 101X

Attached to the above letter is a form notice printed on heavy paper stock and intended to be distributed to district parents and other interested citizens for their use. The notice reads:

NOTICE TO:
PRINCIPAL OF ________________ SCHOOL
SUPERINTENDENT AND MEMBERS OF ____________ BOARD OF
OF
EDUCATION, DISTRICT AND SCHOOL NURSES, CLASSROOM INSTRUCTORS, SCHOOL ADVOCATES, AND TO COUNSELORS FOR THE PUPIL NAMED BELOW.

You are hereby notified that __________ is not allowed by the undersigned to participate in, be subject to, or instructed in any training or education in sex and/or sexual attitudes, the theory of evolution unless it is equally balanced with the creationist's facts and viewpoint, attitude change or development including role reversal, meditation, intropersonal questioning, psycho-drama (role playing), introspective examination of social and cultural aspects of family life, group therapy or group criticism of self, family or Christian values, T grouping and all forms of sensitivity training, situation ethics, the Occult, the undermining of Christianity including school curricula that contains blasphemy and/or profanity, Eastern Mysticism practices and exercises and all of its derivatives (Yoga, Transcendental Meditation, etc.), the teaching and/or comparison of religions, or any combination or degree thereof, without the consent of the undersigned by express written and signed permission.

The prohibition asserted hereby includes, but is not limited to, any exposure to the above kinds of education or training, whether by visual or audible communication, and whether or not by group therapy or activity, television, radio, slides, moving pictures, books, magazines, newspapers, or any printed publications whatsoever, sound reproduction, discussion leader, or any other form of communication.

If removal of this child from any class or meeting or assembly is necessary to meet the above requirements, any damage (including loss of credit), whether it be emotional, physical, mental or otherwise caused by this separation or removal shall be deemed to be the personal and/or collective responsibility of the parties to whom this notice is sent and/or listed above, resulting in possible appropriate action.

This notice and the contents hereof are to be effective as of the date below until expressly revoked in writing by the undersigned or until that day the above named child is no longer under the domain of the above-named personnel.

DATE__________ BY__________
(Parent, Guardian or Adult having custody and control of the named child)

PLEASE PLACE THIS IN OUR DAUGHTER'S PERMANENT FILE.

U.S. Supreme Court Reports, Vol. 10L, Ed. 2nd (US 372.373.374) Decision June 17, 1963, *School District of Abington Township, Pennsylvania* v *Edward Lewis Schempp*—Pages 844–914 incl (374 US 203–320 incl) Decisions, Opinions and Annotations (p. 847, headnote 937) (p. 849 footnote 1); (p. 850 footnote 2, 3); (p. 850, 374 US 206); (p. 861–862, 374 US 228–229); (p. 895, 374 US 289); *p. 896, 374 US 289); (p. 897, 374 US 291–292); (p. 898, 374 US 293, 294, 295), et al.*

The decision cited above is the case of the *School District of Abington Township, Pennsylvania* v. *Schempp.* In this decision, the U.S. Supreme Court held that if a parent or child objects to certain materials being taught, the child cannot be removed from the class because that would violate his constitutional rights.

The court further decided that the objectionable course or material would have to be removed. In the case cited, the question of prayer and religion was involved, but this precedent can be applied with regard to sex education or any other objectionable course or materials.

STUDY QUESTIONS

1. You are Mr. R. Jones, Principal. What action, if any, would you take on this communication?
2. One month after the receipt of this letter, Mr. Lunt comes to see you because his daughter, Gloria, has reported to him a disturbing piece of news. One of her teachers has tried to explain the differences, religious and otherwise, separating people in the Middle East: Jews, Islamic Arabs, Shiite Iranians, and the Palestine Liberation Organization. He requests that the teacher cease and desist from this instruction until he has had an opportunity to review the materials himself and to consent to the resumption of the unit. What answer do you give to Mr. Lunt?
3. Mr. Lunt is apparently speaking as a member of an organization. Is this communication an attempt to censor the school curriculum, or is it a legitimate right of parents to control what their children learn?

INDEX